Footprints Across America

About the Author

Michael McMonagle was born in 1953. A graduate of University College Dublin and University of Dundee, he has worked in community development and as a manager of children's services within the Health Service Executive. He is currently a director of the Lifestart Foundation and chairperson of Tir Boghaine Teo. His interests include sea kayaking, cycling, hiking, wildlife, trees and conservation. He lives with his family in Mountcharles, County Donegal. His previous travel book is called *Walking the Back Roads: A Journey from Donegal to Clonmacnoise* (Appletress Press, 2008).

FOOTPRINTS ACROSS AMERICA

Retracing an Irishman's Journey During the Last Great Gold Rush

Michael McMonagle

ORPEN PRESS

Published by
Orpen Press
Lonsdale House
Avoca Avenue
Blackrock
Co. Dublin
Ireland

e-mail: info@orpenpress.com
www.orpenpress.com

Paperback ISBN 978-1-909895-00-3
ePub ISBN 978-1-909895-28-7
Kindle ISBN 978-1-909895-27-0

Printed in Dublin by SPRINT-print Ltd

For all emigrants and refugees who, like Micí Mac Gabhann, have crossed a 'bridge of tears' in their lives.

Acknowledgements

Travel writers always carry a debt of gratitude to strangers they meet along the way. This book would not be possible without them.

Friends and family have helped shape this book. Special thanks to my family Terry, Eoghan, Aoife and Cróna, and to the observations of Kevin Montgomery, Dr Aisling Gillen, Fatemeh Movahedi, Keith Corcoran, Marie Sundberg, Winnifred McNulty, Richard Boggs and Catherine Breslin.

All at Orpen Press have done a great job in bringing this book to fruition, especially Eileen O'Brien and Elizabeth Brennan.

Thanks to John Hearne who edited this book with a discerning and sympathetic eye.

Seán Ó hEochaidh brought the story of Micí Mac Gabhann to the world. This enriched our understanding of the Irish emmigration story. Valentin Iremonger brought the story to a wider audience through his authentic translation of *Rotha Mór an tSaoil* into English.

The author is grateful to Horslips and Barry Devlin for permission to use a quote from their song, 'The Wrath of the Rain'.

'Where have they gone to, those faded faces,
Those fierce moustachioed men?'

Contents

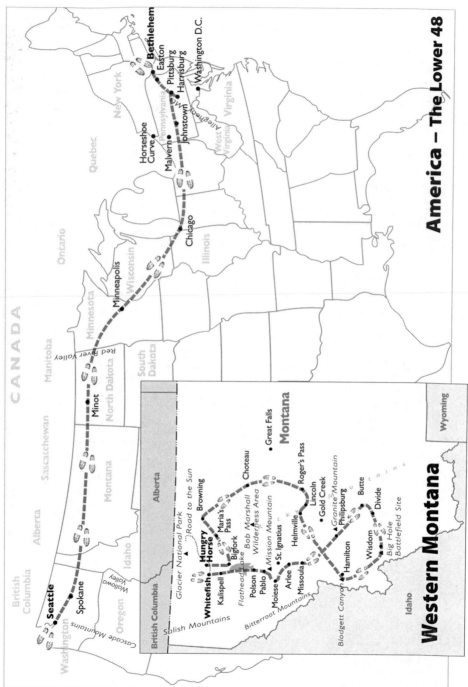

America – The Lower 48

Western Montana

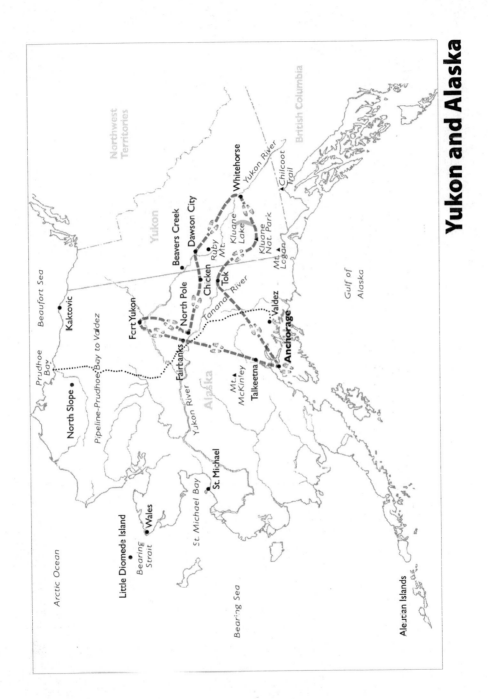

Yukon and Alaska

Preface

On a bright March day, I was walking with my son, Eoghan, through the rugged terrain of West Donegal. We had left Magheroarty on the coast and were heading for Derry, fifty miles away. With the cone of Errigal at our backs and the bleak craggy bulk of Muckish Mountain in front of us, we stopped for something to eat at a place called 'The Bridge of Tears'. Traditionally this was where emigrants from West Donegal bade farewell to family and friends when leaving for America. The group would halt just before the bridge, while the emigrant would cross alone. Family and friends would watch until he or she disappeared from view, knowing that it was unlikely they would ever see their loved one again.

A book called *Rotha Mór an tSaoil*, translated as *The Big Wheel of Life*, had brought me to this place. It was a book that had grabbed my attention as a boy, and had kept me awake during Irish class. It was full of adventures in remote and spectacular locations, places a boy could only dream about. It documented the life of a man called Micí Mac Gabhann, who in 1885, aged nineteen, took his courage in his hands and left to seek his fortune in America. He too walked across this bridge, leaving behind kith, kin and hard times on a small, stony farm at the edge of the Atlantic. Along with countless others in a Europe hit by war, poverty, religious persecution and the effects of industrial revolution, he was drawn by that beacon of hope – America.

Rotha Mór an tSaoil tells the story of Micí's journey from Derry to New York and on to Pennsylvania, where he worked on the canals and in the famous steel mills of Bethlehem. The lure of silver and copper brought him across the Great Plains to the Rocky Mountains of Montana where he spent eleven years mining in Granite, Butte, Gold Creek and on the slopes of Old Baldy Mountain. When he heard that there was gold in the Klondike, he gathered his few belongings and made his way to Seattle. From there he took a steamer north to the mouth of the Yukon River in Alaska, then journeyed for another two thousand miles by boat and on foot to Dawson City in the Klondike.

He had many escapades along the way, and met people from all parts of the globe, including Native American tribes, miners, chancers and bandits. He experienced extreme cold, frostbite, dangerous working conditions, grizzly bears and mountain lions. He crossed one of the most pristine wildernesses on earth, and learned how to survive.

Boom and bust were as common in Micí's time as they are today. The 1890s in America were often called 'the reckless decade'. Banks collapsed, businesses folded and, in the hard times that followed, people suffered desperately. This was the end of the frontier era. The 'Indian Wars' were coming to an end, the Native Americans were being forced onto reservations, the buffalo were being slaughtered and the golden era of the cowboy dawned and dwindled. Then, as now, the same big wheel of life kept on turning.

I had decided to give life to my dream as a boy. I was going to chase Micí's fading footprints across America and onto the Klondike. His dream was fuelled by the prospect of gold and silver. Mine, by curiosity and a desire to glimpse the wonders he encountered and to see how the world he passed through had changed.

I crossed America by bus and train, drove around Montana, hiked in the mountains and took a train to the port of Seattle. I flew to Anchorage, Alaska and travelled by train, small plane and minibus to the Klondike. I cycled in the hills in search of Micí's gold claim and kayaked on the Yukon River. I followed my nose on the journey and, as a consequence, interesting new worlds and people opened up to me.

This is my story.

Road to Bethlehem

'Your ticket is out of date.'

'What do you mean, out of date?'

'You were scheduled to travel on the 1st of October and today is the 2nd.'

'That can't be true.'

The check-in assistant handed the electronic ticket back to me, pointing out the dates. Sure enough, there it was in black and white. Flight Continental 231 – Dublin to Newark, 7.00 a.m. October 1st.

'I can't do anything about it', she said, 'you should talk to the people at the Continental Airline desk over there.' She pointed to a row of desks in the distance.

As I trundled over, a myriad of thoughts rushed through my mind. How could I have got it wrong? How could anyone arrive a day late for their flight? Was it the travel agent's fault? Yeah, blame someone else for my own mistake! What will I do now? When I got to the desk, there was no one there. My mind raced. It might not open for hours. Where are people when you need them? Is there anyone else around I could talk to? Every moment seemed like an eternity.

Eventually, a stewardess came to the desk. She smiled and asked how she could help. I explained my case. 'Can anything be done?' I asked.

She took my ticket and logged on to her computer. After a few moments she frowned and said, 'It gets worse. Since you didn't turn up for your flight yesterday, they've cancelled your return flights from Seattle. It's airline policy.'

Now the machine in my head started pumping. Oh my God, it isn't only about getting another flight to Newark, I'll have to get a flight home from Seattle as well. Can I afford it? Can I afford not to? She asked for my passport.

'Let me see if anything is possible here.'

After a few minutes at the computer she looked up at me with a conspiratorial smile and said, 'I shouldn't be doing this.' She printed off a new document and handed it to me.

'I've booked you on the flight this morning and have reinstated your return flights at no cost … enjoy your flight.'

There is a God. She works for Continental Airlines.

I then faced what I anticipated would be the equally tricky prospect of US immigration pre-clearance, conveniently located in Dublin Airport. I had been warned to expect a tough passage because I had visited Iran twice in the previous year. An American friend had told me, 'lose your passport bud.'

I joined the queue expecting to be called aside. At the booth, the immigration officer took my passport and told me to press my thumbs into fingerprinting pads. He leafed through the passport, looking at me over his glasses with a quizzical eye. 'This is it', I thought.

'How can you afford to take six weeks off work to go travelling?' he asked.

I mumbled an excuse. He pushed his glasses back onto the bridge of his nose, issued the visa and waved me through.

§

Mící and his cousins, Jim Anthony and Tom Ferry, each paid four pounds and ten shillings for their berth on board a ship from Derry to New York, barely a step up from the coffin ships that transported people in famine times. Conditions were desperate. Ten people packed into a small cabin with hard benches for beds. The food was inedible and the tea made from dirty water. As they passed Tory Island, Mící and his cousins turned towards home for the last time. Mící could feel the deck shuddering under his feet as the boat heaved on the waves. Despite being born beside the sea, he was not a sailor. Retreating below deck, he was seasick the whole way across the Atlantic. The only thing that made the journey bearable was a little drop of medicinal brandy given to him by a steward.

I had the luxury of a whole row of seats to myself on the airplane, but no medicinal brandy. I awoke with a start from a long sleep on the descent into Newark, to be confronted with different views out either side of the plane. On my side, the dominant impression was of a vast waterway, trees and abundant nature, verging on wilderness, with sporadic settlement. On the other side, I peered into the sun at the grey concrete sprawl that was New York, its detail hidden by the glare. The irregular jagged teeth of skyscrapers carved sharp, intimidating shapes out of the sky. I could see a power station with columns of white smoke rising.

These were the two sides of America.

I wondered what Mící felt when he first saw New York. His view was more up close and personal than mine. Standing on the deck, he would have felt the wind whipping into his face, carrying the scents of river, city and sea. Shrieks of gulls and the groan of the boat would have intermingled with the hubbub from the city's docks: shipwright's hammers, the clanging of iron foundries, the whistle of steam engines and the hollering of wagon drivers, hawkers, riggers and sailors. He would have seen palls of smoke climbing from long black chimneys, and, from the teeming shore, the gunk of the city being washed out to sea. Steamers, tugs and sailboats would have been coming and going to Staten Island, where oceangoing ships lay at their moorings, all with banners showing their name and destination.

The Statue of Liberty, that mother of exiles, then in the early stages of its construction, promised a land of welcome and hope to every immigrant. Its inscription read, *'Give me your tired, your poor, your huddled masses yearning to breathe free.'* In contrast, two famous islands hinted at a grimmer reality. On Governors Island, a fortress and gallows would have been visible to all on board. When hangings took place, the public scrambled to obtain prime views from riverboats that charged handsomely for the trip. Both the lunatic asylum and penitentiary, housing the 'mad and bad', were built on Blackwell's Island, better known as 'the island of wretchedness'. A sign on the Iron Gate onto the island warned, *'The way of the transgressor is hard.'* Mící however, upon finally 'gazing wide eyed' at the skyline of New York, was inspired to quote Wordsworth: *'Dull would he be of soul who could pass by, A sight so touching in its majesty.'*

When Mící's boat lowered anchor, passengers were loaded onto barges and taken to the immigration centre where they were numbered and examined. Immigration was a relatively simple operation for Mící, as he was young, fit and English-speaking. He stepped out onto American soil, one of many restless faces from a hundred nations that would reshape a country where both opportunity and geography seemed boundless.

Irish people played a significant part in the scramble to fill this vast emptiness. In the century from 1815 to 1915, the Irish constituted the second largest immigrant group after Germans; five million Irish to seven million Germans. In the year 1851 alone, a quarter of a million Irish arrived, most of them settling in either Boston or New York. By 1855, one-third of people living in New York were Irish-born.

Though predominantly from rural backgrounds, the Irish flocked to the cities. The land was associated with too many bad memories; farming was left to the Germans, Swedes and Norwegians.

A welcoming committee waited on the pier for newly arrived Irish immigrants. It consisted of dapperly dressed scoundrels, scheming to defraud them of their money and meagre possessions; smiling politicians and their lackeys, out harvesting votes; and clergy intent on ensuring that the Catholic faith prospered in a land of many temptations. They all recognised that this was the moment when the immigrant was most susceptible to their agenda. A politician called Plunkitt claimed, 'The poor are the most grateful people in the world, a favour is never forgotten.' Micí though, like many an immigrant before and after him, benefited from a pre-existing network of contacts to help ease his way into a new life. His network pulled him directly to Bethlehem and Easton in Pennsylvania where a friend called Frank Ferry had arranged lodgings for him with a family originally from Cloughaneely, just a stone's throw from his home in Donegal. Micí observed that the family had barely a shoe to put on their foot, as the husband had lost his health working in Bethlehem Steel.

§

On arrival in Newark airport, I found the Easton bus stop in a remote part of the airport complex, and was surprised that I was the only person waiting. Wondering if I was in the right place, I shouted over to a traffic attendant directing taxis to the front of the airport building.

'Is this the bus stop for Easton?'

'What honey?'

'The bus to Easton in Pennsylvania?'

'Yeah honey, all buses to Pennsylvania stop there. There should be one along shortly.'

An hour later, the bus arrived. The driver, who wore an officious-looking hat tilted on his head, took my luggage and put it in the hold. On hearing my accent he asked the question that was asked of me at least a thousand times, 'Where are you from?'

On the bus, I watched the countryside slip by. It was like watching a movie: sleep centres and furniture stores, car sales showrooms and truck showrooms, all interspersed with fast food America – Taco Bells, Subway, McDonalds, KFC.

I drifted to sleep.

I arrived in the historic town of Easton, which the Lenape Indians called Lechauwitank, 'The Place at the Forks'. However, Thomas Penn, the son of William Penn, founder of the State of Pennsylvania, must have had difficulty pronouncing Lechauwitank. When ordering the construction of a town here in 1752, he named the town Easton, after his wife's estate in England. During prohibition times, Easton was a speakeasy town where liquor flowed, brothels thrived and nightlife only dissolved with the dawn. People flooded here from New York, especially after boxing contests in Madison Square Garden. The boxing tradition has continued, as Larry Holmes, a former world boxing champion, is Easton's most famous current resident.

I walked around the town that afternoon. Beautiful old cut-stone buildings and tree-lined avenues suggested a grand past. Later, I heard that Easton was one of three places in the United States where the American Declaration of Independence was read in 1776. However, I could now sense a tough side to the town. There were boarded-up stores, graffiti and signs warning people not to loiter outside houses. A group of tattooed, muscular men congregated around a bar door and a hint of unruliness hung in the air.

Ann, a local shopkeeper, said she wasn't giving up despite the decline. 'We shop owners are working to put Easton back on the map.' She then invited me to a garlic festival taking place the following day. 'You'll love it. All sorts of food with garlic. It's being opened by Larry Holmes.'

The following morning, mizzling rain dampened the atmosphere at the garlic festival in Easton's main square. A variety of stalls belonging to local farmers, food producers and shops waited expectantly on the advancing hordes. The sizzling aroma of garlic-infused meats wafted in the air and the band, playing on the back of a trailer, tried their damnedest to raise everybody's spirits. The bandleader, a guy with bushy grey hair and a beard, kept telling garlic jokes in between 70s hits, while women dressed as 'Garlicula' went around scaring the children. I bought a delicious honeycrisp apple from a stall manned by three Amish women in their late teens.

As there was no sign of Larry Holmes, I went to catch the bus to Bethlehem, just five miles away.

§

Bethlehem felt more prosperous than Easton, with a wide variety of shops, hotels and historical sites, and a vibrant street life. I found a building with a sign on it that said 'Historic Bethlehem'. Climbing the steps, I opened the door into a large hallway where a friendly face popped around a doorway and told me to come on into the office. There, Megan, the young and enthusiastic coordinator of the centre, introduced me to the history of the town.

A group of Moravian immigrants bought four thousand acres of land in this spot in 1741, transforming it within a few years into a thriving centre of living, learning and industry.

I wanted to know how Bethlehem got its name. Megan told me that on their first Christmas in America, the immigrants' dwelling house was separated from the stable by only a thin wall. At service on Christmas Eve, the choir used the stable as their base and such was the passion of their singing that it melted the hearts of everyone who heard it. As the town had no name, they thought it appropriate to call it Bethlehem.

Megan introduced me to Richard, who took me on a quick tour of the Gemeinhaus, the first wooden building erected by the Moravian immigrants.

He said that the Moravians were wise in their choice of missionary base. The land around Bethlehem was fertile, rich with lumber and contained a plentiful supply of water. By 1750, they had established forty industries and installed the first municipal water supply in the United States, using hollowed-out tree trunks as pipes. Filled with idealism for the common good, their communal regime of work and prayer played a large part in their success.

They believed that people who share the same situation develop strong bonds. For this reason they organised their community into 'choirs', groups that lived and worked together, based on their sex, age and marital status. Thus, single, married and widowed women formed separate choirs, as did men with the same status. Children remained with their mothers for eighteen months. They were then placed in nurseries until they joined children's choirs at age four. This system freed up adults for economic and missionary work.

The Moravian community dominated life in Bethlehem until the steel industry arrived in the mid-nineteenth century, bringing other nationalities into the area and diluting their influence.

When I asked directions to the Bethlehem Steel site, Megan told me to 'cross the Fahy Bridge'. Anticipating my query she explained, 'It's named after an Irish cop, shot there in the 1960s.'

Walking across the Fahy Bridge to South Bethlehem I could see the spires of numerous churches silhouetted against the verdant slopes of the Lehigh Valley. They demonstrated the power of religion and ethnic identity in the lives of the people who immigrated here to work in Bethlehem Steel – Russians, Poles, Slovaks, Greeks and Mexicans, to name but a few. From the middle of the bridge, I viewed the brooding chimneystacks of the old steel plant, which dominated the valley below. Those sixteen-storey, black, rusting furnaces, located beside river and rail, have been an indelible symbol of this community for two centuries.

A small, stout, elderly man with a baseball cap and a rucksack on his back walking towards me suddenly hollered. 'Look!' He pointed excitedly at something behind me. I turned; a hawk, disturbed by the commotion, took off from a lamppost and swooped low over the Lehigh River towards the steel mill.

§

Dave Murphy loved to talk. Sometimes in mid-sentence he would pause, his face furrowing into intense concentration as he searched for a word or thought. Nearly seventy, retired, divorced, disconnected from his children, he lived alone in a bed-sit.

'I'm a teacher', he said, 'my last job was in Israel during the first Gulf War.'

His smile grew when he heard I was visiting Montana. His niece lived there. He insisted that I accompany him to the library so that he that he could give me her contact details. The library was his social centre, a place where he connected with the world. He had neither friends nor family in Bethlehem.

At the library, he rummaged in his rucksack and brought out notebooks and a wad of papers. From this paper maelstrom, he produced a thick black Filofax notebook into which he had filled, in small handwriting, thousands of names; his lifetime of contacts. Shuffling through the pages, he said, 'I keep rearranging this book.'

He doggedly searched through the Filofax for at least thirty minutes. I fidgeted, anxious to be on my way. Finally, he found the name, address and a possible phone number. I asked him when he was last in contact with his niece. They hadn't been in touch for years, but he earnestly insisted, 'Tell her you know me.' He then added me to his bulging contact list.

Before leaving, I asked the librarian about Bethlehem Steel. I expected a book, but she summoned a local historian. Irene had olive skin, black hair and flashing eyes. She was reared in the shadow of the chimneys. She said that the opening of the steel mills there in the mid-nineteenth century heralded the arrival of the industrial revolution.

When Micí arrived to work in the mills, he entered a world where workers laboured in brutal conditions for twelve hours a day, seven days a week with every second Sunday off. The work was dangerous. Machinery maimed and killed many; it was estimated that 10 per cent of the workforce were injured every year. Gas and dust damaged lungs and lugging heavy loads caused strangulated hernias.

One of the worst jobs was charging the furnace. This involved men standing on a wooden platform on top of the chimneystack, with only leather aprons to protect them. They fed the monster while intense heat, cinders, smoke and carbon monoxide rose from the furnace below.

It was a different story for senior management. Irene told me that when managers arrived in their luxury cars, a 'spotter' rushed out and hunted the workers out of the way to ensure an uninterrupted journey to the office. These managers were paid wages and bonuses that were generous even by today's standards.

In time, Bethlehem Steel had its own police force and medical centre, and grew to become the second biggest steel plant in the world. It flourished during the First and Second World Wars, before entering into decline and finally closing in the mid-1990s. Bethlehem steel was used in most of the big engineering ventures in American history, including the Golden Gate Bridge and the Empire State Building. Workers came from all over the world to work there and each nationality ran a specific department within the steel plant.

Irene said, with a grin, that she was 'living proof' that all of these communities eventually got together, as her background was part Italian, Greek and Portuguese.

The old steel site now covers over one hundred acres and is full of warehouses and chimneystacks falling into ruin. The plan is to turn part of the site into a casino and some of the older buildings and chimneystacks into a historical museum. Irene said that they wanted to maintain the 'historic sense of place' but combine it with a viable economic future.

I re-crossed the bridge, eager to get a close-up of Bethlehem Steel. I found my way down some steps and walked along a back street in the direction of the mill. All was quiet until I heard a racket of music and voices coming from a second-floor balcony above me. I could see lots of bobbing heads, talking, drinking, shouting and laughing. A party was in full flow in an Irish pub.

In total contrast, a line of about two hundred people came around the corner and began walking towards me. They were organised into sections of twenty people of all shapes, ages and ethnicities. At the head of each section, a person carried a placard on which one word was typed, 'PRAY'.

On hearing the racket from the drinking party, a middle-aged woman frowned with disgust.

'This is great', I thought, 'I've landed plumb in the middle of a protest against revelry.' But no, the walkers kept going on their silent way, snaking along the street until they disappeared around another corner. A person handing out leaflets followed the procession.

'What's this all about?' I asked.

'It's a Christian prayer walk open to all Christian faiths.'

I wondered afterwards, 'Why only Christian?'

I continued to the old steel mills, and it was only then that the sheer scale of the buildings became apparent. The warehouses, built of stone and brick, were the size of football pitches inside. I looked into some of them. Windows were broken and wind and rain could sweep through. Weeds grew in cracks in the floors and birds had established colonies in rafters and crevices. Despite their size, these buildings were overshadowed by the gigantic furnaces that once ate fire and belched out black and orange smoke which cast a hulking shadow over the valley and the people who lived there.

Irene had told me that there was a memorial garden to those who had died in Bethlehem Steel, so I went looking for it. I liked South Bethlehem; students mingling on steps, older people chatting outside a church, children laughing in a playground and skateboards screeching on railings. Buying food in a local bakery, the woman there told me that she enjoyed life so much that she sang every day as she baked.

In contrast to this vibrancy, the memorial garden was extremely quiet. The centrepiece was a statue of a worker levering a length of steel into the air and from whose feet spread a circular brick courtyard. Each brick bore a name such as Brady, Murphy and Crowley. Many other nationalities were represented.

To be remembered in this garden, families had to pay for the brick. If Mící had died here, I wondered if anyone would have remembered him.

He worked for a year in these steel mills before he tired of the fact that 'everyone was trying to get more out of you than the next person.' He wasn't too happy to find himself an unvalued and expendable cog in an industrial wheel turning for someone else's benefit. It was time to move on.

News of a silver mining bonanza in Montana provided impetus and hope for a better future. His cousin Jim Anthony had gone there six months previously. Now, Mící and his cousin Tom Ferry would follow. The family he stayed with, as a parting gift, furnished him with a basket of food that sustained him during the weeklong train journey across America.

§

On my return journey to Easton, two men got onto the bus. The first had a weathered face, a grey beard, friendly eyes and strong arms. He wore a lumber jacket and a yellow bandana. The second was a small, wiry man with a moustache and hard, watchful eyes. He carried a hammer in a tool belt. A feeling of unpredictability and even violence emanated from him. Both men were covered in dust after a hard day's work.

I asked the man with the yellow bandana how things were in the area.

'Times are tough and lots of people are only getting the minimum wage.'

'How much is that?'

'It's $7 an hour. You need a couple of jobs to survive and they're hard to come by now.'

'Maybe the presidential election will change things?'

'None of them are any good! They're all assholes. If Obama gets elected, he'll be shot and if McCain wins, he'll die of a heart attack. It looks like Obama unfortunately.'

The thin man smirked and interjected, 'He won't last.'

The man with the bandana pointed out the window, through the evening gloom, at all the buildings and warehouses.

'This was all farmland. I used to ride my motorbike through the cornfields. Now everywhere between New York, New Jersey and Philadelphia is all built up.' He added, 'I lived one block away from Larry Holmes. Now that's a man you could admire. He was a great fighter. Did you know he defended the world title twenty times and was the only man to knock out Muhammad Ali?'

'He was robbed in the fight with Spinks', said the thin guy animatedly.

'He won that fight clearly', said the man with the bandana.

We talked about boxing for the rest of the trip. On getting off the bus, the man with bandana said, 'We're going to bingo now.'

I went to pack for my trip by bus and rail across America.

2

Easton to Harrsiburg

Breakfast time in Easton, waiting on a connection to Harrisburg. I had always associated the Greyhound bus with the freedom of the road, and was eager to be off.

People arrived in dribs and drabs. The bus time came and went. Thirty minutes later, worried that I might have missed it, I asked a father and son who had been waiting with me if they were going to Harrisburg. They were. I paced the pavement back and forth.

A long hour later, spirits rose when someone spotted a bus heading our way. It was a false alarm. It wasn't even a Greyhound bus. A passenger went into the ticket office to enquire, but the receptionist had no news. Shortly afterwards, there was a flurry of activity when a bus stopped at a junction about seventy metres down the street. Everyone grabbed their cases and our motley crew hurried in the direction of the bus, led by a long-legged young man whose stride devoured the street. The driver must have got a shock when he saw this tidal wave of bodies heading towards him. He waited warily, his body a bulky barrier on the bottom step.

'Where y'all going?' he asked.

Every man jack of us was going to Harrisburg.

'I'm going to Allenwood', he said, 'the bus to Harrisburg will be along shortly.'

Before we could say anything else, he jumped into the driver's seat and took off down the road. We trudged back up the hill to the bus station.

Two more hours went in aimless waiting. Occasionally, somebody would go back into the ticket office, but there was never any news. I paced up and down. Some people drifted away. I kicked pebbles at imaginary goalposts. Hope dissipated and people didn't bother to look up the street anymore.

I needed to use the bathroom, but the bus station had no facilities. The receptionist told me to use the restrooms at a nearby shopping centre, 'just around the corner'. I hesitated. It would be just my luck that the bus would arrive and depart while I was away. But I needed to go. Asking the father to keep an eye on my bag, I rushed around the corner. There was no sign of any shopping centre. A saviour pointed out an obscure, unsigned, side entrance. Had I still time to go? I vacillated, but nature prevailed. I charged through the doors into the centre and found the bathroom. After the pit stop, I sprinted back. On reaching the corner, I was relieved to find everything as I had left it. Hoping no one noticed my fluster, I slowed to a casual stroll.

'This Greyhound bus service has gone to the dogs' I said to the father and son. I don't think they got the joke.

Impatience overcame me and I too went to clarify matters with the ticket receptionist. It's a bit like boys trying to fix something that's broken. Everyone has to have a go, believing he has the magic touch. When I entered, the receptionist threw her hands into the air.

'I've no idea what's happening.'

'Is there anyone you can call?'

'I've tried calling but no one knows anything. This company never keep you informed. Last week the Harrisburg bus didn't call here at all and people were left waiting all night.'

Thinking I might cut my losses, I asked, 'Is it possible to get a refund?'

'Not here. You'd have to get it from Greyhound central office.'

I didn't bother to ask her how this was to be done. Back outside, I kicked some more pebbles and thought that if this happened in Ireland, there would be hell to pay. It would be all over the media. Here, people who travelled by bus were of little consequence.

Spirits rose when the mother of the family arrived with a basket of sandwiches, which they shared with me.

When everyone had given up hope, someone pointed at a bus coming up the road.

'Is that a Greyhound bus?' he said.

It was, and it was coming toward us. Then it was going right past us. If this was it, we were nearly past caring. It was five hours late. About two hundred metres up the street, the bus stopped and started doing a U-turn, blocking traffic in both directions. It returned to the station and jerked to a stop. The driver, a tall grey-haired man with a driver's stoop, emerged. He shouted, 'Anyone for Harrisburg?'

He was nearly swamped in the charge. I asked him if he could open the luggage door, as I wanted to load my bag.

He replied, 'No you cain't, it needs a taag to go in there.'

'Where will I get a tag?'

'Try the ticket office.'

I again abandoned my bag and rushed back to the office to be confronted by a queue. I excused myself and asked the receptionist for a tag. 'We don't do those tags here', she told me.

'What?'

'There isn't usually a problem', she said.

When I returned, the driver was unmoved. 'It cain't go into luggage without a taag.'

There was no way that I wasn't getting on board, so when the driver turned his back, I dragged the bag after me into the bus. Inside, I was confronted by an animated group of passengers.

'That driver is loco', said a youngish, roundish man pointing to his head with a twisting finger.

A woman sitting behind him said, 'We went in circles around New York and two hours later ended back at the bus station from where we started.'

'He's from Georgia', said someone, as if that explained everything.

'It's his first day on the job in New York', said another, 'it's ridiculous to send out a newcomer on the route.'

I put my bag on an empty seat directly behind the driver. If he braked hard he would have to deal with the consequences! Two other people followed me onto the bus with large cases, which they humped on top of mine. This made me feel better. There's nothing worse than being the sole offender.

We reached the next town without further incident but once we entered the town, pandemonium broke out again. The Chinese woman beside me hopped up out of her seat and pushed past me, shouting in panic, 'Driver, Driver, you're going the wrong way!'

She pointed out the direction in which the bus station lay. The driver had a problem. He was on a one-way street and it wasn't possible to do a U-turn. He did the next best thing, swinging left at the next junction onto a narrow street which ran parallel to the street with the bus station. An empty carpark lay between us and station. The driver, deciding that the shortest route between any two points was a straight line, drove the bus up onto the pavement, smashing the branches of newly planted trees.

'Oh my God!' shrieked the African-American woman sitting in front of me. 'This driver is crazy. Get me off this bus!'

After much scraping and shaking, we arrived at the back of the bus station. The driver dropped some surviving passengers off before loading up with new victims. He then bumped us once more over the kerbing back onto the street.

Sitting across the aisle from me was a serene older woman in her seventies. Despite looking thin and frail, she had a strong voice. 'I started this bus journey in Nova Scotia and I'm going to Albuquerque. I do this journey and back twice a year to see friends. I love to travel by bus, particularly at this time of the year. I can see all the leaves as they change colour.'

'Did you ever think of flying?'

She pointed to the ground saying, 'Noo, I want to stay down here, and anyway, I'm not in a rush anywhere. This way, I can take my time and suit myself. If the bus is late, it makes no difference to me. Anyway, even if you're late, there's a good chance that the next connection will wait. I've never been stuck yet.' She turned to me and asked, 'Have you ever been in Albuquerque?'

'No.'

'It's beautiful. But I don't like Pittsburgh, too many high places there.'

Yes, I thought to myself, you can get lost in a city. The space between cities is of more interest.

She was right about the transport system. On arrival in Harrisburg, our bus was met by Greyhound staff who arranged onward trips for the passengers.

I planned to stay in Harrisburg for a day before going on a three-day trip by train to Whitefish, Montana. As the train and bus station were combined, I booked my train ticket and on a whim decided to stop for a night in Minot, North Dakota. I also got the name of a cheap Harrisburg motel that might have a room.

It was dark when I left. Walking down a street in the direction of the river, I became aware of a man walking behind me. He was a small Latino in his forties, hard and muscled with a chiselled face. I asked him if he knew how to get to the motel. He gave me directions in a deep voice and fell into stride beside me.

'Are you from Harrisburg?' I asked.

'Originally, but I've been working in Florida for the last few years. I was laid off and returned here. I'm homeless now and living on the street. I've had nothing to eat all day.'

'Have you family living nearby?'

'Yeah I have, but I don't have much contact with them' he replied, shrugging his shoulders.

'Can you get unemployment benefit?'

'I can, but it takes weeks to kick in. There's nothing while you wait.'

I gave him a few dollars, but was struck by the inequity; I was going to a comfortable bed and he was going to sleep on the street. He wasn't alone in this either. On the walk to the motel I saw many homeless people huddling down in doorways and back alleys.

I walked for fifteen minutes through a riverside park to reach the motel. The path was good but poorly lit. A glow came from the river on one side and yellow streetlights on the other. It created a shadowed luminosity, which filtered through the trees. I walked quickly, with a wary eye. A guy on a bicycle came towards me and passed by. I reached the motel and sighed with relief.

Next morning, I walked into town. Harrisburg, lying on the east bank of the Susquehanna River, is the capital of Pennsylvania and has a population of fifty thousand people. In the past, it was strategically important in terms of transport, war and industry. Fertile land drew many German farmers to its hinterland.

The nuclear power station Three Mile Island, site of the most serious nuclear accident in US history, is a few miles away. It was also near Harrisburg that Joseph Smith founded the Church of Jesus Christ of Latter-Day Saints, also known as the Mormons.

I set off to visit the State Capitol building, where the Pennsylvanian General Assembly sits, and found a commotion outside it. A few hundred young people were cheering and waving placards and banners. I hurried to catch the action, but was disappointed when the crowd began to disperse. I approached a group and asked them what was going on.

A youth of about fourteen, wearing a baseball cap and green jersey, said, 'We are part of a campaign against smoking in public places.'

A small girl of about six or seven, with a freckled face and earnest eyes, smiled at me.

'I spoke at it', she said.

'Well done!' I said. "You're great to talk in front of so many people.'

She nodded, her smile broadening.

'What did you say?'

She looked to a woman in her forties, who gave her permission to talk further.

'I said how smoking was bad for our health and makes us sick.'

'Yes, cigarettes make people cough a lot.'

Her mother elaborated, 'All the kids have been campaigning for this for the past five years and now Pennsylvania is the twenty-fourth state in the US to endorse the policy of no smoking in public places.'

I told them that we had successfully introduced this ban some years previously in Ireland.

'Yes we've heard about the Irish ban. You guys led the way. We hoped that our central government would do the same and establish it nationally but they wouldn't. The option we were left with was to try to do it on a state-by-state basis. We're proud that with these kids' help, we've achieved this.'

She emphasised the Irish connection by telling me that her surname was Kelly.

'We are probably related', I said, 'my grandmother was Kelly too.'

'Well it's nice to meet a long-lost relative.'

'Which of us is lost?' I laughed.

In the museum next to the Senate building, I came across another long-lost relative and famous Pennsylvanian – Grace Kelly. Her picture hung on the wall beside other famous Pennsylvanians like Jimmy Stewart, along with many people I'd never heard of.

Leaving the museum, I wandered around Harrisburg and was struck again by the numbers of solitary men hanging around on street corners and in small parks. I saw an old building with the sign 'YMCA' on it and thought that they might give me a perspective on the homeless situation. I climbed the steps and entered a large, circular reception area. I introduced myself to a woman behind the information desk and delivered a speech which I thought would elicit immediate and enthusiastic cooperation. She just pointed to another desk. 'That newsletter over there will tell you what we're doing', she said.

I persisted. 'Do you provide accommodation for homeless people here?'

'We cater for seventy-four men in our accommodation. Some of them are here years. Others leave once they get themselves sorted out.'

She began to warm to the subject. 'When their circumstances improve, they're expected to pay rent, but we never ask people to leave. If it suits them here, they can stay, though most people prefer to get their own place eventually.'

'Do homeless men on the streets use your services?'

'They must go to the mission first and ask for help there. They try to get them a suitable place, or they might end up here. We're full at the moment though.'

After leaving the centre I crossed the Walnut Street Bridge out to an island on the Susquehanna River. The bridge is known as 'Old Shaky', which might be explained by the fact that most of it was swept away in a flood in 1996. The wide and shallow Susquehanna River got its name from the Native American tribe, the Susquehannock, who lived here for five thousand years before European colonisation in the seventeenth century. Their final remnants were wiped out by a group of Scots/Irish frontiersmen called the Paxton Boys in the eighteenth century.

§

That night, a local Democratic senator appeared on television, promoting 'food banks' for the poor. Accompanying television shots showed volunteers handing out food in a local charity shop. According to the senator, the need for this kind of action was increasing, as many people 'don't know where the next meal is coming from'. He emphasised too that this charity work had nothing to do with government. Local farmers leave the corners of their fields untouched during harvesting. This is then 'gleaned' for food banks, leaving thirty-five tons of produce per year in the local county.

The senator quoted the Bible, 'When you're blessed, you should share this blessing with others.'

He said that the main beneficiaries were older people unable to survive on pensions, working people who were still below the poverty line and also those who had recently lost their jobs.

In 2007, charitable donations from people and corporations exceeded $300 billion according to the Giving USA Foundation, which tracks philanthropy across the United States. It's an impressive figure. Americans donate substantial sums to charitable causes, but there is fierce resistance to and suspicion of government involvement in catering for people's needs. The fear is that they might waste money on the undeserving poor!

§

Travelling always means waiting. It is as much part of the journey as moving from place to place. A story can inhabit the space between events more powerfully because, with silence, it has time to germinate.

The early morning train to Pittsburgh was late. The harder one waits, the slower time goes by. You notice every tick of the clock. An old African-American woman with incredible presence and poise, and a man of similar age walked towards me. The woman was tall, with a serene face, long neck and tapered, artistic fingers. She was dressed simply in a black hat and plain coat. She walked painfully and slowly with the aid of two sticks. The man walking attentively beside her was strongly built with soft eyes. They sat down on a nearby seat, exchanging quiet words and gentle laughter. After a while, the man stood up and asked her a question. She shook her head, smiling. When he left, she started to hum. The music rose unself-consciously from the depths within her. It was her soul speaking and, perhaps, the soul of generations. The tone, like a cold mournful wind, hinted at sadness and loss. I closed my eyes for a while and let the sound enter deep within me, stirring frontiers within my own frozen land.

A little while later the man came back and, taking her hand in his, they murmured to each other before lapsing into silence. She started to hum again, and its sound seemed to envelop the two of them in a blanket of common memories. The world of noise around them continued; people talking, laughing, crying, coughing and sneezing. Mobile phones rang, people came and went, children ran and slid, luggage wheels rumbled across tiled floors, newspapers rustled, soft drink cans snapped and hissed and money tinkled. They seemed oblivious of all of this.

Then the public address system joined in, announcing that the train to Pittsburgh was five minutes away. The woman pushed herself to her feet with difficulty. The man put his hand on her back, more as encouragement than help. Once standing, like an accordion stretching, she drew herself erect, taking a moment to get her balance. She then walked painfully, but still gracefully, with her two sticks across the floor. At the entrance to the door leading to the platform, they embraced quickly. Tears came into her eyes. He walked ahead of me down the ramp to the platform. When he reached it, he stopped and looked back. She was still there. He climbed aboard.

3

Harrisburg to Chicago

Trains have an appeal about them, a certain magic, a passport to a new life or a new adventure. If you are going on a long journey, there's a sense, mostly mistaken, that you can shake the dust of the past from you.

A conductor welcomed me aboard the two-story Superliner carriage on the west-bound Amtrak train. I climbed to the upper level and found a seat for the relatively short trip to Pittsburgh. I had travelled through America by many modes of transport, but this was my first time on an American train.

In my boyhood imagination, I'd had many daring adventures on them. I was thrilled to be heading west, following in the frontier footsteps of a host of miners, soldiers, homesteaders, clergy, ranchers and businesspeople who shaped the west. In a sense, it was the train that united America.

What was Mici Mac Gabhann's experience of his six-day train journey to Montana in the late nineteenth century? He got little sleep on the journey, as trains were dangerous to travel on. Even though his pockets were not 'too heavy', he had to protect his personal belongings, his little bit of food and indeed his life from the dangerous people who roamed the trains. 'Scores were being murdered', he said in his book. He was heading into frontier land where laws were weak and where the powerful prospered.

§

A shrill whistle sounded and we were off to Pittsburgh. The rail line followed the route carved by the river, which was wide and shallow with rocks visible, like stepping stones, all the way across. The train rumbled along, blowing its whistle before it came to each small settlement. The countryside was heavily wooded with glimpses of dappled autumnal sunlight flitting through to the forest floor. Fleeting images appeared. A man stood fishing in a river, his line a swirl of energy in the stillness, seemingly alone in a wilderness of wooded hills. Little towns came and went: Lewistown, Huntingdon, Altoona and a place called Tyrone. They mightn't have changed in scale much since Mící's time. An imposing wooden church stood in the middle of the forest beside a secluded village, its wooden steeple conducting prayers to the sky. On a distant hillside, you could see the first autumnal colours as the land began its retreat towards winter with one final show of splendour.

We came to an industrial town called Johnstown. The river turned dirty brown. Warehouse after grimy warehouse stood upon its banks. The chimneystacks of old mills disturbed the contour of the sky. I overheard snippets of a conversation.

'A lot of people drowned here in a great storm in 1936.'

'What happened?'

'The river burst its banks and swept people away.'

'I never knew that.'

This wasn't the first drowning tragedy in the steel town of Johnstown. On 31 May 1889, shortly after Mící passed through, two thousand two hundred people were killed or drowned out of a total population of thirty thousand. Two things caused the flood. Firstly, the town had grown rapidly; the riverbanks had been narrowed to facilitate building; and houses sprung up along the floodplain. Secondly, fourteen miles upriver, a dam had been built at Connemaugh Lake, which lay 450 feet higher than Johnstown. This lake was a fishing playground for the rich of Pittsburgh who had bought it and built summer houses around its shores. They neglected however to adequately maintain the dam.

At 4.07 that afternoon, the inhabitants of Johnstown heard a low rumbling growl, which grew to an earth-shattering roar. The dam had burst, releasing twenty million tons of water which swept down the narrow river valley, forming a surge sixty feet high and travelling at forty miles an hour. One can only imagine the impact.

Some bodies were never found; remains were still emerging from the ravelled earth five years later. It was the greatest flood tragedy in American history.

The conductor announced that we were coming to the famous 'Horseshoe Bend, with spectacular views'. When I asked him about its history, he replied, 'I don't know too much about it but I know you Irish did a lot of it.'

The Alleghany Mountains were always an obstacle for the railways, forming a seemingly impenetrable barrier to the expanding nation. They are five hundred miles long and a hundred miles wide, with an average height of two and a half thousand feet. The Lenni Lenape Native Americans called the range the 'Endless Hills' as they seemed to stretch forever in wave after wave of wrinkled ridges.

A railroad engineer called Thompson developed a horseshoe design for crossing the most difficult part of the range and 450 Irish immigrants, using pick and shovel, built it over four years. They were paid 25 cents each for a twelve-hour day.

The route was of such strategic importance that the Germans actually tried to sabotage it in 'Operation Pastorius' during the Second World War. They realised that if they could destroy the railroad at Horseshoe Curve it would dramatically affect the American war effort. Ultimately however, the saboteurs were betrayed, arrested and executed long before the curve came under any serious threat.

To celebrate the fact that the Irish built this stretch of railroad, rain started to bucket out of the heavens. Visibility disappeared and all I could see were the lights of cars on the road below. It was dark when we got into Pittsburgh and we had to wait there for our connection to Chicago for four hours.

§

An older woman collapsed heavily into the seat beside me and pulled out the leg support. 'That's better', she said, with a sigh, as she sat back, legs stretched out. She was small with determined brown eyes, bottled red hair and a lime-green dress. She was travelling to Omaha, Nebraska to see her son for his fiftieth birthday.

'How long will you stay?'

'One week. I always say, one week a guest, two weeks a pest.'

'I must remember that', I laughed.

The seat extension for my legs didn't work properly. I couldn't get my feet in a comfortable position like the woman beside me. I noticed her swollen ankles.

'Long journey?' I asked.

'Yep. I come from the Alleghanys, way up there in the Boonies. I'm twenty-five miles from the nearest town and shops. It takes a while to get anywhere.'

'There's plenty of wildlife up there?'

'Yep, there's wild critters in the hills and forests. Bears, coyotes, cougars.'

'Your pets wouldn't be safe then?'

'They surely wouldn't. Last fall when in the kitchen, I heard a scratching noise at the screen door. I thought it might be one of the cats. When I went out to let her in I saw this big bear on my porch. He must've smelled the sausages. I screamed so loudly that he bolted upright and hit his head on the awning. He scared himself and ran away, thankfully.'

After a while, she confided, 'I had a big argument with myself about whether to take this trip to Omaha because I have a daughter who is sick.' Tears came but she continued. 'It started some time ago with fainting fits. She'd get over them, but after a time they became more severe. They then found out that her lungs were collapsing due to an infection and they've put her into an induced coma. I went in every day to the hospital and sat beside her, but I'm not allowed to speak to her or touch her. She's only forty-four.'

'That's tough.'

'One day I stroked the back of her hand. The nurse told me not to, because they want her condition stable to find out what's wrong. The doctor told me to go see my son. He said I could do nothing for her there. I took their advice, because I've not seen him in a long time. This country is so big.'

§

The railway station in Chicago is like an airport, with shops and restaurants on different levels and bustling lines of people gathering and dispersing. Tired after a night tossing and turning on the carriage seat, I decided to comfort myself with a scrumptious breakfast. When my plate arrived with one slice of toast I was dismayed.

'Is there any chance of more toast?' I asked.

'Where are you from?' was the reply, as if this had an important bearing on the request. We chatted for a few minutes. This seemed to do the trick.

'Would you like one or two more slices?'

'Two', I said thankfully.

I sat where I could watch the world, feeling the invigorating charge of strong coffee. Afterwards, I pulled my case to the rest room. There, I became aware of a sturdy shape beside me trying unsuccessfully to coax water out of the faucet. He pressed and turned everything to see if water would flow, all to no avail.

Having encountered the same problem in the past, I told him, 'Stick your hands under the spout. Water will come automatically.'

'Jaysus. Modern technology', he replied.

It suddenly dawned on us that we had the same accent.

'Seamus', he said offering his hand, 'I'm from Buncrana.'

Seamus was bald and barrel-chested with a round red face and a moustache. An aura of openness and cheeriness emanated from him. He collected his rucksack and guitar and we returned to the café.

'I'm going to stay with a friend of mine who owns a bar in San Francisco', he told me. 'I might do some gigging for him if it suits. I like playing folk, blues or country rock. We get a lot of Irish there. Hold on until I get a tablet.'

He searched in a pocket, brought out two tablets and downed them.

'I've problems with my stomach since my treatment for cancer. I'm better now but I've to keep taking medication. I'd a few tough years there. I'm also an alcoholic, but I'm off the drink for years now, thanks to Alcoholics Anonymous.'

When some spilled mayonnaise left a stain on his T-shirt, he asked me to mind his things while he changed.

When he returned he said, 'You came when I needed something. A higher power sent you.'

'A what?'

'In Alcoholics Anonymous, we believe that there's a higher power which helps us when we specially need it. You've got to be open to it though. Before you came along, I was thinking of going for a drink. I was telling myself, one would do no harm, though I know in my heart, I'll not stop at that.'

'That's the first time I ever heard of the higher power.'

He produced a book called *The Twelve Steps*. 'That's my bible.' A little later he asked, 'Are you carrying much money?'

'I'm carrying a good bit, but I took my laser card as well.'

'I've four thousand dollars with me but I've no card. I carry it in a bag above my balls, a place where I hope nobody can find it.'

'People might think you've enormous tackle!'

'Jaysus, we shouldn't be talking about money in public', he said, indicating a young man at the next table who seemed to be listening to our conversation.

Seamus remembered the story of Micí Mac Gabhann from school. 'The bit I remember was the fight with the Connemara man and how he shut him up with a slap.'

When we parted company, Seamus said to me, 'A higher power sent you. It'll come to you when you need it too. That's the way it works.'

4

Chicago to Minot

I boarded the Minot train and ambled downstairs to the snack carriage. There I met Amy, a confident red-headed woman in her mid-twenties. She was the only customer and didn't seem surprised when I asked to sit beside her. There's an informality in train travel that allows people to cross barriers easily. We watched the fertile Wisconsin countryside slip by as we talked. Her job as an agricultural scientist involved visiting farms and telling grizzled farmers how they might improve their anti-pollution efforts.

'It ain't easy being a woman sometimes, telling farmers how and when to spread fertilisers and talk to them about septic tanks, especially when you're young. They think you're wet behind the ears.'

'What sort of crops do they grow here?'

'Soya beans and corn mainly. We also grow wheat, oats, cranberries and tobacco.' She added, 'Some people in this neck of the woods creep into the middle of cornfields to plant marijuana. Because they're not growing it on their own land, they can't be prosecuted. The police send out helicopters and spotter planes to identify sites and trap them when they're harvesting.'

She laughed and shook her head, 'They don't need planes to spot marijuana. It grows taller than corn. It's visible from the roadside long before harvesting. The police have to be careful when they arrest someone because marijuana grows wild alongside creeks and in the sides of fields. They have to catch them in the act.'

'And people go to the bother of trying to plant it when they can pick it naturally?'

'Yeah, it's a bit strange I suppose, but they would need to know where to look for it.'

'Look!' she said, pointing at a large, blood-red lake in a field.

'They're harvesting cranberries there. When the berries are ripe, a machine shakes them off the bushes. They then flood the area, the berries float to the top and they're pumped onto a truck.'

Later, I met a tall man with black glasses standing at the back of the observation carriage.

'Where are you going?' he asked.

'To Minot.'

'I'm getting off there too. What in the name of God brings you to Minot?' he asked, giving me a sceptical look.

'I heard so much about North Dakota as a boy', I said, 'I thought I should at least set foot on its soil when passing.' Thinking I needed more reasons, I added, 'and Minot is situated near to the middle of the North American continent.'

He looked suitably unimpressed. Steve ran his own book-selling business. He sourced rare books for clients and 'charged them handsomely for the privilege'. Laughing, he said that most of his clients could find the books online if they put their minds to it, 'and at a much cheaper price too'.

One notable thing about living in North Dakota, he said, was the continuous westerly wind blowing across the plains, rarely at less than thirty miles per hour.

'That wind drives many people mad here.' Shaking his head he continued, 'It certainly applies to most of the guys who struck it rich in the oil boom. They haven't learned how to spend their money yet. They still drive around in battered pick-ups, dressed in old overalls.'

'Is there much oil here?'

'There's enough oil there to last us decades. It's deep down and hard to get to, but technology is improving all the time. They have drills now that can go deeper and move sideways as well.'

I asked him about Minot.

'Minot is prospering because of oil and the air base. It's a safe place with little or no crime. When I leave home, I don't have to lock my doors. A neighbour keeps an eye on the place. Where are you staying?'

'Don't know, I'm sure I'll find a motel.'

'I would ask you to stay with me but getting you in for the early morning train would be a problem. I'll give you a lift to the motel from the station if that suits you?'

'That's great.'

Night closed in and I blessed my good luck that I had two seats to myself. I could curl up as if in bed. Why pay for a sleeper carriage at nearly one hundred dollars when you can have this? I got two pillows from the attendant and settled myself with blankets and hat for insulation. It seemed like an instant later when a touch awakened me. I looked up blearily at an athletic woman standing above me, saying something unintelligible.

'What?'

'I think this is my seat.'

'Sorry', I mumbled, shuffling back to my own seat. I'd forgotten that trains stopped at stations in the middle of the night.

§

Katy had served in the American military, then resigned, married an Icelandic man and went to live in Iceland. We found common interest in cycling and kayaking. She had even cycled in Iraq.

'Was it not dangerous?' I asked, imagining an American soldier cycling along, dodging bullets and bombs.

'I cycled in the Baghdad Green Zone in temperatures of up to 120 degrees in full uniform, flak jacket, helmet and gun slung over my shoulder. It was generally safe.'

She told me that in their spare time, soldiers also liked to go fishing. 'Saddam and his son Uday had ornamental lakes near their love palaces, which were all inter-connected. The area was known as Little Venice. Saddam stocked these lakes with many varieties of fish. Most soldiers are country boys who grew up fishing. It helps them escape from everything, even though they had to throw the fish back in. The lakes were toxic.'

'A soldier's life isn't easy, I suppose?'

'No, and it's not good for the soul either.'

Early the following morning, I stirred out of an uneasy slumber and shuffled to the observation carriage, hoping for a glimpse of the dawn. There were others there with the same idea, all wrapped up and shivering in the cool air. I settled down to wait. It was too early to talk to anyone.

Soon, an intense, red orange filled the pre-dawn Minnesotan sky and suffused the landscape with magic and colour. In the distance, a dark strand of spectral trees provided the only contrast between plain and sky. Cornfield after endless cornfield flowed by, followed by fleeting images: isolated farm houses and barns; a village with a solitary car moving up the street; a steely grey stream; a graveyard full of white crosses; a pick-up truck speeding along a dirt track, throwing up a cloud of dust; tractors, lights glaring, out harvesting the plains. The intensity of sky waned and other colours started to appear; warm oaten colours of ripe grain, intense green alfalfa grass, autumnal hues on the occasional stand of trees, and patches of light blue and aquamarine in the sky. Then, like an emerging God, the sun appeared as a golden globe at the edge of the eastern plain. I turned around and looked out the window to the west. The dark train-shadow about a quarter of a mile wide galloped across the plain with us. I watched it for a few minutes as it glided over small hills and bluffs, across cornfields and houses. It touched everything but affected nothing.

Flocks of small birds with energetic wings flashed low across the surface of the plain. My heart responded and my being lightened. What a great way to travel.

The train announcer called out, 'Next stop, Minot, North Dakota.'

§

'Those damn m****r f****rs', said Steve, his face glowing with anger.

'What happened?' I asked.

From inside his 4X4, Steve yelled, 'Some jerks have nicked my radio and cassette player.'

'Crime-free Minot', I thought to myself and said, 'God that's awful.'

Steve searched the jeep to see what else might have been stolen. 'That's a relief', he said, holding up a box of books and CDs, 'they didn't touch these. Some of them are irreplaceable.'

'That's good', I said, searching for words.

'They must've been disturbed', he said, 'or they were stealing to order. It shows you, there are bad apples in every box.'

'Are you going to ring the police?'

'There's no point.'

After a moment's reflection, he changed his mind. 'I might have to report it to claim insurance.'

After finishing the necessary phone calls, in a better humour, he asked me, 'Fancy something to eat?'

'Sure do.'

'We'll go to Denny's Diner. They serve a great breakfast.'

We drove onto the main street. The four-lane highway rose away from us on both sides, flowing through the town, following the contours of the rolling plains.

'Just look at that', said Steve, pointing to extensive road works on the northerly part of the road, 'they always start digging up perfectly good roads at this time of the year, just to spend their yearly budget. It's such a waste. That road was finished last year. Now look at it! Nonsensical!'

Denny's Diner was populated with truck drivers, retired couples and working men with padded check shirts and baseball hats. The smell of coffee was good. We ordered bacon, eggs and hash browns. Steve came to North Dakota from Florida, he told me. There could hardly be a greater contrast between the two states.

'I came here to get some peace after my divorce', he said, 'I guess I've lots of that here. I get up and turn on the coffee and the computer and both are on the go all day. I live online. I keep myself to myself here, except for a few neighbours. My best mates are my two dogs. I'm looking forward to seeing them again. A fortnight is a long time to be away from a dog.'

Breakfast over, Steve insisted on helping me search for a motel. We finally found one about two miles outside of town on the far side of the road works. Good deed performed, Steve departed with a friendly beep.

Walking back into town, I was reminded why walkers are nearly an extinct species in America. No provision had been made for pedestrians at the road works, so I was forced to scramble for half a mile on a rough earthen bank to avoid traffic. I then continued past the train station until I reached the Scandinavian Heritage Park. This park, referred to as the jewel of Minot, was constructed to honour the contribution of the many Scandinavian people who flocked to the Midwest and helped build America. A Norwegian five-storey wooden stave church that looked to me like a flying dragon dominated the park. Sitting there, I saw an enormous brown plane climbing so slowly into the sky, it looked like it might stall. It was a B52 bomber.

Later, someone told me, 'When one of those boys takes off, the whole place shakes.' I shuddered at the thought of its dark potential.

That evening, in the local bar, everyone was riveted to television screens, playing bingo. I sat beside a guy with a scarred cheekbone, tattoo and moustache. He was definitely not the type of person you would see playing bingo in Ireland. Luck didn't go his way. He banged the table and scratched his head when each round of numbers was called. Game over, he downed his beer and departed.

I eavesdropped on a conversation between middle-aged women behind me. These were definitely the type of women you would see at bingo in Ireland and they were discussing Daniel O'Donnell, of all people. I jumped up and said hello, telling them that I was Daniel's neighbour! With much jocularity and pride the women showed me pictures on their phones of them posing with Daniel. They told me that they attend Daniel's concerts all over the US. Two of them said they were going 'on pilgrimage' to Daniel's home place in Donegal, and both threatened to visit me as well. And I thought that I was the first Donegal man in Minot!

§

Minot's existence is inextricably linked to the railway. The railroad magnate James J. Hill pushed the Great Northern Railway across the plains in a race to get to the west coast, but had to stop for the winter in 1886, leaving all of his workers stranded in the middle of North Dakota. A tented city of five thousand people sprung up overnight. Because of the speed with which this encampment was established, it was named 'Magic City'. Why would anyone subsequently decide to call the town Minot, when it already had a more interesting name? Well, it helped that Henry Minot was an investor in the railroad and a personal friend of Hill.

The next morning I left, dragging my case behind me. Everything went fine until I came to the roadworks. It was impossible to step aside on that narrow traffic lane with a case in tow. There was only one thing for it. Waiting until the lights on my side turned red, I went to the top of the queue and when the lights turned green, I started walking. The only way past was to run over me. A few of the cars started hooting but I ignored them, and after some minutes, I got to the far side. What people in the waiting cars thought, when they saw a stream of traffic coming towards them, all following a man pulling a case, is anyone's guess.

5

Minot to Whitefish, Montana

The landscape out of Minot rolled, with lots of small mounds and bluffs. Occasional small lakes materialised, on one of which some optimistic soul had built a small pier for a boat. The soil got poorer; the landscape, a hungry brown with splashes of green. We passed a single oil derrick nodding away in the landscape, and a few gravel pits appeared as scratches on the skin of the land. Near a small ranch house, horses galloped away from the approaching train. We passed a ghost town with a ruined church, embers of life long dead here. The Great Plains, similar to rural areas the world over, are becoming increasingly depopulated, not that very many ever lived here in the first place. They are now an insipid shadow of what they once were, even when Mici crossed them.

What's the point of travel if one can't time travel as well? So I took as my guide to life on the plains a man who rode them often – General George Custer.

His first task was to teach me to ride a horse. That took a virtual second. I chose a rangy mustang, having read about how tough they were in cowboy books. As we rode off, I pointed at a ridge, 'I thought the Plains were flat.'

'Well son [he's much older than I], most people think that, but if we start from the centre of the Great Plains, we'll see ridge after ridge, fifty to five hundred feet high, stretching out in front of us like immovable waves upon an ocean, for a thousand miles.'

We topped a ridge and we saw buffalo moving northwards in a single file. The line seemed to have no beginning or end.

'Why are they moving like that?'

'That's the thing that surprises a fella. The dominant male leads, because he's the most powerful and has knowledge of the landscape. A buffalo trail is only ten inches wide.'

'Does he have to mate with all these females?' I said, indicating the seemingly endless line.

'He might have some help in that department', he laughed, 'but only after he picks his own harem. Do you see that depression in the soil?' He pointed to a hollow about ten feet wide and about a foot deep.

'Yep.'

'That there's a wallow. It's created by a buffalo bull in springtime, pawing the soil to get rid of grass. In this way he challenges a rival bull to fight. The winner takes the wallow and the harem. A wallow is really a buffalo pleasure resort. It not only enhances rights to females, it also gives him the benefit of being able to roll and get rid of vermin, and the freshly turned soil helps to cure wounds. Wallows are plentiful in the plains. It's my estimation that there's between one and three in every acre. When it rains, wallows fill up with water, as all the buffalo activity compacts the soil. Indeed many travellers have reason to be thankful for wallows, as they often contain water when the creeks run dry. Can you notice anything else about them?'

I always hate it when someone asks me a puzzle. I shook my head.

Custer rubbed his hand through his mane of hair. 'Look at all those gadflies and hoards of mosquitoes. This stagnant water creates ideal conditions for flies. The worst of the lot is the buffalo fly. Thin-skinned animals like horses will stampede to escape from them. The buffalo is lucky; its shaggy coat withstands the attack.'

'Those darn pesky gnats are real irksome' I said, practicing my American.

He ignored my efforts.

'Nature always looks for a balance, and wherever you've swarms of flies, there are also multitudes of starlings to feed on them. I've seen starlings perched on cavalry horses, from neck to tail, eating any fly that came near.'

'Where are you going after this?'

'I'm going up by the Little Big Horn.'

He sat ramrod straight in his saddle and his eagle eyes focused on something far away. He pointed in a westerly direction, 'Can you see the mirage over yonder?'

I gazed across the landscape and saw what looked like a war party of Native Americans, galloping across the Plains.

'Is that really a mirage?'

No answer. When I turned around, there was no one there. I peered into the easterly sun and through the glare, I thought I made out the hazy image of a horseman with flowing blonde hair, galloping away in the distance.

I shouted after him, 'I wouldn't go near the Little Big Horn if I were you!'

§

A small, thin woman with a weather-beaten face sat down beside me in the observation carriage. Lynn had brown, thinning hair and kept fiddling with the clasp of her handbag. She opened it up and brought out a small perfume bottle and a bag of hard sweets. Offering a sweet with a bandaged hand, she told me that she was travelling to visit her sister.

'My parents had sixteen kids and I had six. I've drifted apart from all of them. They don't want anything to do with me. My sister is the only one of my kin that I get on with now. She's always glad to see me, because she needs to get a break from her family. I take her out for a few beers.'

'What's it like to live in North Dakota?'

'It's all right, except that the cops make your life a hell here. I was done for DUI by them.'

'What's DUI?'

'It's driving under the influence. Cops here are always looking out to fill their quota at the beginning, middle and end of the month. There's only one week in the month when they leave you alone.'

She went on. 'The best week in North Dakota is when the Devil's Run is on. People show off their old cars. There's a big festival for a week. Lots of fun, eating and drinking. The cars go on tours to different places. If you're interested in a hot-rod car, Minot is the place to come in May. Parties every night.'

I gazed out at the vastness of the Great Plains and thought about how they had changed since Custer's time. The native grasses, buffalo and wildlife had largely disappeared. Now, grain is grown to feed the masses of people and animals that wander the earth. It's a type of agriculture that's oil dependent. You wonder whether it can survive into the future. Oil-based fertilisers preserve the soil's productiveness and all aspects of grain production are mechanised, with the minimum of human labour. One harvester has the same capacity as hundreds of horses and perhaps thousands of men. As long as oil continues to flow, the machines will continue to churn out product. The now-exhausted soil is forced into doing what it doesn't want to do. Environmentalists now say that 50 per cent of the plain's topsoil has disappeared since the arrival of the white man.

I heard someone say, 'We are in Montana now.' Montana is the fourth largest state in the Union, four times the size of Ireland, but with a population of only one million. It's a state of two parts: two-thirds prairie and one-third dominated by the Rocky Mountains. Montana is regarded in America a bit like Donegal is in Ireland – remote and beautiful.

For me, Montana was a place of magic, the home of the cowboy and the Native American. The Blackfeet, Sioux, Nez Perce and Shoshone live there. Reputedly a place of physical grandeur, featuring the mighty Missouri River, the Bitterroots, and the Yellowstone and Glacier National Parks, I felt elated at the thought of spending some time exploring it.

As I stared across the prairie, lost in my own thoughts, a long-haired man asked if he could sit beside me. He had intense brown eyes and a long scar down one cheek. He asked, 'Are you Irish?'

'Yes.'

'I heard you speaking earlier and thought that I'd like to talk with you. My name is Terry Clark. I'm of Scots/Irish descent.'

Terry worked for a Californian company that specialised in salvaging sunken submarines and other shipwrecks. He would go anywhere in the world at a moment's notice.

'My girlfriend doesn't like this job of mine, because I can be away for quite a while. We're now thinking of moving to North Dakota.'

I wondered why anyone would leave sunny California for the cold, windy climate of North Dakota.

'That'll be a change', I said.

'Yeah, but California is too crowded and North Dakota is where my people, the Métis, come from.

'The Métis?'

'Métis are the descendents of Scots/Irish fur trappers who moved into the Great Lakes area early in the eighteenth century. The tribal peoples who lived there at the time were the Cree and the Ojibwa.

They got on well because both sides were interested in trade. The Indians were interested in tools and weapons and the trappers were interested in fur. In time, the trappers started to live with women from the tribes and benefited a lot from their traditional knowledge. We've our own culture and language. It's called Bungee and it's a mix of Gaelic, Cree, Ojibwa and French. It nearly died out but we're trying to revive it. Can you speak Gaelic?'

'Yes, a bit.'

'Many people ask me if I speak Gaelic, and I'm embarrassed to admit that I can't. It motivated me to take Irish Gaelic classes in California.'

As part of pursuing his Scots/Irish identity, Terry had bought twenty kilts and sporrans. At over a thousand dollars an outfit, it was a considerable investment.

'I've bought bagpipes too and I'm taking classes in them. My aim is to set up a small business, dressing up and playing bagpipes at events. I think a lot of people would enjoy the spectacle.'

He told me that the traditional lands of the Métis included the Red River Valley and parts of Manitoba, Minnesota and North Dakota.

'The Métis living in Canada are recognised officially as a tribal people but the Indian Council in the US won't recognise us because they have a rule that qualification for tribal status requires a person to have more than 50 per cent Native American blood. That's impossible for us.'

'You have a rich history.'

'Yes. In the eighteenth and early nineteenth century our people, both men and women, carried furs from Canada to Minneapolis on carts over what were called the Red River Trails. It took about two months to get there and the same to get back. During the journey, the drivers usually slept under the carts.'

Later, an athletic girl in her mid-twenties sat down beside me in the observation carriage. She wore a colourful knitted jumper, hiking trousers and a blue headband that tied back long, fair hair. She started reading a book that clearly gripped her.

Later, when she laid it aside, I inquired what it was. 'Something by Kierkegaard', she replied. I'd heard of him, but that was all.

'He was a Danish philosopher and also a theologian. I enjoy reading his books.'

'What's interesting about him?'

'Well, he believed we should live our lives with passion in everything we do. I believe that I should live my life with real passion and commitment. Kierkegaard felt that sometimes religion or the rules of society limit us by trying to make us conform. Instead we should celebrate our uniqueness.'

She told me that her name was Ingrid, her parents were Swedish and she had one brother. She had landed her dream job in a wilderness park in California, and had quit her old job to take it up but, while packing for California, her prospective employers informed her that they weren't filling the post because of a cut in funding. It meant that she was homeless and jobless.

'That's awful.'

'No, it's a good thing. It lets me concentrate on looking for something I can be really passionate about and also to take another qualification. In the meantime, I'm crashing in a friend's apartment and looking for a waitressing job. That will keep me going until I figure out what's the future. I would love to own a small piece of land to take care off. I hope that it'll happen before I'm thirty.'

We spotted the Rocky Mountains on the horizon, but at that distance, they had an ephemeral quality about them. They could have been mountains, plains, clouds or indeed the sky.

The mountains spurred Ingrid to tell me about how she and a group of friends climbed four peaks in the Rockies in one day and camped there for a week. She said that she had 'floated outside time' for a while. She was a person comfortable with silence and only spoke when she had something to say. She talked about nature, her assignments, her beliefs and how established religions had lost contact with important values.

A Vedic sage once said, 'If you have the fire of soul, it is reflected in the shining of your eyes.' As Ingrid talked about her love of nature, I felt the truth of those words and felt too a twinge of remorse that I hadn't applied myself with sufficient commitment to our environment. Sometimes we think we have forever, but time marches relentlessly onwards.

We came to a town which seemed to have been dropped incongruously in the middle of the plains, full of small, prefabricated houses, some of which seemed to be deserted or in disrepair. Perhaps the route of the train presented an unflattering view.

We pulled in at the station. This was Browning, the main town on the Blackfeet tribal reservation. As a solitary elderly man with long, black hair disembarked, his eyes lifted and met mine. I resolved then to someday revisit Browning.

The Rocky Mountains spread out in front of us as far as the eye could see in either direction. Clouds and snowstorms played with the rays of the evening sun, creating wondrous patterns amidst the mountain peaks. In the foreground, the oaten-coloured plains were speckled with Black Angus cattle, for which the snow-capped mountains formed an impressive backdrop.

It was getting late, and now it became a race to reach the mountains before darkness descended. We were approaching Glacier National Park, a part of the Rockies, supposedly one of the most beautiful places in North America. We sat, hoping against hope that the light wouldn't desert us before we got there. When you think like that, fate usually conspires to produce the opposite. The darkness enveloped everything and no matter how intently we peered, our eyes couldn't pierce the gloom. Spectacular mountain views lay shrouded from view. The darkness blinded us, until the lights of Whitefish appeared in the distance.

6

Whitefish and Flathead Reservation

'It's not fair they've a car', I muttered, having spent a forlorn hour trundling my case down the dimly lit streets of Whitefish. The four motels I had tried had all been full.

'The Canadians are in town', I was told.

This motel was my last chance, and as I approached the car park, a car passed me and pulled up in front of reception. A couple got out. I quickened my stride, but my contrary case wobbled and then somersaulted on the uneven surface. Cursing, I righted it, but the couple beat me to the door. We squeezed into the reception area, a box about seven feet square. An overweight young receptionist sitting behind a cramped counter dragged her listless eyes from a small television.

The news was good. There were two rooms available. Formalities speedily completed, she turned her attention back to television.

The following morning, the receptionist was still watching TV, a mug of steaming coffee encased in her fingers.

'Gosh are you still here?' I asked.

Her eyes livened a little.

'No, I start at six in the morning.'

'You work a long day.'

'I start at six in the morning and work until ten at night.'

'Sixteen hours! You must've tomorrow off then?'

'No, I work six days. I get Tuesdays off. I use it to catch up with the housework and spend some time with the children.'

As I left, the television blared out an advertisement for shampoo, featuring a smiling woman whose hair bounced as she walked.

Outside in the cool sunshine, I was exhilarated by the view of the mountains. These weren't the high Rockies, just minnows of seven or eight thousand feet, but I decided in any case to hike to the top during my stay. My immediate priority however was to rent a car, to follow

Micí's trail around Montana. My luck was in, as there was a car rental centre opposite the motel. A slim man in a brown suit welcomed and then shocked me with his quote for a three-week rental.

I thought the tourist office in town might have a list of car rental agencies but, when I arrived, it was closed. While I gaped in the window, a small, round, energetic man with an engaging grin emerged from the estate agent's office next door and said, 'You look like a man in bother, can I help?'

When I explained my story, he ushered me into his office. 'I sometimes cover for the tourist office when they're closed on a Saturday', he said, 'I'll sort you out.'

'It's my lucky day you're open.'

'I work every day to get away from the wife', he joked.

When I told Bill about the price quoted earlier, he shook his head. 'Daylight robbery.' He picked up the phone. 'I have my own contacts. We'll see what we can do.'

He dialled a number and passed me the phone. The price quoted wasn't much of an improvement. Bill shook his head. With one failure under our belts we phoned the next company. The owner said he was 'half Irish'.

'That's good', I said, 'half Irish means half price.'

Bill laughed and gave me the thumbs up. My patriotic plea however failed to produce a reduced price. After more phone calls, it appeared that a price cartel existed. Bill, however, wasn't giving up.

'I've one more contact.'

The owner of this company was part Irish too and he quoted a price half the rate of his competitors, albeit for an older car.

'If it gets me from A to B, I'll take it.'

Bill popped up beaming from his chair and clapped me on the back, saying, 'I knew we'd get a deal.'

The word 'we' impressed me.

Whitefish is a lively tourist town. In a downtown art gallery, I met a red-headed artist called Rusty. Her eyes lit up when she heard I was Irish. I asked her about the local Native American reservations. She told me there were two: the Flatheads to the south and the Blackfeet across the Rockies to the east. The Flatheads were the third richest reservation in the country and were what she classified as 'Plateau Indians', who lived on uplands and had a horticultural and river tradition.

'They even grew tobacco', she said. In comparison, the Blackfeet tribal people who lived on the Great Plains came from a more nomadic hunting tradition and were renowned warriors and horse people.

'The Blackfeet Reservation is a lot poorer and there's lots of "attitude". You can expect trouble if you go there.'

'Why is that?'

'Drink and drugs', she replied.

'Do many Native American artists exhibit here?'

'Native American artists never show their art in Whitefish, though we're ideally placed, halfway between the two reservations. Native artists go straight to super stardom, such is the demand for their work. They get big money in large galleries in Santa Fé.'

Later, while waiting on my food at a nearby café, I read an historical pamphlet on the history of Montana. If you're a Native American in Montana, your roots go back twelve thousand years. When the Native people encountered the first white men, they could have had little idea of what was ahead of them. The discovery of America ushered in an era of intense competition between the superpowers of the time, France, Britain and Spain. The Hudson Bay Company, one of the first corporate entities established on the stock market, was granted a monopoly by the British Crown, backed up by British military might, to extract wealth from the new frontier.

The following morning, I prepared to walk ten miles by road and trail from Whitefish to the top of 'Big Mountain'. If Mící were with me, he would think it foolhardy to expend such energy unnecessarily. I, however, enjoyed the feel of walking up that mountain, the strain of the slope against my legs and the raised level of my breathing. I didn't meet bears or wild cats but a few encounters with wildlife stood out. Walking through a narrow, straight piece of the trail with tall trees on each side, a raven flew straight towards me at head height. When it neared me, it nonchalantly rose above my head with a guttural call. A shiver went down my spine and my scalp tingled with the strangeness of the encounter. The raven flew high up and over the trees, disappearing from view. Later, I spotted a small bird hanging upside down on a tree trunk, probing for insects. He walked down the tree head-first. I thought initially it was a bird doing yoga but afterwards I found out that it was a nuthatch, a bird that likes to feed upside down.

Half way up the mountain, a feeling of aloneness took hold of me. I felt disconnected. I stopped beside a clump of tall, quivering aspens. Looking to the sky, I watched two ravens wheeling high in the air near a mountain peak; even they were connected. A gentle breeze arose and the rattle of aspen leaves sounded like the patter of light rain on a tent. A cascade of yellow leaves drifted down in a mesmerising flurry. Then, as if by magic, the aspens fell silent. I could see only one leaf trembling. My phone shuddered in my pocket. It was a text from my daughter. The world felt connected again.

I ate lunch on top of the mountain and watched smoke rising straight into the air along the Flathead Valley. The deep blue of Whitefish Lake seeped through a green haze of conifer trees. You could see the snow-capped Rocky Mountains of Glacier Park in the distance. What could be better than this?

That night, before bed, I read over the Indian prayer that I saw in Whitefish Museum. It began:

O' GREAT SPIRIT,
whose voice I hear in the winds,
and whose breath gives life to all the world, hear me!
I'm small and weak; I need your strength and wisdom.

The following morning, with thoughts like thunder, I paced around my bedroom. I'd been trying to contact the car rental agency for one hour without success. I finally got through to the owner, Don, at 10.15 a.m.

'Ahh the Irishman. Are you ready for the road?'

I thought to myself, 'I'm ready for the last hour', but I replied, 'I sure am.'

'I'll pick you up in fifteen minutes.'

Forty minutes later a tall, rangy man with a moustache and a disarming grin walked up to me in the motel. 'Are you the Irishman?'

I thought to myself, 'There must be more than a bit of Irish in you too, if your time-keeping is anything to go by.' I nodded and we introduced ourselves.

When we pulled into his garage, he showed me the rental car, a small, cream Dodge looking forlorn amidst the splendour of surrounding cars. The twinge of disappointment I felt heightened when I saw 100,000 miles on the clock. I wondered if I might get stuck in the back end of nowhere. Don's radar must have been working, because he said, 'This is a great machine. I've never had a moment's trouble with it.'

Remembering a name from a cowboy book, I named my new steed 'Crusty'.

My first planned stop was the library in Kalispell. On finding it, I climbed the steps to two impressive wooden doors that refused to budge when I pushed. Puzzled, I stood back and looked around. A short, thoughtful-looking man with a heavy black jacket and a colourful box hat sat at a picnic table in front of the library.

He looked up and said, in a soft voice, 'It's closed. It's Columbus Day. I thought it was open too.'

On hearing I was Irish, he said, 'I'm proud to be a 100 per cent third-generation Norwegian.'

He was from a Quaker farming tradition. His ancestors, who left Norway because of religious persecution in the nineteenth century, were enticed to America by the prospect of acquiring free land. He told me, 'Did you know that the Norwegians were the first Europeans to reach North America?'

'No, it was the Irish', I indignantly replied, 'St Brendan the Navigator, an Irishman, was the first.'

A lively debate ensued on whether the honour lay with St Brendan in the sixth century or with a guy called Eriksson who landed in Newfoundland via Greenland at the end of the first millennium. Though we couldn't agree, it seemed an appropriate discussion for Columbus Day.

I drove south along Flathead Lake, the largest freshwater lake in western America, which is bounded by the Mission Mountains on its eastern shore and by the Salish Mountains on the west. My destination was Polson, a town on the Flathead Indian Reservation. My interest in the place had been stimulated by Mící's accounts of the Flathead tribe's tribulations in his book. About halfway through the sixty-mile journey, I entered the reservation. Houses here seemed to have been tossed into the sky before landing haphazardly, facing in every direction. It reminded me of Gweedore, where Mící came from. Feeling at home in this apparent anarchy, I crossed the bridge into Polson.

In the first motel I came to, I received enthusiastic handshakes from the owner, Suzanne, a woman with a strong face, and from Kay, the thin, dark-haired Native American receptionist. Suzanne and her husband bought the motel when they moved to Polson from Nebraska. 'It's such a beautiful place to live', she said, 'Look at that!' She pointed at the lake and the backdrop of high mountains. 'Who could ask for more?'

I asked what it was like to live on the reservation.

'Two mayors and two police forces. It's total confusion.'

She told me that there was an ongoing conflict between the local tribal council and the Governor of Montana regarding water rights, gambling and taxes; in short, about anything of any value.

'Politicians are like diapers, they should be changed often and for the same reason.'

Later, walking the main street in Polson, I passed an environmental department building. Acting on impulse, I went in and asked a bemused receptionist if she could give me any information on environmental issues in the area. Seeing her confusion, I joked, 'You must get lots of enquiries like mine.'

She burst into friendly laughter, shaking her long, jet-black hair. 'No, you're the first.'

She thought for a second. 'You need to talk to Tom McDonald or Dale Becker. Their office is about five blocks from here. Hold on, I'll ring to see if they're there.' She returned a few minutes later and said, 'They're expecting you.'

Dale Becker was a tall, well-built man with an easy-going demeanour and a check shirt. With a warm handshake he asked, 'Coffee?'

He told me that the climate in the Flathead Valley was milder than the rest of Montana because the lake acted like a hot water bottle. That made it an attractive place to live, but it brought its own environmental challenges, such as preserving water quality.

He told me that his favourite fish was the cutthroat trout, but that the fish was having a difficult time in Flathead Lake. An alien species of trout called the mackinaw preyed upon it.

'With a name like that', I said, 'you'd think it'd be the cutthroat that would devour the mackinaw.'

He laughed. 'No, the mackinaw is much bigger, but anglers love the cutthroat because they fight hard on the rod.'

'Why is it called the cutthroat?'

He shook his head. 'To tell you the truth I don't know. Perhaps the red markings on its jaws?'

'Is anything being done to protect them?'

'Not enough', he replied, 'angling events are held each year to try to catch as many mackinaw as possible. This helps, but it doesn't solve the problem. It'd be difficult to eradicate the mackinaw, now that they're established in the lake. You'd have to hit their spawning grounds.'

Introducing a species such as the mackinaw for sport was a type of environmental vandalism. The mackinaw doesn't replace the cut-throat in the food chain because it lives deep in the lake, not on the surface, and it spawns in the lake, not in the surrounding streams like the cutthroat. This affects a whole range of wildlife including the bald eagle, the osprey and the grizzly bear. Birds have adapted to catching the cutthroat but cannot dive deep enough to catch the mackinaw. Grizzlies are affected because they get a large part of their seasonal diet from catching cutthroat in streams.

Dale, on a roll, told me about the hobo spider. It came from Europe aboard ship, making its first landing in Seattle in the 1930s. From there, it spread into the Flathead Valley, where it had no natural pred-ator. The spider carries a painful sting.

Hobo spiders and mackinaws are not the only immigrants. The cherry picking season brings many Mexican migrants to the Flathead Valley. Dale said that this caused conflict locally. Having seen first-hand the poverty of rural Mexico, he could readily empathise with the desire to flee to the US.

'It would be better to invest in the Mexican economy than to build big walls on the border', he said, 'and that wall is a disaster for wild-life too.'

I left shortly afterwards to spend the evening in a café overlook-ing Flathead Lake, watching the day surrender to the encroaching night. Pondering Dale's comments about the Mexican wall, I reflected that, for a country built on immigration, the belief that there should be no more of it existed in every era. There was no Mexican wall in Micí's time, but Micí arrived into an anti-Catholic world inhabited by organisations such as the 'Know Nothing Party', a secret society com-prised of white male Anglo-Saxon Protestants alarmed at the influx of so many Irish, Italian and German 'papists'. When questioned about their anti-Catholic activities they always answered, 'I know nothing.' In time, they were subsumed into the Republican Party.

The present-day Mexican crisis has been caused in part by the North American Free Trade Agreement of 1994, which allowed heavily subsidised US agribusiness to flood the Mexican market with cheap food, driving many off the land. Following the agreement, illegal Mexican immigration into the US increased by 500 per cent. The grimmest statistic of all is this: six thousand men, women and children have died in the attempt to enter the United States since that date. Others have joined drug gangs to help supply the US drugs market and, as drugs come north, guns go south, leading to violent chaos in Mexican border towns.

I pondered how like Micí these Mexican immigrants are. They too are forced to leave a land that can no longer support them. Each crosses his or her own bridge of tears to undertake a perilous journey, to eke out an equally perilous subsistence in the US.

§

At breakfast, Suzanne told me that 'the blood rule' was one of the biggest issues on the reservation. To qualify for tribal status, you had to have 50 per cent Native American blood. In olden times it didn't matter. You were a member if accepted by the tribe. One consequence of this blood rule is that if the tribal partner in a mixed marriage dies, the spouse is left homeless, because property cannot pass out of tribal hands.

Two separate health systems existed on the reservation: one, free, for Native Americans and a private/public scheme for other ethnicities.

Suzanne asked me if I would like to talk to someone in the tribal council in Pablo. 'I know the tribal president', she said, 'he's a good man.'

Pablo was ten miles away. Here, the architecture of life on the reservation was to be seen everywhere: children's bikes lay against fences, three men talked together on a doorstep, junk, trucks and old caravans littered backyards, plank sheds were filled with cut logs, satellite dishes pointed to the sky, a fat cat on a Perspex roof watched two men pushing a car. There were vegetable gardens, flower pots, barbeque bays, children's swings and assorted dogs wandering around. These were the tribal people Micí encountered most frequently during his time in Montana. He empathised with their plight, despite the fact that he was part of the river of change that swept across their lives.

The multi-storey glass-fronted tribal council building was decorated with Native American designs. It stood out amidst the single-storey prefabricated wooden houses and trailer homes. I entered a bright reception area and was guided to Rob McDonald's office. Rob, the council's communications officer, was tall with brown stubble tinged with red. He welcomed me with freshly brewed coffee. Placing his own coffee cup beside an Apple laptop, he eased his frame into a chair, telling me that he'd been working as director of communications for two years.

'I've been hired to get the tribal point of view out there. We haven't been good at this up to now. The tribal people have turned their face away from their critics and haven't engaged with others outside their community.' He shook his head. 'This approach hasn't worked for us. We are blamed for everything, from petty crime to drugs, and when the tribal council takes economic initiatives, our motives are always questioned. That's why it's important to get our story out there.'

'How do you do it?'

'I use television, radio and the print media generally. I also attend meetings in local communities, to act as a public face for the tribes.'

'What sort of reception do you get?'

'It varies. People don't think I'm a tribal member because of my looks. When I tell them that I work for the council, some people are shocked and spend the rest of the evening being overly polite. It'll take time to build allies.'

He filled me in on the history of the reservation, where three tribes live together: the Salish, the Kootenai and the Pend d'Oreille. Collectively, they are known as 'Flatheads'. The traditional lands of the main tribe, the Salish, consisting of twenty-two million acres, lay one hundred miles to the south in the Bitterroot Valley. It was here that the tribe encountered the Lewis and Clark expedition in the early years of the nineteenth century. Lewis and Clark had been commissioned by President Thomas Jefferson to explore the unknown western lands. They were the first white men to come through the area. To the Salish, they were little more than visitors passing through. They had no idea that the expedition was branding the land for their sponsors. Waves of settlers followed, bringing disease and oppression with them.

In 1891, while Mící was still in Montana, the army arrived and force-marched the Salish people on their 'trail of tears' from their homeland to the reservation in the Flathead Valley, leaving behind their homes, their holy places and the graves of their ancestors.

Chief Charlo described the experience:

What's he? Who sent him here? We first thought he came from the light, but he comes like the dusk of the evening now, not like the dawn of the morning. He comes like a day that has passed, and night enters our future with him …. His laws never gave us a blade nor a tree, nor a duck, nor a grouse, nor a trout. No; like the wolverine that steals your cache. You know he comes as long as he lives, and takes more and more, and dirties what he leaves.

The skulduggery did not end there. In 1910, the Homesteading Act opened up the reservation to settlement by whites. The ensuing land rush left tribal peoples with only 20 per cent of the 1.2 million acre reservation.

'We are changing that now', said Rob, 'we are buying up land as it becomes available. The tribe has now achieved 70 per cent ownership.'

'It must be costly to buy all that property.'

'Yes, but the tribal council has made it a priority.'

To fund these purchases, the council raises finance from a variety of sources, including power generation, forestry, federal grants and tourism. I told him that I had heard his was one of the more prosperous reservations. He laughed. 'We still have 30 per cent unemployment. There's a lot more to do.'

§

Little did I realise when I reached the trendy village of Bigfork, on the other side of the lake, that I would be confronted by a name from history class in primary school. I entered a sculpture gallery and met an elegantly dressed woman. When she heard that I was Irish, she told me that her maiden name was Mary Meagher and wondered if I had ever heard of her ancestor, an Irishman called Thomas Francis Meagher? I surely had. Our schoolmaster had imprinted this name into us. Meagher was a leader of the Young Irelanders. A fierce proponent of physical force as a way of removing British influence from Ireland, he was given the name 'Meagher of the Sword'. He had led a doomed rebellion against the British in 1848 and, when captured, was sentenced to be hung, drawn and quartered.

Unrepentant, he promised the judge, 'My Lord, this is our first offence, but not our last. If you'll be easy with us this once, we promise on our word as gentleman to try better next time.'

Meagher was given the opportunity to make good on this pledge. Because he was of the 'gentleman class', his sentence was commuted to banishment to Van Dieman's Land, or Tasmania as it's known today. From here, he made his way to the US where he led a succession of Irish regiments on the Union side in the American Civil War, including the '69ᵗʰ Fighting Irish'. We had learned in history class that the objective of fighting in the Civil War was to develop military expertise to return and fight the British. When this didn't happen, the Irish school curriculum lost interest in him.

Mary Meagher filled that blank by telling me that after the Civil War, he became acting Governor of Montana.

'He faced many problems here, but the biggest was being a Catholic in a Protestant and Mason world.'

He tried to bring in legislative reform and religious freedom, but met obstacles at every turn from the powerful families and from the media. Thomas Francis Meagher died on a riverboat at Fort Benton. Mary maintained that vigilantes controlled by the 'big families' in the state murdered him.

§

'Welcome to my store, Creative and Native. I have authentic craft items from one hundred Native tribes across the United States and I feature fifty local artists as well.'

Jill was a small, vibrant woman in her fifties with sharp and engaging eyes. Her shop was full of items that held a fascination for the young boy in me: bows and arrows, tomahawks, drums, medicine balls, dream catchers, horsehair belts and my favourite, miniature paper bark canoes. Jill lived most of her life outdoors and believed that the natural world provided all that we really need.

She told me, 'One of my aims is to teach folk what life was like and what it can be still.'

She was immersed in tribal lore and told me that the commonly used names of tribes are not their real names. Navajo, for example, is a white man's word meaning 'little thief'. The tribe's real name is Diné, which means, 'We the People'. This erroneous labelling applied to other tribes too, including the Blackfeet, Sioux, Cree and Flatheads.

Jill told me that a white bear has a spiritual significance for many Native Americans. It's a sign that 'the creator hasn't forgotten them.'

Apparently, every tenth black bear is born white. She told me that the white buffalo is even rarer. It's only accepted as white when it sheds three times and the fourth coat is still white. For some tribal people a white buffalo is associated with the 'next coming' and is the most sacred animal one could meet. It will bring healing, greater unity and transformation into the world of Native peoples.

She inquired if any animal had entered my consciousness in the previous few days. I told her about my encounter with the raven.

'When were you born?' she asked. When I replied, she said, 'That's interesting, raven and bear are associated with your birth date. An encounter with a raven in your consciousness means that you're going through a transformation in your life, out of which you'll grow stronger.'

'I hope I don't meet that bear!'

'You might call one to you. It would add to the significance. This is the time of the year that you have to watch out for the bear and other critters. They're all getting ready for hibernation and they're eating anything and everything .... Whatever happens, the bear smells it, the eagle sees it and the deer hears it.'

7

St Ignatius and Missoula

I left the following day for Missoula, where Micí first set foot in Montana. I planned first however to detour via the bison range and St Ignatius Church. The road towards the bison range was straight and flat with white crosses on the roadside, marking where road deaths had occurred. These memorials were effective in their simplicity and equality.

I passed wetlands, shimmering water, textured by reeds and grasses, coloured dark brown, russet and gold. I took a picture of an advertisement on a saloon gable in a village called Charlo. It said, 'Branding Iron Bar and Grill, Home of the Mission Mountain Testicle Festival'.

'What the heck is going on here?' I thought, wondering if I was safe in such a place. I later found out that it was bulls' testicles that they were celebrating.

A saloon owner later described the ceremony, 'I skin the testicles when they're thawing because the membrane peels like an orange. After that, I marinate them in beer, bread them four times and deep-fry them.'

People are then expected to eat them, along with copious amounts of beer. They've even re-branded them as 'oysters'.

When I reached the gates of the bison park at Moiese, I spotted another peculiar bar sign, advertising buffalo jerky (dried meat) for sale. 'What's this?' I thought, 'we're outside a bison range dedicated to the preservation of buffalo and they're selling buffalo meat at the gates?'

Did you ever meet someone who cheerily imparts bad news? The woman in the reception area of the bison range told me with a smile that only half the range was open, adding that the buffalo were grazing in the closed part.

'They close that road in winter as it's dangerous because of snow and ice.'

In Irish terms, this was a T-shirt day. The only snow or ice to be seen was on top of distant mountains. The receptionist tried to soften the blow. 'You might be lucky. There could be a few buffalo on this side, and there are lots of other animals.'

The park was crisscrossed with gravel roads used for viewing wild-life, but there were no buffalo to be seen.

I did see a small herd of pronghorn antelope grazing at the base of the small range of hills that ran through the centre of the park. They were bedecked in striking displays of white and tan, with white rumps. What advantage can a white rump give an animal that's a possible meal for a variety of predators?

Beside a river I spotted a bald eagle. A thrill ran through my body as I watched it; they're such majestic birds. It landed on top of a tree on the riverbank and looked positively regal, silhouetted against the snow-capped mountain peaks, watching the landscape intently from its perch.

Up to forty million buffalo once roamed over the vast, unfenced American prairies. The tribal people used every part of the buffalo. Meat was preserved in different forms for later use. Hides were used for tepees and clothing, and the bones transformed into knives, carving tools and war bonnets. This careful management of the buffalo ended when the professional buffalo hunter came to the plains around 1870, resulting in the near extermination of the species by 1885. This was part of a concerted campaign, promoted by government, to clear the plains of buffalo and consequently of the tribal peoples in order to make it safe for white settlement.

The buffalo were inadvertently saved from extinction by the efforts of Walking Coyote, a Flathead Indian who collected a small herd of orphan calves. Walking Coyote had left the Flathead area with his wife to work for a fur trading company in the Blackfeet area, east of the Rockies. He lived with the Blackfeet and married a woman from their tribe. This was legitimate under Blackfeet rules, as a man could take as many wives as he could support. In contrast, the Flathead tribal rule, influenced by the Jesuits in St Ignatius, was 'one man, one wife'. Some years later, a homesick Walking Coyote decided to return home. The only problem was the prospect of a public flog-ging for contravening the rules of church and tribe, so he brought a peace offering of buffalo calves in the hope of buying forgiveness. The Jesuits however were more interested in flogging than buffalo. This ultimately worked to Walking Coyote's advantage, because he kept the calves and, when the herd increased, he sold them to two ranchers, Michael Pablo and Charles Allard, for two thousand dollars. This stock was later sold to both the US and Canadian governments, as they belatedly sought to preserve the species.

The buffalo is a magnificent animal, and can weigh up to 2,500 pounds. They look cumbersome, but appearances are deceptive. They can travel at speeds of up to 35 miles per hour and can clear a fence like a horse when in full stride. They can also be surprisingly nimble and light of foot, a skill perfected in many mating and territorial battles.

Leaving the park, I drove to St Ignatius Jesuit mission on the southern end of the Flathead reservation. The present church was built in 1891, with brick made from local clay. When I went inside and knelt down, I was struck by the colour and brightness of the church. Light poured into the building through large, beautiful stained glass windows, while paintings and frescoes adorned the walls and ceilings. People were continuously coming in to pray or to have a look around. A white man was telling two five- or six-year-old Native American children a story about one of the paintings. Pointing to a picture he said, 'Jesus invited all his friends to a meal to say goodbye. Can you count the number of friends he invited?'

One of the boys pointed his finger at the painting and, with an earnest face, started to count. Four smiling Hutterite women – a sect not unlike the Amish, but more colourfully dressed – came in and lingered before a small altar bearing two statues, a large statue of a sermonising Jesuit priest and a humbler one of Sacagawea, the Shoshone woman who guided and translated for the Lewis and Clarke expedition.

The Jesuits, in the person of Father DeSmet, came to the Salish tribes in the Bitterroot Valley, opening a mission there in 1840. In 1854, he opened St Ignatius mission in the Flathead Valley, coordinating the churches' efforts with the government's plans for a reservation there. The Salish character impressed DeSmet. He described them as 'generous, honest and hospitable', and feared that greedy white people might corrupt them. The Jesuits were trying to create the ideal society in a virgin setting, one that might allow the tribes to work 'productively' within Jesuit values and culture. Of course, the tribal people would have to change a bit in the process. They had to give up their nomadic culture and end all wars and conflicts. They should work for their living in agriculture and forestry, pursuits which matched the Jesuits' idea of fruitful, honest labour. They had to give up polygamy and their old ceremonies, especially the warlike sun-dance, and adopt a new morality on sexuality, euthanasia, education and abortion.

§

I arrived late on the outskirts of Missoula and stayed in an anonymous motel. At breakfast, a solitary mood possessed me. This solitariness seemed pervasive; there wasn't a hint of mumbled conversation between people seated at six breakfast tables.

As I was staying a few days, I went in search of a more central motel, which I found beside the library.

The receptionist told me, 'Be sure and call into the Irish shop across the road.'

'Where is it?'

'You can't miss it. It's the place flying the Irish flag, called Celtic Connections.'

I crossed the road and went into the shop. A fair-haired young woman of about twenty smiled and said, 'Hiiii!'

'Howya', I replied. When she heard my accent her mouth opened in shock and she hopped up and down clapping her hands. I don't think I ever had this effect on anyone before.

'Where are you from?'

'Whitefish', I replied.

'Nooo you're not, you're from Ireland. I would love to hug you!' she said, laughing. 'Would you like a cup of tea?'

'I would love one.'

'Well, I'll make you a cup of Barry's tea', she said, going behind the counter and getting a teabag out of a container.

'I'm just back from Ireland and I'm missing it', she said.

'Sounds like love', I replied, laughing.

Bingo! I'd hit the nail on the head. Her heart was closely connected to an Irishman she met while on an exchange programme between the University of Montana and University College Cork.

Jackie gave me the tea and said it was 'awesome' that I had called. I felt that I didn't deserve such a welcome but it's great to be around unbridled enthusiasm. 'Here's Michele now', she said, greeting the well-dressed, brown-eyed woman who entered the shop. Michele was the owner, also a former international swimmer who swam competitively against Michelle Smyth, the Irish gold medallist from the Atlanta Olympics.

We talked for a good hour and when I was leaving Michele asked, 'Would you like to go out for dinner with Jackie and I? I was going to cook soup at home. How boring is that?'

'I wouldn't like to put you to too much bother', I said, and they seemed to accept this.

Once outside, I realised that I had acted ungraciously. A debate raged within me and, surprising even myself, I went back inside. 'I'm sorry but I'm an awful eejit. If the offer is still open I would love to go to dinner.'

Michele smiled and said, 'When you said no, I thought the floor would open up and swallow me.'

Later, as we entered the most popular restaurant in town, Jackie waved to a man at a table and said, 'Come on, I'll introduce you to Professor Emmons.'

David Emmons was a slightly built man with grey hair and twinkly eyes who spoke with passion and ease. You could sense a great enthusiasm within him for learning. Coincidentally, some years earlier, he had been involved in the making of a documentary on Mící's adventures in America. During our discussion, I told him that I had visited the Flathead reservation because the tribe was mentioned frequently in Mící's book.

He laughed. 'Mící mightn't always have got the name of the tribe right when he mentioned particular incidents. They might have been Flatheads, Blackfeet, Crow, Nez Perce or some other tribe.'

I thought that wasn't too surprising as I'm sure the tribal people were not certain when they looked at a white man whether he was Irish, English or German. David said that Mící, generally speaking, showed 'a wonderful understanding' of the difficulties encountered by tribal peoples, because he was able to compare their ordeal to the Irish experience of oppression. He said that such understanding was rare at that time, even among Irish immigrants.

At dinner, I learned that Jackie was making a CD featuring Irish songs such as Raglan Road and Caledonia, and that Michele talked about living in Ireland for years before deciding to open a business in Missoula. She said that wages were low in Montana. This applied even to prestigious jobs, in the university or hospital, as the combination of size, remoteness and low population made it difficult to take in enough income to adequately maintain Montana's infrastructure.

After dinner, Michele drove us to the university to meet an Irish lecturer from Cork called Toirdealbach O Riordan who worked there as part of a cultural exchange programme with University College Cork.

Toirdealbach was a gregarious man, possessing a canny Cork eye and a passion to speak Irish at every opportunity. This eagerness fell on barren ground as I shook my head in bafflement at his every Irish probe. He found it difficult to believe that a Donegal man could scarcely remember a word of his native language. I felt a fraud. Any ability I possessed disappeared into a black hole and the more pressure I felt, the farther it receded. Toirdealbach loved Missoula and had settled happily there with his family. I asked him what he missed most about Ireland.

'Cork hurling', he replied. When following Cork, he felt part of a close-knit community participating in an enthralling story. There was nothing in Montana that celebrated summer quite like championship hurling. Maybe he hadn't heard of the Mission Mountain Testicle Festival.

The following morning, I met a couple of panhandlers on the street. The man, a tall Native American with long, grey hair and a beard, had a lived-in face and a twinkling eye. His partner, a rotund younger woman, had a more calculating eye. A rangy dog lay beside them on the pavement, chomping biscuits.

'Nice dog', I said.

'His name is Brat', smiled the man.

'He's getting well fed.'

'A traffic warden gave us biscuits for him. I've had him since he was a pup.'

My prejudice against traffic wardens shrivelled. The dog observed me with a droopy, watchful eye as the woman's hand stroked his head.

'Are you from here?' I asked.

'No, we're passing through. I'm from North Dakota and my wife is from Idaho. We got married last week.'

'Congratulations, I hope you have many happy years', I said, dropping a dollar into their hat.

Missoula has a liberal aura. In a local coffee bar, funky music played in the background and the aroma of scented candles and unidentifiable herbs filled the air. Customers were young; the men dressed in sandals, scarves, T-shirts and fancy hats. The women wore colourful clothes – a mixture of long flowing dresses, berets, striped trousers and expensive tops. They all carried that essential accessory, an Apple laptop. Conversation about Buddhism, technology, art and literature filled the air, and cheap coffee, at a dollar a mug, lubricated the vocal cords.

Later, as I took a night-time walk, I noticed a commotion around an art gallery. It was jammed with people, and more were milling around the door trying to get in. A famous photographer, William Albert Allard, was launching a photographic exhibition. I squeezed into the room, which was hung with selections of Allard's cowboy photographs.

Allard, a man in his sixties, wearing a dapper cowboy hat and boots, stood in front of me.

'They [the cowboys] didn't give a shit that I was from *National Geographic*', he said in a strong, confident voice. 'What mattered was that I tried to live their life, ride a horse, lug my own saddle, sit at the campfire. That got me accepted and gave me the chance to take good pictures.'

He said his images portrayed all aspects of cowboy life: its toughness, bleakness, loneliness and camaraderie. Each scene he shot, whether steer wrestling or shooting pool, showed the person behind the activity. One photograph that stood out in my mind was of a cowboy astride a horse galloping across oaten-coloured plains that stretched towards mountains in the far distance. The vastness of this landscape was accentuated by the fact that prairie and mountains only took up one fifth of the photograph. The rest was big, blue Montanan sky.

What made a good cowboy, he said, was the same as what made a good photographer. You had to care passionately about your work. A good photographer should have the ability to see possibilities for photographs 'at the edge of situations'. He favoured working in the early morning and at 'the time between dog and wolf', his definition of dusk.

He bemoaned the thinning of American life to considerations of just profit and efficiency. This demeaned all public, private and creative work. The only possible antidote was to do something that you cared deeply about.

8

Philipsburg and Gold Creek

Micí didn't delay long in Missoula. He travelled by local train to Philipsburg and from there walked to the top of Granite Mountain in search of work in the biggest silver mine in America.

I drove out of Missoula at dawn. A winding river and train track accompanied my route through wooded mountain valleys. The sun was shining and life was good. Country music poured from every radio station, all telling of love, lust and loss in heartfelt voices. A laugh bubbled out of me and I started to sing. That's another advantage of being in a car like Crusty; it's a non-judgemental buddy.

The countryside flattened out, but snow-capped mountains were still visible in the distance. This was cattle country. Black Angus herds speckled the prairie and signs such as 'Hogan's Ranch Suppliers' appeared on the roadside. Horses of all colours and shapes roamed in paddocks, and a rider on a black horse cantered across an open range. Large wooden barns of varying and imaginative designs dotted the landscape. Oval shapes, circular windows and steep-pitched roofs indicated the ethnic roots of the ranchers who first settled here.

I drove into Philipsburg along a wide gravel roadway and parked in the middle of the town. I was struck by the vibrancy of the place; it reminded me of Dingle. There were brightly coloured buildings and people out on the street talking, drinking and shopping. Country music blared out of saloon doors. A pick-up truck pulled in beside me with a load of logs, a chainsaw and an Alsatian dog in the back. A young couple, both dressed in overalls and baseball caps, got out and went into a store, leaving the truck unlocked behind them.

When I entered the 'Sapphire Gallery' on the main street, a shopkeeper with fair hair and adolescent energy must have labelled me a tourist, because she herded me into an adjacent 'mining' room.

'You can mine sapphires here', she said, showing me bags of gravel and stone stacked in a corner. 'People are often very lucky.'

The prospect didn't tempt the gambler in me. My priority was to walk up a mountain to the old ghost town of Granite, where Mící lived and worked for seven years, so I asked for directions. Blushing, she replied that if I had a 4X4, I could drive almost to the top. I shook my head, explaining that I wanted to walk. She arched her eyebrows. 'Make sure to take bear spray with you.'

'Bear spray?'

'A spray you can use if a bear attacks.'

'Does it work?'

She just smiled.

Wandering through the maze of gravel roads on the edge of town, I found the sign indicating the track to Granite. With a sense of history prodding me, I followed the shopkeeper's instructions and started walking 'five miles straight up', through a canopy of evergreen trees. As I walked the empty road, her words kept coming back to me. What would happen if I encountered a bear here? I could be attacked and eaten and no one would be any the wiser. No one, not even my family, knew I was here.

I had heard that bears can get a bit grumpy if surprised, so I started coughing loudly. Feeling foolish, I changed tack and started singing a favourite childhood song, 'Come Down the Mountain Katie Daly'. Luckily, no bear with that name responded.

After a while, I got sick of making noise. In the midst of a seemingly empty wilderness, thinking about bears and expending energy unnecessarily seemed counterproductive.

Occasionally, the veil of dense trees would pull back to give glimpses of distant snow-capped mountain peaks and, in the foreground, wooded hills thatched with winter white. As I climbed higher, snow gathered in sheltered clearings and on old rusted barrels, remnants of busier times, which were scattered around the mountainside. The sky was grey. The day was getting colder and soon the ground was carpeted white. The snow squeaked underfoot and I grabbed a knobbly fir stick to act as my third leg.

I saw the rusty remains of the old cable line, whose suspended cable buckets were used to carry silver ore from mines in Granite to mills at the bottom of the mountain beside Philipsburg. It was the only indication that this quiet road was the same busy road that Mící walked in the 1880s and 1890s.

Dean A.L. Stone described life on this road in the 1880s in the *Mineral Independent*:

> This was a busy highway. It was teeming with life its entire length. Great teams strained up the long grade, laden with supplies for the thousands of people whose homes found resting places between the great boulders of granite .... It was thoroughly busy, every foot of it and it was busy for nearly every one of the 24 hours ... ceaseless was the movement of the endless line of cable cars and down below the great stamps beat incessantly upon the stream of ore which poured beneath them, hammering out the wealth which the rock contained. It was the greatest silver camp on earth.

The road remained the same but the texture of silence cast a cloak over the mountain. No echo of the past emerged. I came to a weather-beaten sign, 'Welcome to Granite'.

The town of Granite came about by accident. In 1875 Eli Holland, out hunting, found a rock scraped by a deer hoof, exposing the silver underneath. When its value was confirmed, he staked a claim on Granite Mountain. Developing the site was difficult, so he offered an experienced Irish miner called McIntyre 25 per cent of the claim if he sank a fifty-foot shaft into the mountain. Sinking such a shaft through granite in an inhospitable environment was not easy. McIntyre thought he had completed the job but, on measurement, the shaft was found to be only forty-nine feet deep. Holland demanded that he finish the drilling, but McIntyre insisted that he'd never walk up that 'damned hill' again. It was later established that if he had sunk the shaft another foot he would have owned a share in the richest silver mine in the west.

Holland sold a controlling share to Charles McLure, who assembled a team of investors from St Louis to develop the mine. Granite was a hazardous place to work. It consisted of steep mountainside, hard rock and forbidding weather. People jeered at what appeared a foolhardy undertaking, and when the early finds were not encouraging the project ran into financial problems. At one point, McLure had to offer a thousand shares in the mine to purchase a horse from a local farmer called Griffith. A couple of years later Griffith sold his shares for fifty thousand dollars, and the horse became known as the fifty thousand dollar horse.

Granite was to become the greatest silver mine in the United States. Between 1882 and 1893, it produced forty-five million dollars in silver and paid a hundred thousand dollars a month in dividends. The silver boom had begun.

The town grew quickly. Mining neighbourhoods included Finnlander Lane, Cornish Row and Donegal Lane. Magnolia Avenue was more grand. Doctors, mine managers and other professionals lived there. Locals soon renamed it 'Silk Stocking Row'. By 1889, the town boasted a public school, a bank, a hospital, a fire station, a bathhouse, eighteen saloons and a three-storey hotel. Those who wanted to keep up with the news read the *Granite Mountain Star* newspaper. Entertainment for the workers included a roller-skating rink, a library, a ballpark, a red light district and a five-mile bobsled run, which connected Granite to Philipsburg.

§

Around the next corner, I caught my first glimpse of Granite. Before me stood two massive, decaying humps of tumbling timber, slowly rotting back into the mountain. These were the skeletal remains of the mining mills that once made silver ingots out of Granite dirt. Below these buildings, it looked as though a gigantic badger had scraped out the earth, as extensive mine tailings, on which no vegetation had ever grown, toppled down the mountainside. These scars were testament to the scale of the mining.

I crunched my way through snow to old shapeless mills. The sun broke through, creating a temporary thaw. Melt water seeped through rotting planks and ran off rusted pieces of tin, falling drop by drop upon stone floors. A sign, situated beside an innocuous hole in the ground, indicated that this was the famous Ruby mineshaft, from which great riches had come. It might have looked innocuous, but it ran 1,800 feet into the earth, which is the approximate height of the highest sea cliffs in Europe. At a depth of one thousand feet, horizontal tunnels fanned out for miles in each direction.

Micí described the first time he went into one of these mineshafts and the shock that he experienced having to walk for a mile and a half through tunnels before reaching his workplace. When he arrived, he found miners at work boring holes, into which they inserted explosives. There must have been a collective holding of breath as the charges were detonated and the mountain shook from the ensuing explosion. Micí said 'that his heart was in his mouth with the fear' of being in a little dark hole far underground, with a whole mountain over him. Being new and unskilled at mining, it was Micí's job to worm his way into these holes, and, in the faint candlelight, heft dirt and stones into cars to be taken out of the mine to the mills. Micí soon adapted and became oblivious to danger, describing it as like going to the well for a bucket of water at home.

There was more to mining than digging and Micí learned the skills from a Cornish foreman. He showed him how to identify silver-bearing rocks, set explosives, extract silver from rock, use drills and prop up the mine. Micí soon settled in and, along with six friends, he built a small cabin on top of the mountain, where they lived 'quite comfortably' for seven years in this self-contained world.

On the main street of Granite I saw the remnants of the derelict Miner's Union Hall, an ornate three-storey stone building, once the social centre of this bustling town. I tried to visualise streams of people entering in all their finery for dancing, concerts, travelling theatre, operas, billiards and cards. The highlight of the social calendar was the New Year's Eve Ball, which carried a $3 entry fee, the equivalent of a week's wages.

I followed another trail through the trees, trudging higher up the mountain through knee-deep snow, secure in the knowledge of being able to retrace my steps. Fifteen minutes later, I came to a standstill. The snow had obliterated any clue as to what direction the trail might have taken.

I did a standing meditation. I closed my eyes, holding my hands out in front of me as if hugging a tree and blocked out everything except the sounds, smells and taste of this remote spot. After a while, I became aware of a digging and a grunting noise coming from farther up the mountain. It was strangely rhythmical in the cold, still mountain air. Curiosity and fear pulled me in opposite directions. I decided to investigate and crept towards the noise, each step a loud crunch. As I approached, the noise stopped. The silence brought a feeling of foreboding and I asked myself what the heck was I at. On my own, on top of a mountain, probably pushing my nose in where it was not wanted. I retreated.

Granite had only one reason for its existence. When that reason disappeared, so did the town. In 1893, the Sherman Silver Purchase Act, which compelled the US government to buy silver to boost the economy, was repealed. The price of silver collapsed and most of the silver mines in the west shut down. The bubble burst. The big wheel of life turned and jolted Mící and his friends onto a new and uncertain path.

The mine closure decimated people's lives. Virtually overnight, the town emptied of all its citizens, leaving this hulking presence decaying on top of the mountain.

Next, a rumour spread that the bank in Philipsburg was about to go bust. When the crowds arrived, they withdrew every penny and lodged it in the post office. The little post office, which measured nine foot by twelve, had never seen such business and by evening every inch of the floor was covered in gold, silver, money, cheques and bags of coins.

Economic depression affected all of the western states. Over 50 per cent of the banks in Montana went bust in the year following the crisis of 1893. Mící had saved some money but not enough to make any real difference to his life. As he walked down the mountain with his friends, he had to make a decision. What to do next?

§

The following morning, two elderly women, probably sisters, were hard at work serving breakfast to a room full of hungry customers. The smells of coffee, bacon and eggs – which were being cooked beside the counter – filled the diner. Both women were thin and stern looking. One cooked, preparing omelettes, bacon, hash browns, eggs and pancakes, while the other took orders and did the serving.

When she came to take my order, I asked the waitress about the history of mining in Philipsburg. She looked at me with no-nonsense eyes and nodded towards an old timer who was sitting at the counter.

'Roy there will be able to tell you all about the mining. He knows anything there is to know about it.'

Roy looked up at the mention of his name. He turned to me and asked, 'Is it mining you're interested in?'

'Yes.'

'Well I'm the oldest miner in the area and I've seen it all over the years. What age do you think I am?'

'Seventy-five?' I ventured.

'I'm ninety-one' he replied.

'You're never that age.'

'I am.'

Roy B. Hamilton had the vigour of a man twenty years younger. His chiselled, weathered face was etched with the trials of life but his mind was as clear as a bell. He still had a big appetite – I'd watched him polish off a big breakfast earlier – and a strong voice that came from deep within his chest. He told me about his holiday in Europe.

'The government sent me on an all-expenses trip in the forties. London in the Blitz, North Africa, Italy, France and the Rhine. It was some adventure, but a time that I wouldn't want to repeat. Life should be about work and gals.'

On seeing the cutting look from the waitress, he said, 'I was married for fifty-six years. That took up a lot of the gals part.' He changed gear. 'You'd like to know something about mining?'

When I finished telling him about Micí, he said, 'Hold on there, I've something outside in the truck that will be of interest to you.'

With that, he climbed stiffly from his stool, but, once pointed in the right direction, he headed off at a brisk pace. Moments later, he was back with a book of photographs. 'This will give you an idea of what mining was like years ago.'

With veiny hands, he placed the book down on the counter and awkwardly thumbed through pages showing pictures of Granite and the people who lived there. Above the caption 'Miners of the Granite Mine 1891', a group of men stood in formal pose. All were dressed in suits and waistcoats, fine hats and strong shoes and wore impressive handlebar moustaches. There wasn't a pick of extra flesh on any of one of them. I wondered if Micí was there, staring out at me.

Roy had pictures of Granite taken from an adjoining mountain. Granite Mountain, stripped of trees for construction and to fire the mills, looked nothing like it does now. Perched on top, the town looked like a pimple on a bony nose.

'Five thousand people lived in Granite in its heyday', said Roy, pointing to a picture of gentlemen resplendent in top hats standing on the snow-covered main street. In full flow, he indicated a picture of horses and carts with water barrels on board. 'There wasn't much of a natural water supply in Granite. It had to be ferried there every day on carts.' Other pictures showed teams of horses pulling huge carriages and mules ferrying packs of firewood. 'It was tough on those horses. They had to pull heavy loads through snow, muck and mud. Trucks didn't come to these parts till the 1930s.'

Roy worked as a metallurgist in the mills. Originally the mills were built beside the mines, but soon they built bigger ones further down the mountain and transported the ore on a cable tramway, the remains of which I'd seen earlier on my hike. The ore was crushed in the mills by hundreds of giant stamps. When it was finely ground, salt and water were added and it was crushed again. The solution was put into barrels with mercury, which then amalgamated with any silver present. When the amalgam was heated, the mercury burned off, leaving pure silver behind.

'It took five pounds of mercury for every ton of ore', Roy told me, 'the mercury was brought through a cooling device that recovered most of it.'

'Could you reuse the mercury?'

'You could if you were stuck, but they always preferred to use fresh mercury.'

This was an improvement on earlier mining methods, when the amalgam was heated in a pan and the mercury released into the atmosphere, or into the lungs of the miner.

A man with a friendly smile and red check shirt came over to Roy and greeted him warmly. He sat down and introduced himself as Gary. When Gary heard I was from Ireland, he smiled and said, 'My wife is from Waterford, would you believe that? She was in here a little while ago talking to me and my friend. You must have seen her; she was sitting right here.'

I asked him where he had met a Waterford woman.

'It's a long time since she came here', he said, 'tell you what. Go down to the shop and ask for Susan Flynn. Flynn is her maiden name. She'll get a big surprise.'

Roy chipped in enthusiastically, 'Her shop is just two doors down. It's the charity shop.'

In this way, a plot was hatched and, after one more coffee, I headed off. I found Susan Flynn's shop and seeing no customers inside, I opened the door to a tinkling bell. A reddish-haired woman looked up, whom I recognised immediately as the woman in the breakfast diner.

'Is Susan Flynn here?' I asked.

A surprised look came into her eyes and she tentatively said, 'That's me.'

'Do you not remember me?'

'Are you Irish?'

'Yes I am. I've been living for 25 years in Donegal but I'm originally from Waterford. I used to know a Susan Flynn there.'

A worried look came into her eyes; not the response I had been expecting. I immediately thought I should explain that the two rascals at the breakfast counter had sent me on an errand. She laughed when she heard the plot.

'I was worried that you might be an old beau from my past. I'll kill that pair.'

'What happened to your Irish accent?'

'I've been living so long in Montana that it's mellowed, but I still think it's there in the background. At least they all tell me that.'

With that, the doorbell tinkled again and a group of serious shoppers came in.

'Call in later for a chat', Susan said.

§

There must be something in the air in Philipsburg that produces vitality in old age as the woman in charge of the museum, though not quite as old as Roy, had the same spark in her eye and spring in her step. I arrived as she was opening the museum doors.

'You shouldn't have opened just for me', I said.

'There might be a few more along later after you', she laughed.

As she talked, she moved about, turning on lights, opening doors and getting ready for the day. I was the only visitor and I roamed around the museum at my leisure. When I returned to reception she told me of the lone miners who still work on Granite Mountain.

'For a lot of these guys, it becomes an obsession. They give up everything else to work at mining.'

As I drove out of Philipsburg I glanced back at the town, nestling in a rich valley surrounded by three mountain ranges. Living as I do

beside the sea, the place seemed to me like a proud, lone limpet cling-
ing tenaciously to a rock at the edge of a wild ocean.

§

Micí Mac Gabhann and his six friends were unemployed when they
left Granite. With no easy resolution available, they decided to try
prospecting. Armed with pick and shovel they ventured into the
Garnet Mountains and began work near 'Old Baldy Mountain'. They
built a cabin in the foothills and laboured long hours in a variety of
locations in search of wealth.

One evening, after they discharged dynamite in a small mine, their
eyes were taken by the shine of gold in the candlelight. They let out
a lusty cheer, hugged each other and rushed to tell their mates. All
night long, they celebrated by drinking whiskey. The next morning,
one of the men, Owen Mac Neelish, was nominated to travel the fifty
miles to Philipsburg to get the find valued. It was in the middle of
winter and snow lay heavily all around. The only way Owen could
travel was on Norwegian snowshoes. The way Micí tells it in his book,
you would think that he was going down to a neighbour's house for
the loan of a shovel, rather than heading fifty miles across a wilderness, confronting dangers at every turn. The remaining six men set to
work, with understandable gusto, mining gold nuggets.

When Owen returned, 'one look at his face' told them that all was
not well. The gold was too rough and dark and, in consequence, was
virtually worthless. Desolation set in on the small camp. They didn't
have enough food to survive the freezing winter, so they decided to
return to Philipsburg, which is where they were when they heard the
cry, 'There's gold in the Klondike!'

The group did not have enough money to send everyone on the
journey northwards, so they decided to send three people ahead as
scouts, one of whom was Micí's cousin, Jim Anthony. Micí wasn't
lucky in the drawing of lots, so he left for Butte in search of work.

§

I drove into Gold Creek, where Micí also prospected for a while. It
consisted of five houses, one closed shop, a large, deserted red brick

building and a school. There wasn't a person to be seen. A sign proclaiming 'Brown eggs for sale' pointed down a narrow gravel road, running parallel to the railway line. The road was as straight as an arrow but there wasn't a house anywhere in the immediate vicinity. It might be quite a journey to find those eggs! The fields before me had subtle shades of colour running through them: creams, greens, browns and yellows, all blending into one another and bounded by a sprinkling of autumnal trees. Hereford cattle and big round bales of hay freckled the prairie, corralled by traditional log fencing. I urged Crusty on up a gravel road, as I half expected Gold Creek to open out into a more substantial community. It didn't. All I found were three signs. The first one said, 'Thomas Herefords, Total Performance Kind'. The second, 'Griffin Hollow Barns', and the final sign in the middle of a field said, 'Cheese for sale'.

I got out of the car to savour the quietness. Two horses stood beside a fence while flocks of black crows together with a large herd of Black Angus cattle shared the next field. The dirt road stretched straight across the plain before disappearing into the forested foothills of the mountains.

On the way back, I passed Gold Creek School, a small white building with a green roof. A mural of galloping horses titled 'Home of the Mustangs' was painted on the wall of the school. Looking out across this prairie, you could easily imagine herds of wild, untamed mustangs galloping. I liked that place, perhaps because of the combination of prairie, faraway mountains and the idea of mustangs running free. I galloped off on my trusty steed, in pursuit of Mici, in the direction of 'Butte, America'.

9

Butte, America

'Don't tarry in the United States, come straight to Butte.' This was the message to many Irish immigrants in the late nineteenth century. The journalist Edwin Dobb once wrote, 'Like Concord, Gettysburg, and Wounded Knee, Butte is one of the places that America came from.'

Butte is a sprawling town situated on a honeycombed hump of Montanan mountainside, underneath which lie a maze of tunnels stretching for a total length of 2,700 miles. Sitting a full mile above sea level, it is the highest city in the US, and in its glory days was known as the 'richest mountain on earth'. It was an urban oasis in the midst of a vast rural landscape and was famed for not having a blade of grass or a flower growing. It didn't have time for such frivolities when lots of money could be made digging up the earth. It was also a town where the more primitive capitalist instincts came to the fore; the survival of the fittest, disregard for the powerless, and death and violence were part of daily life. Gold and silver had started the mining frenzy in Butte but in the 1880s it was copper which transformed it into the largest city between San Francisco and Chicago, with one hundred thousand people from all over the world thronging the streets. David Emmons, in his book *The Butte Irish*, said that Butte in the late nineteenth century was amongst the most rowdy and dangerous towns in the US. There were 300 saloons, which were open twenty-four hours, a booming red light district and wide-open gambling establishments. It had Turkish peddlers, palmists, hurdygurdy men, Hungarian opera singers, circus acrobats and countless other opportunists. This was the world that Mící entered when he came to Butte.

§

When Marcus Daly, the founder of the Anaconda Silver Mining Company, uncovered a fifty-foot wide seam of copper, he soon realised that he owned the richest copper mine the world had ever known. Daly was born in Ballyjamesduff, County Cavan in 1841 and emigrated without a penny in his pocket at age fourteen. Twenty-five years later he was wealthy beyond his wildest imaginings. He was a short, dark, stocky man, quick to make both friends and enemies. He was a generous benefactor of the Catholic Church and Irish causes, particularly Charles Stewart Parnell and Michael Davitt. At times, he loved a bit of pomp and entertained visitors regally, but despite all his wealth he remained a man of simple tastes. He loved to eat in the mess with his miners, he would share a hotel room with the 'muckers in the mines' and was never happier than when swapping yarns with Irish companions.

It was known that Daly would never see an Irishman stuck. This helped to create a strong connection between Ireland and Butte, and the Irish flooded here in their thousands, particularly from counties Cork, Mayo and Donegal. Some put down roots and stayed. Some, like Mící, tarried a while before moving on. At the height of the mining, there were ten thousand Irish miners out of a total of twenty thousand.

§

As I drove into town, election posters featuring names like McCarthy and O'Sullivan were plastered on poles and walls. I pondered to what extent elections had changed since Mící worked here. Politics is often about deeply-felt rivalry and the great rivalry then was between the Democrat Irish and Republican Cornish communities. To quote an Irish Democrat of the time,

> 'The elections in thim days was ghastly. It paid a man to be a citizen. Ye could follow the rallies and speakers from neighbourhood to neighbourhood, night after night, and a man could keep blind drunk for three months prior to the election if he'd a mind to.'

In the build-up to the election, every dance hall, schoolhouse and lodge hall were taken over. At each venue there was a fanfare of speakers and politicians, after which they all moved to the next venue in hacks and buggies. They took with them huge billboards and posters caricaturing their opponents as fat, sleazy and greedy. Drink and rhetoric flowed in equal measure and the mutual antipathy inevitably spilled over. On one occasion, a hall was wrecked in a battle between rival supporters.

On Election Day, all saloons closed down to ensure the maximum turnout of electors. People were taken from hospitals and surgeries and special transport was laid on for older people, who were well taken care of for the day. A Cornish miner of the times commented, 'Thee robbing Hirish, they not only 'ave two votes heach on helection days, but thee buggers vote seven years hafter they've been dead and buried.'

§

That night, I went into a small, dimly lit bar, where five youngish men with baseball caps and a blonde woman were sitting around a horse-shoe-shaped bar counter. A young barmaid smiled a welcome. The place was quiet but it was a companionable quiet, as if I had just come into a lull in conversation between regulars. I ordered a beer and sat on a bar stool. When they heard my accent, I became the centre of attention for a while. The barmaid hopped up on a corner of the counter and sat there, Buddhist style. Andy, the guy I was sitting beside, was small, fat and gay and had been working up until recently as an air steward. One of the other guys joked, 'All those air stewards are gay.'

'No they aren't', replied Andy, 'I knew one who wasn't.'

Everyone laughed.

'Have you seen the Scary Mary?' he asked me.

'The what?'

He pointed to the sky, or at least to the bar ceiling, and said, 'The Scary Mary, the statue on the hill.'

It dawned on me that he was referring to the ninety-foot statue of the Virgin Mary which stands on the mountainside, 3,500 feet above Butte. At night, it's illuminated and shines over the town. You couldn't miss it. A local businessman built it to give thanks for his wife's recovery from cancer. Once he started the project, the local community pitched in to help him design it, build it and to lay a path to the spot where it stands. Andy remembered seeing them fly in the pieces of the statue by helicopter. When they were fixing the very last piece in place, one of the cables snapped and the helicopter nearly crashed.

'But why do you call it Scary Mary?' I asked.

'A friend of mine called it that. When he left a bar one night after a day's hard drinking, he looked up into the sky and saw this bright, shining figure looking down at him. He said it was the scariest thing he ever saw. We all call it Scary Mary ever since.'

§

In Missoula, Toirdealbach had told me to be sure to visit Father Sarsfield O'Sullivan when I got to Butte, as he was 'a fount of knowledge'. After breakfast the following day, I walked up the steep hill to the landmark St Lawrence O'Toole Church. It was a quiet residential area with neat gardens. I knocked on doors to find out where Father O'Sullivan lived, but no one had heard of him. I finally spotted a stocky man hoovering up leaves in a garden. I waved to him. He turned off his machine and I asked if he knew where Father O Sullivan lived.

'You've come to the right place', he said, 'this is his house here. I'm doing some gardening for him.'

At the door, I was greeted by a stern woman who didn't seem surprised at my arrival. She brought me along a narrow hallway full of personal memorabilia, most of it related to the Church, then into a sizeable living room which smelled of mahogany. Father O'Sullivan was stretched out on a recliner with a breathing apparatus beside him. His thin body was frail and listless, but he had a keen eye.

I told him my story and he launched into a joke about bishops and bell ringers. He spoke slowly, stopping frequently between sentences, but there was a determination to complete every word no matter how great the effort.

Father Sarsfield O'Sullivan's ancestors came from the Beara Peninsula in County Cork. His grandfather, Michael, was orphaned along with his three younger sisters when their parents died in the 1820s. Usually in these circumstances children are divided and cared for by relatives, but Michael wanted to keep the family together. He approached the landlord, Lord Lansdowne, and asked for permission to build a house for his sisters and himself on an uninhabited and inhospitable little island off the Beara Peninsula called Inishfanard. Lord Lansdowne, though sceptical, granted permission. It wasn't long before five or six other families followed Michael's example and thus a community was established. In time, Michael and his sisters married and Sarsfield O'Sullivan's father, Sean, was born on Inishfanard. Times were tough and Sean O'Sullivan, joining thousands of Cork men, made his way to Butte in search of a better life.

His journey was similar to Micí's, but Sean O'Sullivan stayed in Montana, got married and had three children: two boys and a girl. Sean wrote poetry and taught the Irish language to anyone who might be interested. The family never forgot where they came from and Father O'Sullivan quoted a poem his brother had written about Inishfanard. Upon finishing, he declared, 'Going back to that island was the most moving experience in my life. I had finally come home.'

'Your father certainly passed on his love of his native island', I said, wondering how home could be a place you have never been before.

'Yes, we were lucky though, in that we knew our father. He always spent time with us and passed on the stories.' He shook his head slowly and continued. 'Many children of miners never really knew their fathers because they used to work twelve-hour shifts and came home exhausted.'

While we were talking, a slim middle-aged man swept into the room and greeted Father Sarsfield, kissing him on both cheeks. He re-tied the buttons on the older man's shirt and laughed, 'We have to make sure you're looking presentable.'

Father Greg also lived in the house. He had been away working for a few days. When he went to unpack, Father Sarsfield said, 'Father Greg is a wonderful man. He takes care of me here. He has a brilliant mind. He's in big demand all over the States.'

I felt that I had taken enough of Father Sarsfield's energy. I was appreciative of his willingness to share with me despite his illness. Father Greg came to walk me out. In the hallway, he drew my attention to a framed photograph on the wall, featuring both himself and Father Sarsfield meeting Pope John Paul II.

Smiling, Greg pointed to the picture. 'That was a great day when we met the Pope in Rome. I had much more hair on my head in those days.'

'Well you've a lot more left than I have.'

'I've a theory', said Greg, 'that the first thing we lose is the greatest flourishing of our youth.'

As Father O Sullivan's house was halfway up the hill, I continued walking to the top. I stopped at St Lawrence O'Toole Church and read that it had been built in 1897 with twenty-five thousand dollars raised by miners' subscriptions. I passed lots of small, neat, colour-ful houses sitting in narrow cul-de-sacs. They had once belonged to miners. It was a far cry from Micí's time when these same streets were a putrid soup of muck, rubbish and faeces.

Periodically, I encountered a relic of the mining age, as old fur-naces and mining shafts, each with its own distinct design, poked their heads above the roofs of the houses. Some might think that they are rusting metal monstrosities, but I liked them. They added charac-ter to the town.

The road became a network of gravel lanes churned up by heavy machinery. I walked through this grimy wilderness onto a scalped, dusty hilltop. I saw before me a vast quarry hole, one mile deep and many miles wide. This was a grim, brown mountain moonscape. A yellow earthmover, like a lone soldier ant, crawled about the depths of the hole. The skeleton of this land had been laid bare and any morsel of monetary value had been sucked out. The bones were now being scavenged for any remaining morsel before being discarded in a pile of rubble.

From the hilltop, I could see the Berkeley Pit, a seventeen-hundred foot mining hole, a mile long and half a mile wide. It is slowly filling up with toxic water, causing extensive pollution to the town's envi-ronment and water supply. This water is already at a depth of 970 feet and when it reaches groundwater level at 1,100 feet, it will have the potential to irretrievably pollute the water table. This toxic lake of thirty-seven billion gallons is rimmed by barren rock and is dirty red at the surface. There are no fish, and no sign of vegetative life any-where near. Not even an insect will visit. If you fell into it, it would scorch your skin and burn your eyes. In 1995, a flock of snow geese, whose winter migration was halted by a storm, were forced to land on this toxic lake. The following day, 342 carcasses of these magnifi-cent birds were found on the water. All had been poisoned.

Every cloud has a silver lining. Lurking in the depths of Berkeley Pit are hardy microbes that exist nowhere else on the planet. Researchers have found that these microbes have powerful medicinal properties. Already, they've shown they can improve the treatment of fifty dif-ferent conditions, including ovarian cancer and lung tumours. These microbes literally eat cancer cells.

On this hilltop, there was a memorial to 168 men who died in a fire in the Speculator Mine in Butte in 1917. It was one of the biggest mining disasters in US hard rock mining history. The fire started 2,400 feet into the earth. To face disaster this far below ground must have been truly horrendous. Some of the survivors told of badly burned bodies, 'the soot was up to our knees, several bodies were under the soot. They were all cooked.' But even more horrendous were the deaths of those who survived for a day or two but died of asphyxia. Many left notes for loved ones. One of the letters was from J.D. Moore to his wife:

> Dear Pet, this may be the last message you'll get from me. The gas broke at about 11.15 p.m. I tried to get all the men out, but the gas was too strong. I got some of the boys with me in a drift and put in a bulkhead …. If anything happens to me you'd better sell the house … go to California to live. You'll know that your Jim died like a man and his last thought was for his wife who I love better than anyone on earth …. We'll meet again. Tell mother and the boys goodbye.
>
> With love to my pet and may God take care of you.
> Your Loving Jim

The memorial celebrates the bravery of a miner called Manus Duggan who led twenty-nine men to safety. His words that day are recorded here. 'Now is the time men, we can make it if you muster all the strength you have left.'

Mící came to Butte at the height of its productivity. This was a dangerous world and on average a miner was killed every day. Mící wrote about the pollution caused by the unregulated smelting of ores. The smoke, laced with sulphur, arsenic and many other chemicals, cast a grey black pall that hung over the town and caught in people's throats. For every miner killed or seriously injured, up to three died from respiratory illnesses. Working in hot, unventilated mines and breathing silica dust exacerbated this. Men would come out of 90 degree mine shafts into temperatures of -40 degrees outside. One resident remembered men coming from mines 'covered with sweat and then disappearing in balls of steam'. These men walked home in clothes frozen to them. When Countess Markievicz came to Butte to raise funds in 1922, she said, 'the hospitals are full of men suffering from work in the mines.'

The unheralded heroes of Butte were the one thousand mules that worked in the mines. These poor animals were wrapped up with their legs tied underneath them and then dropped head-first, like an Exocet missile, into the mines. There they would live out their lives in enforced labour. Yet the mules soon learned their rights. They first learned the length of the working shift and no entreaty or bribery would encourage them to work longer. They would pull six cars or none; not one more or one less. Some of the more contrary mules would work for only one 'skinner'. Miners and mules shared one passion; they both loved to chew tobacco. If a person had a plug of tobacco on him the mule would follow him around until he felt obliged to share. There was a report of one mule who, when fed up with work, yanked off one of his shoes in the knowledge he wouldn't be required to work until he was reshod. It may well have been the first recorded instance of 'pulling a sickie'.

Later, while walking around the old downtown, I saw many grand but faded buildings in need of a face lift. Several had hand-painted ghost signs upon their walls advertising the products, businesses and services of long ago, some dating back to the 1890s. Coca Cola featured, as did Wrigley's gum and Babcock's hats and furs, but my favourite was 'Wright's pharmacy – try Hoyers magic linimint'. Many stone buildings were either fully or partially empty, which isn't surprising given that the population has declined from one hundred thousand to thirty thousand people and many businesses have moved from the old downtown to skirt the new by-pass.

In a downtown bookshop, an older woman proudly told me, 'Butte has the number one on its number plate and it isn't going to give it up any time soon!'

She said that the rest of Montana tended to look down on Butte. At a recent high school game, students from Helena took great delight in shouting at the kids from Butte, 'Dirty water! Dirty water!' This was in reference to the Berkley Pit. At the return game the Butte kids had printed T-shirts with the slogan 'Butte – Dirty Water' emblazoned upon them. These young people have learned to make a virtue of adversity.

The next day, part of me was happy and part of me was sad to be leaving Butte. The place is a bit like a favourite old sock, now faded and frayed, containing a strong whiff of history.

10

The Bitterroots

A town called Divide lies south of Butte. It is pragmatically named as it is situated near to the Continental Divide, where water on the west side of the mountains drains to the Pacific and on the east to the Atlantic. There, I crossed railroad tracks and headed west towards a town called Wisdom. The road veered upwards through a narrow valley in the Pioneer Mountain Range, with just room for the road and the thundering Big Hole River. Later, the road led into a more open landscape with forested mountains, rolling hills and a widening river. I passed bars and lodges, many with banners out luring hunters and anglers for the new hunting season. Snow lay in shaded areas, the sky was grey and a scything wind shook the grasses.

I stopped the car on a height overlooking a vast plain and noticed thigh-high, blue-green-purple bushes matting an adjacent hillside, shaking in the wind. It was sage. In the books of my childhood, outlaws always rode through it, or Native American shamans burned it so that its aroma cleansed their surroundings. I picked a piece; it had a sharp, pungent smell. I gazed across the plains to faraway mountains etching jagged patterns into the skyline. A wedge of rain cloud, stretching from the plain to the sky, spread towards me. Soft amber rays of light played around the edges of its black and grey clouds. A few minutes later, the town of Wisdom, nestling about halfway to the horizon, was absorbed into it, dissolving from view. I hoped it wasn't an omen!

I saw a sign for Big Hole National Battlefield Site. Because Terry of the Métis had told me a little of the Nez Perce story on the train trip through Montana, I decided to visit this historic site, which was the location of an infamous battle between the Nez Perce tribe and the US Army. The story of the tribe's war with the US government began in the Wallowa area of northeastern Oregon. This area of 3,145 square miles, comprising mountains, canyons, high valleys and pastures, all drained by the Wallowa River, was homeland to a band of Nez Perce under the leadership of Chief Joseph. The Nez Perce owned the largest herd of horses on the continent and were famous for their horse breeding, especially the celebrated, leopard-spotted Appaloosa horse. The Wallowa area is high in altitude and difficult to access, but it is bountiful. The tribe's pattern was to spend summer at the headwaters of rivers in high mountain valleys and to retreat in winter to the shelter of the deep river canyons. They hunted deer, elk and bear, caught salmon in the Clearwater and Snake Rivers and harvested camas – a bulb that tastes like sweet potato – in the meadows.

In the 1860s and 1870s, settlers moved onto these lands in increasing numbers, leading to disputes. The government's initial reaction was to grant these lands to the Nez Perce as part of their reservation and to compensate settlers for improvements carried out. However, both the settlers and the Methodist Church put pressure on the government to change this decision. The Methodists trenchantly opposed the Nez Perce 'Dreamer' religion, where shamans guided the people through dreams. The Dreamers demanded rejection of the white man's culture and opposed ideas of land ownership and farming. 'Mother Earth' sustained them, was abundant and needed respect. The Methodists believed that such 'heathen' beliefs should be eradicated and joined with the settlers in advocating that the Nez Perce be sent to the Lapwai Reservation in Idaho, to be 'Christianised'. The government ordered General Howard to hold talks with Chief Joseph to 'persuade' him to move.

Talks quickly reached an impasse. Chief Joseph declared that the earth was his mother and nurse. He was made of earth and grew up on its bosom. Mother Earth was sacred to his affections, too sacred to be valued by, or sold for, silver and gold. He would not agree to break his connections with the land that bore him. After unsuccessfully attempting to change his mind, General Howard issued an ultimatum, giving him one month to move onto the reservation or else the tribe would be moved forcibly and all their stock seized.

With great reluctance, Chief Joseph ordered that all livestock should be collected in preparation for the move. However, a few Nez Perce braves, in a drunken spree, killed a number of settlers and the army declared war on the tribe. The Nez Perce, greatly outnumbered, fled. Thus began one of the great journeys by any people in

American History. Eight hundred men, women and children from the Nez Perce left their homelands in northeast Oregon with the intention of moving 1,800 miles through difficult mountainous country in search of perceived freedom in Canada. After minor skirmishes, they outmanoeuvred the army and slipped out of Oregon, entering the Bitterroot Valley.

I drove up to the site's administration centre at five o'clock, as a woman was closing the doors for the day. However, she gave me permission to explore on my own. From outside the centre, I viewed the battle site that lay below in the valley. A small river flowed there. It was bounded by bluffs on three sides, hence the name 'Big Hole'. I drove down to the large car park at the site, where I was the solitary visitor.

The Nez Perce set up camp and, confident of their safety, didn't post any guards for the night. However, General Howard had alerted Colonel Gibbon that Chief Joseph was headed in his direction. Gibbon's scouts found the Nez Perce and, with surprise on his side, Gibbon led his two hundred troops in an early morning attack. The army fired two volleys before rushing upon the tepees, where ninety men, women and children were killed. Pandemonium reigned. Women grabbed their children and ran to the reeds and willows on the river to hide. Some of the Nez Perce returned fire and hand-to-hand fighting broke out. One of the Nez Perce chiefs, White Bird, rallied his braves and gradually the tide of battle turned. The soldiers retreated to a clump of trees, taking up a defensive formation. The Nez Perce pinned them there for nearly a day, during which the tribe were able to escape.

Cat-and-mouse skirmishes between the tribe and the army continued until the final showdown, when General Miles caught up with the Nez Perce in high plains near the Bear Paw Mountains, forty miles from the Canadian border. After a fierce engagement on October 4th 1877, Chief Joseph, troubled by the death of many of his family, friends and colleagues, surrendered, on condition that the remnants of his tribe could return to the Wallowa. Even though General Miles' intentions were honourable, this agreement was later discarded, as his political and military superiors wanted to make an example of 'the Indians' for fear of further rebellions. Chief Joseph and his depleted tribe achieved celebrity status in the media of the time and were feted publicly, but, despite this, they ended up being shunted from reservation to reservation and were never allowed to return home.

The winding path at the Big Hole battle site followed the river through stands of willow and cottonwood before opening into a wide meadow. In the distance, I could discern a circular encampment consisting of bare lodges with tepee poles looking like bleached, bare bones in the fading light. This camp was sheltered against the elements. You could imagine camping here, listening to the wind and the river talking. This is now a shrine to the tribe and hanging on the poles of the tepee lodges were feathers, ribbons and medicine bags. Chief Joseph's lodge was lavishly adorned. I stood inside a lodge where three women were killed. The breeze murmured, the river rustled on by and the sound of the medicine bags beat their drum in memory of long ago. A strange emotion filled me. It had elements of sadness, futility, serenity, gentleness and forgiveness. Time had passed and this site had turned from a place of pain and suffering to a sacred place where the balm of nature and reverence for memory soothed old wounds.

I returned to Crusty and, in the gathering gloom, I headed for the Bitterroot Valley. Snow fell as I ascended the icy road on Chief Joseph's pass. For mile after mile, I was the only vehicle on the road. At the top of the pass, I came to a T-junction. To the right was the Bitterroot Valley, and to the left a signpost said, 'Welcome to Idaho'. Like a person who claims they have visited a country if they've been to the airport, I turned left and crossed the Idaho state line. Duly satisfied, I turned back and headed down another steep pass into the Bitterroot Valley. Precipitous gorges lay on either side and whole mountainsides of trees had been blackened by fire. At the bottom, the countryside opened out into a fertile valley floor, bounded by two tall mountain ranges, the Bitterroot Range to the west and the Sapphire Range to the east. This sheltered valley is similar to a desert. It gets just fifteen inches of precipitation per year, while the mountain ranges get one hundred inches. It's ideal; water with little rain! I entered Hamilton in darkness.

'That day would skin you.' The words of my mother came back to me as I stepped out into the early morning light in Hamilton. A powdering of snow lay on the ground and a bitter wind swept up the street. I searched for shelter and found it in a warm, well-stocked bookshop owned by Russ Lawrence, a slim man with trim beard, round glasses and a blue shirt. I asked him if he had any books on the natural history of the area and quickly struck paydirt. He whisked me to a bookstand where his own book on the Bitterroots had pride of place. In two shakes of a lamb's tail and with a Garfield smile playing on his face, he sold me a personally signed copy.

Having found a treasure trove of information, I asked him where I could go hiking. This elicited a search for a piece of paper on which he drew a map.

'Blodgett Canyon is the most beautiful canyon in the Bitterroots. If you're going on a one-day hike, this is the one for you. Be careful. I hiked there last week and I didn't see any bear but I did meet aggressive elk. Most of the time you'll not see or hear anything. Most animals will try to avoid you.'

It was the word 'most' that worried me, but at the same time I was a little disappointed. What's the point of being in the wilderness if you can't see wildlife … at a distance?

Russ told me that the Bitterroots were named after the Montanan state flower. It is a small plant with purple to pink flowers that grows in the foothills. This begged the question; how did the flower get its name?

'It's because of the taste', said Russ, 'Native Americans eat the roots of this flower and it has a bitter taste. It tastes better when cooked and mixed with berries. They believed if you ate the tap root, it protected you from bear attack.'

'I should find some', I joked.

Lyman and Mary Blodgett were settlers who moved to the Bitterroot area from Utah in 1867 in a covered wagon. Like most other settlers, they were poor people, driven by a mixture of desperation and hope, willing to endure hardship to build a new life for their family. Knowing little of the politics that lay behind the opening of Salish lands for their use, they only saw an opportunity to improve their lives. While they prospered in Montana, they also experienced tragedy. On the journey from Utah, their daughter Polly died, then, a few years later, 14-year-old Mary also died. The girls' parents named Blodgett Canyon in memory of their lost girls. In the great well of despair, people always try to hold onto something solid that will help them identify with a fading form.

The car park and adjacent camping site at Blodgett Canyon were empty. I got out of the car into cold, glaring sunlight. The surrounding vegetation was frozen stiff. There were two signs. The first said, 'This is Bear Country'. The second sign warned all hikers to be on the look-out for a particularly aggressive bear. As I headed off on the trail through trees, the ground crackled, loud in the stillness, under my feet. On each side I could glimpse sheer canyon walls rising in places up to four thousand feet. Those grey granite walls of rock were spectacular. Even to get to the base of them would be a chore, as you would have to cross forest, rough boulders and scree. This was real wilderness.

There was evidence of fire everywhere, as vast tracts of forest within the canyon had been burned, leaving black, charred remains of trees. I walked through two miles of such devastation, but when you looked closely you could see seedling firs and aspens painting new greens and yellows into the landscape. Wildfire plays an important role in the life of the ecosystem here. It detoxifies and clears out decadent growth, recycling nutrients. However, encroaching human habitation has complicated the matter and fire suppression is now the policy.

As I climbed, the snow thickened, but as the sun climbed higher the snow began to melt, causing glistening water drops to congregate at the edge of pine needles, before dropping to the canyon floor. Silence descended on the mountain, except for the occasional warning calls of small birds. I saw paw marks in the snow and immediately thought, 'mountain lion'. I laughed and told myself not to let my imagination run away with me.

A river accompanied me up the canyon. When I couldn't see it, I could hear it, channelling its way through rock. I came across a still section in the shade of aspen and pine, where the river's surface glimmered green, black and dark blue. It was a beaver pool. I stopped to look at that jumble of wood, its lodge. A ripple spread across the pool, lifting a small leaf as it went. On a bridge across the river, I saw the paw marks again, and looked down the course of the river. The white of its tumbling waters blended with the light snow on its banks. Bare fallen trees were scattered haphazardly over its surface, like matches fallen out of a box. Straight, straggly fir trees provided a frame that drew the eye down along the river into the valley below. I could see the altitude line of the trees drawn along the face of the mountains and, above this, the tough terrain of sheer cliffs, cave, boulder and scree formed a rugged and challenging environment. I imagined what it would have been like to play cowboys here, under fire from dry-gulching varmints. What fun we could have had in a setting like this. Our parents wouldn't have seen us for weeks.

I walked for another thirty minutes before I stopped and retraced my steps to Crusty. It was time to head towards Browning.

11

Cowboy Country

Lao Tzu once said, 'A good traveller has no fixed plans and isn't intent on arriving.'

As I drove along with a light heart, I was accompanied by beautiful mountain scenery, flowing rivers and wooded mountainsides. Perhaps I wasn't as free as I felt, but I was content. Country music, with hearty refrains extolling hay barns, pick-up trucks and the 'chi-chi-choo' of trains, played on the radio. I passed many ranches, some with the traditional log fencing still in evidence, though most used utilitarian wire fencing. Ranching has moved on since Mici's time, when the cowboy achieved his greatest flourishing.

An early pioneer said, 'Montana must become the great grazing country of the United States.' Up until the 1880s, only a few, small, family-owned ranches existed to supply the local market. However, with the extermination of the buffalo and the removal of the Native American tribes, the rich grasslands of the prairies were taken into public ownership and thrown open as a free resource for exploitation. This enticed a new breed of rancher, the corporate investor from the eastern states and Europe. This group of people wouldn't know one end of a steer from another, but by 1884 these absentee corporate ranchers and their 'ranch managers' packed a sea of longhorn cattle, driven from Texas, onto the range. Their intention was to make a rapid return on investment. There was no consideration for the land, the animals or the people working for them.

Soon, warning voices in the press claimed that there were too many cattle on the plain, that the grass was too closely grazed and there was no shelter or feed for animals in bad weather. This whole edifice, built upon a foundation of sand, was swept away with the arrival of the Kissineyooway in the winters of 1886 and 1887. Kissineyooway is the Cree word for 'it blows cold' and it certainly blew cold that winter.

The temperatures dropped to a low of -63 degrees. Snow was piled into high, sharp-edged drifts. If an animal stepped into one, its flesh would be cut to the bone. There was no grass. Up to five thousand head of bawling cattle, eyes crazed with hunger, invaded the new town of Great Falls, eating trees and rubbish in a vain effort to survive.

In Harper's New Monthly, Julian Ralph wrote, 'The cattle owners are in Florida or the South of France in the winter; but their cattle are in the wintry fields …. The poor beasts die by the thousands – totter along until they fall down, the living always trying to reach the body of a dead one to fall upon.'

The Chinook wind, or the 'snow eater' as the Cree call it, arrived in March and brought relief from freezing temperatures. It was only then that scale of the disaster became evident, when the ranches started their spring roundup and found rotting carcases littered across the plains. Up to 70 per cent of the cattle were wiped out, compared to the usual winter loss of 10 per cent. This brought ruin, especially for the bigger corporate ranches that had made no emergency provision. Thus ended the ranching boom, immortalised in fiction through cowboy stories, but which in reality lasted a short number of years.

Through this entire story, it was neither the rancher nor the investor who claimed the popular imagination, but the cowboy. He rode a horse where he wished, engaged in dangerous physical adventure and was apparently unconfined. These things made him the heroic projection of people's desires.

The depiction of the cowboy heroes as square-chinned Caucasians is suspect as, in reality, the majority were either Mexican or African-American. The word 'hero' wasn't something the cowboy had much time to think about. He worked long, monotonous hours with little sleep in conditions ranging from searing heat and dust to extreme cold, all for a few dollars a week.

§

I drove east along the Blackfoot River and reached Lincoln as evening gathered in. Lincoln is a long string of a town, straddling the main highway, with businesses, motels and bars spread at intervals along it. For a small town, it had an amazing array of signs, all clamouring for your attention. I selected yet another anonymous motel and afterwards went for a walk down a gravel road leading to the Blackfoot

River. I passed an estate of small, red, wooden houses with wild deer scampering about in their gardens, their tails flashing like white beacons in the twilight. Further along, three horses grazed in a grove of birch and aspen trees, all glowing in the bronzed, slanting light. A Palomino horse trotted over and put his head over the wooden fence. I patted him. The drought-ravaged river, little more than a trickle, was lost in the grand landscape of large fields, many adorned with mahogany barns, that stretched away into the wilderness.

Back in the motel room, I turned on the television and was shocked that nostalgia flooded through me when I heard, of all things, a British accent. Needing a drastic remedy, I took the age-old solution and went to the pub. I sat at the bar and met a man called Lenny, who sported a dapper moustache, and his wife Mary, who had a shock of blonde curls. They were ranchers.

Mary said she was half-Irish and half-German and declared that she was going to Ireland for her fortieth birthday in a few years' time. She wanted to know if she would be able to ride horses on the beaches in Ireland, as she had seen on television. Mary's sister-in-law, Sharla, came over. Dressed in denim blue and holding a bottle of beer, Mary introduced her as 'my greatest friend'. Sharla had been raised hunting and had been taught how to skin, clean and cut a deer as a child.

'I can do it better than most men', she said. Every hunting season, she and her husband kill four deer and one elk. 'It keeps us eating for five months. We've meat every day. I'm teaching my kids now the way that I was taught myself.'

A cowboy called Kenny filled me in about the rodeo. The most entertaining event was the wild-cow milking, where cowboys have to chase and lasso a cow, then milk her. Whoever can collect the required amount of milk in the quickest time is the winner. It sounded like great fun but I wondered about the cow.

Mary asked me if I had ever ridden a horse. I told them that I had only ridden donkeys. To their great amusement, I told them about one really mean black donkey that always made a beeline for trees in an attempt to knock me off on low-lying branches.

Later, an elderly man called Tom came over as I was talking about the deer I had seen.

'Doggone it', he said, 'those darn deer get everywhere.'

Everyone laughed. When I asked Tom how he was, he puffed up and said, 'Pretty darn good, seeing that I'm eighty-nine.'

I looked at him in disbelief. He was lean, active and erect. I wanted to know how he kept young.

'Plenty of hard work, plenty of whiskey and plenty of fun', he said, to the further amusement of those around him. He must have thought that I could do with some help keeping myself young, because he shouted to the barman to give me a shot of whiskey, which arrived despite my protestations. More whiskeys followed, from a variety of sources. After a while, the barman started to worry that I might be getting young too quickly. He whispered to Mary as she was buying another whiskey, 'Don't go too far, I think he's had enough.'

Mitch was a moustachioed hunter who favoured archery because of the satisfaction he got in manoeuvring to within thirty metres of the prey. He liked to get close to ensure that the animal was killed instantly. He had even shot two bears with arrows.

'What does bear meat taste like?'

'Most people don't like the meat. They think it's too strong. It's all in how it's cooked.'

He explained how he cooked palatable bear meat; something about marinades, the use of garlic, putting the meat in jars and the use of pressure cookers. I jokingly suggested Guinness for the recipe and he obligingly replied he might try it the next time. I was curious about what a bear's temperament was like.

'A bear is a mixture of a dog and a pig, only bigger.'

Mary asked if I would be staying around for a few days. When I said no, she said it was a pity, as they would have liked to invite me for dinner the following evening.

'I love to cook', she said. Then she had a bright idea. 'You should visit my uncle in Helmville. He's eighty-two. He'd love to meet an Irish person. He'll probably give you so much whiskey that you mightn't be able to go further tomorrow.'

Full of enthusiasm, she wrote down his address and made me promise to call. She told me that Helmville was located in a remote mountain valley and that 90 per cent of its population was Irish.

On returning to my room, the sense of nostalgia had disappeared.

The next morning, despite the whiskey, I woke up hungry and went to the local diner for breakfast, joining a group of men sitting at the breakfast counter. All were dressed in the usual western garb: jackets, boots, padded shirts and baseball caps. A rather grouchy waitress shoved a menu at me. Behind the bar two posters proclaimed, 'We hate tree huggers' and 'Tree huggers suck'.

I tried to talk to the young man beside me but he was more interested in listening to jokes about sex and discussing trucks and hunting with his mates.

On leaving the café, I debated. Would I visit Mary's uncle in Helmville or go straight to Browning? I visualised knocking on some stranger's door, announcing my arrival to startled people who would probably wonder what I was trying to sell them. Discouraged by the thought, I deciding to proceed to Browning.

I got to the end of the town, then changed my mind. I told myself not to be afraid of making a fool of myself. After all, what was the worst that could happen?

I turned the car and went searching for Helmville amongst minor roads and lost valleys in the middle of Montana. An hour later, I found the few houses that made up the village and stopped to ask directions to the 'Geary Ranch' from a young woman manoeuvring two babies and a dog into a car.

'Which Geary is that?' she asked; seeing my face she continued, 'Yes, there's more than one Geary.'

I told her the name and she pointed. 'Go along this road and take the first right, followed by the first left.' She then started to give me another set of directions in case I should get lost.

I threw my hands up in horror. 'I'm a man. I can't cope with too much detail.'

She laughed and said, 'I'm Irish too', as if this were a further explanation.

I turned left onto a dirt road. On one side, Black Angus cattle grazed a prairie that stretched to the mountains, and, on the other, there was a large gravel pit. The ranch entrance was directly opposite rodeo grounds which contained an impressive-looking stand. A sign showed the admission prices for the rodeo: adults $5 and children under six free.

I hesitated momentarily at the entrance, before driving up the tree-lined avenue towards distant ranch buildings. I kept telling myself I hadn't come all this way just to turn back. I drove into the ranch-house yard. On the right hand side were three sizeable, mahogany-coloured barns and on the left a house set amongst some trees. A large log pile lay outside one of the barns with a shiny hatchet wedged in a log.

Everything was quiet and there was no one to be seen. I parked beside a pick-up truck.

I clunked my way up steps onto a porch and knocked on the front door. The noise created a commotion but not the one I expected. A large Airedale dog with a lean, muscled black and tan body jumped off another porch and came racing towards me, barking loudly. He stopped beside me and sniffed my shoes and trousers. Still no response from inside. Feeling relief, I gave the door one last knock. At this, the dog dashed in through a flap in the door and resumed his barking inside. Where my knocking had failed, this racket succeeded and a slightly perplexed, brown-haired woman opened the door. She looked at me with a strong, level gaze as she listened to my story, which seemed a little implausible, even to me. I squirmed, knowing that my only possible salvation was my Irishness. I apologised for arriving unannounced.

'Don't worry about that. Come on in. My name is Moe.'

We went into a small dining room where a man sat reading the paper and drinking coffee. Bill, a wiry eighty-two-year-old, gave me a quizzical look and invited me to sit down at the table. I sat with my back to the wall. The dog, duty done, lay down beside the log fire. They told me that I was the second stranger who had come knocking on their door that year. The first, also from Ireland, had been looking up relatives in America. It took Bill a few moments to remember the name of the place the stranger came from.

'Ballyduff. That's where my ancestors were from. Have you heard of it?'

I shook my head. Moe remembered a clue. 'Something to do with crystal?'

'Waterford Crystal. Is it County Waterford?'

'Yes, that's it', said Bill, 'that guy appeared at the door just like you.'

I asked them what they knew about Irish connections with the area. Bill said that a group of people had come from Ireland and had started mining gold in the mountains. They found enough to buy land in this valley in the 1860s.

'The families have stuck together in this community ever since.'

'They must have struck it rich', I said.

'No, the only ones who made money were the merchants.'

I laughed and thought that with this reply, there was no doubt at all but that Bill had Irish blood in his veins. I could understand why these families 'stuck together', as in this landscape of infinite skies, endless plains, extreme weather and towering mountains, you needed all the help and support you could get.

Such a landscape demanded practical, problem-solving skills for survival. It's a world far removed from suburban America, and I could see how, in Bill and Moe's eyes, I might be perceived as a cosseted representative of a suburban world, dipping into their experience. As their ancestors had mined gold, I mined information.

They had two sons and one daughter. Their tone warmed as they talked about them.

'The army are paying for the oldest boy to do a PhD', said Moe.

'What's he studying?'

'It's a system for the early identification of water contamination, especially in relation to terrorist threat.'

According to Moe and Bill, the government was especially worried that the water supplies of many cities and towns were vulnerable to attack. A defensive technology was needed to counter the threat.

Their other son had served twice in Iraq and had won three Purple Hearts for bravery. He was injured on the first tour when he saved his troops in an ambush. He made a good recovery and went straight back to Iraq. He then got an award for inventing a more effective method of quickly moving heavy field weaponry around the battle field. This made it safer for troops because it wasn't as easy to pinpoint their position.

'I work in the forestry department', said Moe, 'and it's full of rules. We can't sell timber because some group or other, whose only concern is to preserve every snail in existence, will sue us. They've no idea of the wider picture. Timber needs to be felled and sold to maintain healthy forests and keep people in jobs.'

She said forests in Montana were already under stress because of drought, and that the pine beetle had attacked and killed weakened trees, leaving a trail of devastation across the state. Older trees were especially vulnerable; trees that could have been logged at an earlier stage if that had been permitted.

'Those environmental people, they're making rules 'bout everything', said Bill.

§

On my way back to Lincoln, I saw one of the most magnificent wild places in the United States, the Bob Marshall Wilderness. If many people touch the earth with a heavy hand, we are fortunate that some have a somewhat lighter touch. One of these was Bob Marshall. The wilderness called after him is one million acres of soaring peaks, surging white water and shiny snowfields, where the spirit can fly with eagles.

A book Marshall read as a boy called *Topographical Survey of the Adirondack Wilderness* sparked his love of nature. Though the title would hardly grab your attention, its descriptions of nature and wildlife created a fascination for wilderness within him. After graduating in natural studies, Marshall became a forester in Montana and immersing himself physically in the wilderness; he undertook hundreds of tortuous treks. This involved scaling mountains, snowshoeing across plateaus and scrambling through canyons and rivers, all with a heavy pack on his back. He lived for a year in an isolated Eskimo village in Alaska. In his own words, it was 'the most glorious year in my life'.

He said, 'The inhabitants of Koyukuk would rather mush dogs with adventure than to have the luxuries and restrictions of the outside world.'

On his return, he studied for a PhD and produced a work which became known as 'the Magna Carta for wilderness'. He called for spirited people to fight together for the freedom of the wilderness, because without it 'there would be countless souls born to live in strangulation.' He battled, with others, to develop wilderness areas containing neither roads nor logging activity. His movement resulted in the addition of 5.4 million acres to the nation's wilderness system. The Bob Marshall Area contains miles upon miles of pristine forests, where bears, wolves, wolverines and cougars roam, undisturbed by man.

However, the heavy hand on nature is never far away. There is now a campaign to allow oil and mineral companies access to the area. The struggle for the remaining wilderness goes on. It is a recurring battle that needs to be fought by successive generations.

I stopped at Rogers Pass and watched birds of prey circling. In January 1954, the temperature here was measured at -70 degrees, a record for the United States.

On the far side of the pass, the terrain started to change. Trees faded away and the landscape opened up. The road rolled along open prairie with long, straight ascents and descents. A cold wind had risen and swept across the land, shaking any blade of grass standing tall. I stopped at Dearborn River and, even sheltering in the gully, the air was biting. Hibernation had come early for the bare, skeletal trees that hunkered down in this river gulley. Grey clouds rolled across the sky, threatening snow, and my mind sunk into deep loneliness. Whereas the peaceful shade of solitude can revive mind and spirit, the melancholic mind creates despair that wallows in self-pity. I knew however my melancholic incarceration would pass.

Subdued, I turned along Route 287 towards Augusta and Choteau, only to be confronted by mile after mile of road works. For hours, Crusty rattled across rough gravel roads, dodging huge earthmovers as it went. The scene became apocalyptic, full of gravel, dust, huge earth-gobbling machines, grey skies, empty prairies and brooding mountains in the distance. I wished I could get out of this misery.

I finally arrived at a one-horse town called Augusta and entered lands dominated in turn by large dinosaurs, the Blackfeet Native American tribe and large ranchers. Some of the most spectacular dinosaur finds ever have been made in this part of Montana. T. Rex and a motley assortment of other scary creatures roamed the landscape for millions of years. It is truly a fitting setting for them.

I crossed the Sun River, once the stomping ground of the Blackfeet Indians, and drove onto Choteau, still undecided if I would continue on to Browning. In a local supermarket a young cashier warned me, 'Don't stay in Browning.'

'Why not?'

'Lots of crazies live there.'

I decided then that I would stay in Choteau that night and go to Browning the following day.

Later, as I searched for the motel room key, the cold wind chased leaves up and down the pathway in rustling flurries before finally corralling them in an eddy of swirling energy. I entered the room and the wind crept in after me. It blew underneath and around the edges of the door and window, making the venetian blinds shiver. I rubbed my hands and waved my arms to get the blood flowing. In the room next door, dogs started to bark. This was a hunter's motel and dogs were welcome. A few signs with pithy sayings were displayed on the dressing table. I liked this one best: 'The two best times to go fishing are when it's raining and when it isn't.'

The centrepiece of the room was a large fireplace, with logs provided. I lit a fire before going out, thinking it would take the chill out of the air, but when I returned the fire had died and the room was full of smoke.

12

Browning and Glacier National Park

There must have been something in that smoke because, driving to Browning the following morning, my eye was alive to beauty. The prairie can seem to be one huge featureless expanse of oaten colour stretching forever. On closer inspection, you become aware of an exhilarating world, and I watched with pleasure as strong winds sent waves of energy pulsing through long grasses, creating interweaving patterns of subtle flowing colours, stretching to the horizon. The Rocky Mountains, to the distant west, looked like an inconsequential afterthought compared to the immensity of the plains.

There was a crisis on the radio. Paul McCartney had lost his head. There was no need to panic though, as it had been found again in a rubbish bin, and the lucky finder had received a four thousand dollar reward. I had thought that McCartney's head would have been worth more, but the fact that it was made of wax probably brought down the value slightly.

I stopped to take a photograph of a solitary green barn sitting in the middle of a vast grain field. In the background, the snowy white tips of the Rocky Mountain Front appeared through a ribbon of lingering cloud. A sign on the roadside grabbed my attention with its thought-provoking message, 'Wildlife Conservancy – Hunters Welcome!'

Something else grabbed my attention. Parked beside an impenetrable wire fence, miles long, was an armoured car and two large 4X4 vehicles with blacked-out windows. Soldiers and men in black suits and sunglasses stood on the roadside, talking. Shortly afterwards I spotted two similar 4X4 vehicles coming along the road towards me. What could be going on here? I pulled into a lay-by to read a sign. No sooner had I got out of the car than another 4X4 pulled up alongside me. The blacked-out window of the vehicle lowered, to reveal two fresh-faced and clean-shaven guys in their thirties, drinking coffee. One of them called out a 'hello' and a few pleasantries were exchanged. Interview over, he closed the window, shuttering out the world. Later, I was told that there was a nuclear missile site adjacent to this road and that if Montana declared itself a republic it would be the fourth-largest nuclear power in the world.

The road ascended to the top of a rolling hill. I got out and gazed at the prairie sweeping away like a flat sea to the horizon. There was a sizeable speckle of dwellings in the distance that I took to be Browning. Those speckles looked like they could be blown away by the wind and reminded me that all physical and mental structures are temporary, no matter how hard we strive to put stamps of permanence upon them. Only two things moved across that vista. A long freight train, far away, snaked its way towards the town and a car, equally distant, headed in my direction.

§

Browning had a feeling of temporariness. Perhaps it was the cultural legacy of a migrant people who once moved with the seasons and the winds, following the bounty of nature. Now, rows and rows of pre-fabricated wooden houses, men drinking on the street and roaming dogs gave the impression of a camp that had stayed in the same place too long.

I drove to a solid square building, the 'Museum of the Plains', as it reputedly provided an informative history of the Blackfeet people. It was closed for the weekend.

Micí mentioned the Blackfeet whenever they flared into his world; when there was trouble, war or they were kidnapping settlers' wives. Like Micí, the Blackfeet were immigrants in Montana, as this area only became part of their territory in the eighteenth century. Their previous migrations brought them from forests in the northeast of the US into Canada and finally onto the Great Plains. At the height of their influence, their territory ranged from the Saskatchewan River in Canada to the Missouri River in Montana, which was a huge area. The Native American tribes, similar to Celtic tribes, were continuously competing for resources, power and territory. In Celtic history we have observed the feelings engendered when one Celtic tribe transplanted another. Animosities were handed down through generations and divided tribes were easily conquered. Similarly, it never dawned on North

American tribes to cooperate, as together they could have mounted considerable resistance to the white man's progress. The only chief who advocated this was Sitting Bull of the Sioux nation, and only when facing imminent defeat. By then, it was too late.

The result for the Blackfeet was the same as for other tribes; confinement to a reservation, where alcohol drowned the loss. The experience of reservation life has been a spiritual disaster for the proud and warlike Blackfeet nation and these problems extend to the current day.

§

I walked into the small reception area of a Browning motel, where a sign invited guests to help themselves to complimentary coffee. The pot was empty. The sound of people talking and a television growling came from the lounge area behind the counter. I knocked twice and finally a young, thin man in his twenties, with long, black hair tied in a ponytail, emerged. He tapped the counter while I asked about a room. He quoted an extortionate price. Seeing the empty parking lot, I made a reasonable counter-offer.

He shook his head impatiently. 'That's the price.'

I persisted, exuding a message of hopeful expectation. He wanted to be somewhere else and with no quick solution forthcoming, he said, 'hold on', and went into the living room, where I heard him talking to an older female.

The details of the conversation were drowned out by the television. He returned and accepted my offer. The paper preliminaries quickly sorted, he handed over the key and disappeared. However, if he thought he was free from aggravation, he was to be disappointed, as I couldn't open the room door with my key. When I knocked on the counter again, he came and stood sideways in the doorway, edging from foot to foot, as I explained my predicament. He huffily told me to go back and wait at the room. A few minutes later a teenage girl with a good-natured smile appeared. She solved the problem.

When walking up the town, I was twice nearly knocked down by speeding cars at junctions, even though the pedestrian lights were green. I could see the people in these cars laughing, taking great amusement at my sudden dash for safety. It probably served me right, as I always jaywalked in America, not understanding why people would wait for a green light when there wasn't a car in sight.

On that short walk, two men asked me for money. One pointed to a white pick-up truck parked across the street, claiming that he needed money for gas to get home.

§

The 'Road to the Sun', as it is known, is a fifty-mile drive over the Rocky Mountains. I planned to drive to the end and back again. However, when I arrived at the gates leading into Glacier National Park and onto the road the following day, I learned that only an eleven-mile stretch was open, due to the threat of snow at higher levels. The drive along these eleven miles was full of spectacular scenery. The mountains were magnificent craggy lumps of rock that towered into the sky above me. They had erupted from the surface countless eons ago and had been carved into their present shapes by moving ice. These imposing mountains combined with the icy-blue St Mary's Lake to create a variety of beautiful vistas that stirred my awe. I drove until I reached a barrier that declared there was no access allowed beyond that point. Undaunted, I climbed over the barrier and walked up the road.

The trouble with mountain roads is that they have lots of tantalising bends. You are drawn inexorably by the lure of the unknown. Two hours later I was still walking uphill. Leaving the road, I scrambled up along a small track and my reward was to reach a narrow gorge, home to a rushing stream. If the Rockies were beautiful in a grand scale, this stream burrowing its way through boulders, with beams of light playing on its waters, was beautiful in a more unassuming way. I sat there and looked at the Rocky Mountains strutting to the sky. The higher slopes looked inhospitable to any form of life, with craggy outcrops, sheer drops, crevices and the wind blowing snow in swirling crescents off the mountain. It's no wonder this terrain had a spiritual significance for the Blackfeet. At one stage, it formed part of their agreed reservation, but was subsequently taken from them when it was decided to open a national park here. Nature too is considered a product. A national park doesn't include the people who feel connected to the landscape.

We risk losing connections with the natural world. Our culture gives no credence to the mystic meaning of a sacred mountain or to the meaning of the order of wild birds in flight. We are losing the capacity to describe the roar of the black wind, the Chinook, the silence of the white cold or the whisper of falling snow. We no longer test ourselves against nature and face its elemental fury in the understanding that it will produce within us some insight into the meaning of our existence.

As evening started to close in, I retraced my steps. Everything was quiet. The tops of the mountains were bathed in the dying golden light of the day while the lower parts were cast in deep, dark shadows. There was something uplifting about being alone in this landscape.

The car was still a few hundred metres distant when a flurry in the trees, thirty metres in front of me, drew my attention. The next few moments became the longest in my life, as out of the undergrowth popped a bear. I stopped dead in my tracks and the bear, oblivious to me, continued across the road. When it got halfway, it must have sensed an alien presence because it stopped, lifted its head and looked directly at me. Those pig eyes bore into mine and its ears pricked forward. I was subjected to intense scrutiny. Time stood still. But this was only a break in stride for the bear because it continued on its way and, with a slight shake in the bushes, it was gone. Everything was quiet again, except for my pounding heart.

I was in a quandary. The bear's path stood between me and Crusty, and my mind filled with all sorts of scenarios, most of them horrible. I scanned the undergrowth and listened for the slightest noise. I thought I should hear it escaping in the distance, or that a chorus of birds would announce the passage of a predator. Nothing stirred. I stood like this for five minutes before advancing, making as much noise as possible. Making noise was like the sudden urge to pray in a crisis. I passed the spot where the bear re-entered the forest and walked briskly on. I reached Crusty and after a moment foostering with keys, I sat inside with a long sigh. A feeling of exhilaration surged through me, which lasted the rest of the day.

Having faced down the bear – well, that's my story – I put the car into gear and, secure in my tin box, I headed back towards Browning. Having been so conscious of bears in my earlier hikes, it was strange that I should encounter one in such an unexpected place. People asked me afterwards if it a grizzly or a black bear and I couldn't honestly answer. One person brought out pictures of both and pointed to the grizzly's distinguishing feature, the hump behind its head. When you see a bear close up in the wild for the first time, who looks for badges of identity?

I arrived in Browning after dark and seeing lights in a church, and recalling my encounter with the bear, I suddenly thought it was time to rejuvenate my religion. My timing was wrong. No sooner had I parked the car than people started to come out. Giving up on religion, I decided instead to go to the casino. It had opened in 2006 and was a joint venture between a private Native corporation and the Blackfeet tribal council. In commercial terms it was a great success and employed over one hundred tribal people.

Inside was a huge space full of people and whirring machines, card tables, roulette tables and restaurants. Women generally played the slot machines while the card sharks headed to small adjacent rooms for serious gambling. It felt like a labyrinth; everyone subsumed in a glitzy world full of tick-tack sounds. Soon, I became conscious that of the hundreds of people in the casino, I was the only white person.

An unusual thing happened then. A thin, middle-aged Native woman came up to me, looked closely at me for a moment, then pressed an object into my hands, saying, 'I want you to wear this for your protection.'

With that, she was gone. I looked at the object in my hands. It was an ornate necklace consisting of silver, wood and coloured beads. At the centre was a wooden pendant with nine small stones embedded into it. It felt heavy as I tied it around my neck. Not wanting to get involved in gambling, I bought a beer. Later, I saw the woman who had given me the necklace sitting in another part of the bar. I went over and introduced myself. Her name was Eva. I thanked her for the necklace and asked her why she had given it to me.

She replied, 'Because I felt the need to and I can always get another from my uncle if I want one. He makes them.'

Eva told me she worked for the tribal council and that much of her work was taken up with legal issues pertaining to the treatment of the tribal people on the reservation.

'We aren't getting our due from the nineteenth century', she said. 'We are taking a class action against the government. You can look it up on the website indiantrust.com.'

Her grandmother came as a child from the Blackfoot Reservation in Canada to Montana. However, the authorities in Montana took her from her family and sent her to state boarding schools in Pennsylvania and Arizona where children were treated like slaves. The philosophy of these 'Christian' schools was to 'kill the Indian and save the child'. Discipline was fierce. All children were forced to do heavy labour and carry out military drills. She told me that this policy began in the 1870s and continued until relatively recently. I asked her about her own family and she told me she had two girls, one married in Alaska and the other, 'lost in the wind'. However, she said that she knew that the girl who was lost would return again when she was ready. There was an echo here reverberating through generations.

An elegant, elderly man called Thomas leaned over to speak to me. Even in old age he was tall, with fine features. His long, graceful hand held mine in a strong grip for the duration of our conversation. Eva told me, after he went back to his friends, that 'He has been hit bad.' A few years before a white man, passing through, had murdered his son and nephew, and his wife had also died recently. Thomas turned to me occasionally, each time pressing my hand firmly. Once, I took back my hand quickly, but he shook his head and insisted that I shake his hand properly. Once, he leaned over to me and said with a smile, 'Everyone is watching you.' It was like he too was an outsider, but with an insider's knowledge. At one stage, I wanted to buy him a drink but Eva told me to put my money back in my pocket saying, 'You shouldn't be flashy about here.'

I told her about my encounter with the bear.

She replied, 'Those bears should be in hibernation by now.'

She explained that their food supply, such as berries and tree shoots, had been destroyed in forest fires in the national park and consequently they were struggling to get enough fat. They would postpone hibernation until they were ready. It seems that these competing instincts made them even grouchier.

A boisterous group of what turned out to be Eva's nieces, nephews and cousins flowed into the bar and greeted her with hugs, kisses and banter. I was introduced to all of them, and where previously I had noticed a reserve when talking with Native people, there was none here. The drink flowed and everyone became friendlier. As it was near Halloween, young adults in fancy dress suddenly crowded the bar. One guy dressed as Elvis strutted his stuff and everyone applauded. Another guy did a Michael Jackson 'Thriller' dance and a few drinkers contorted their bodies in an effort to imitate him. Alcohol continued to flow, even though some people grumbled at the restriction on Native people having no more than three drinks per hour. Eva bade farewell in the midst of this hubbub. The noise level rose and the night hummed with energy. Two grandsons came to take Thomas home but before he left, he stopped to shake my hand again.

One of the grandsons, who was in his twenties, stopped, looked me in the eye and said, 'We don't like whiteys.'

The other grandson pointed to Thomas and said, 'And that's the reason.'

On seeing this, a niece of Eva's called over a tall man in his thirties who was drinking at the bar and said to him, 'Sheriff, make sure you look out for this man.'

The sheriff, like a lot of the Blackfeet people, was an imposing figure, at least six foot six, and broad in proportion. We talked with jaded politeness for a while and he shook my hand before going back to his friends at the bar. Some of Eva's nieces and nephews wanted to know all about Ireland. They were especially interested when I talked about how our country had been colonised and persecuted. They invited me to a party they were heading to later, but I decided to say goodnight. Alcohol is a double-edged sword, particularly in a place that has suffered.

Back in my motel room, I was ready for bed when there was a loud banging on my door. Taken aback, I eventually asked who it was.

A muffled voice said, 'Telephone call for you at reception.'

I thought, 'That's a likely story!' No one knew I was in Browning. I made sure the door was well secured and jammed a chair under the door handle.

Then I shouted back, 'Ok, thanks!'

To my surprise, it worked. After a few more minutes shuffling around on the boardwalk, he left. I was a little worried about Crusty parked outside the door until I realised there was little I could do about it. Crusty had one great advantage though. He didn't stand out in a crowd. I went to bed, feeling on edge, but finally fell asleep only to be roused later when somebody else banged at the door looking to speak to me. I ignored the commotion and the night settled down with only the occasional police siren to disturb the tranquillity.

The next morning, I got up and went outside to see if my trusty steed was ok. All seemed fine with Crusty, and I opened its door to get a bottle of water only to find the water frozen solid. I noticed four men standing in an open barn talking and passing around bottles of alcohol. They were all dressed in heavy jackets and must have been there all night. Thirsty, I went to reception, but the coffee machine was still empty. Disgruntled, I went back to my room. It's always the small things that get you.

A big breakfast and a few mugs of coffee in a local diner helped ease the disgruntlement. I liked this diner. The place was full of nooks and crannies and different levels. When I came in, an old man with a grizzled face pointed to the only vacant table. I took my place near to a young family: mother, father and three young daughters. These girls were always on the go but the waitress, an aunt of theirs, contained them by giving them jobs. The place was humming. People moved between tables talking to people they knew, some young people were glued to mobile phones and a few older people were equally stuck in newspapers. The grub was good. It was a relaxed Sunday morning. I was sorry to be leaving Browning as I felt I had only scratched the surface of the place, but I had to drive to Whitefish to catch a train to Seattle.

13

Browning to Seattle

A long freight train emerged from a tunnel below me. It swept around a curve and trundled on by. The clanking of metal on metal gradually faded away into the distance. A river gushed alongside the railway line, incising its way through a valley of yellow aspen and larch. Above me a mountain, similarly clad in yellow, reached for the sky. I'd driven through the Rocky Mountains via the old secret pass of the Blackfeet nation, now called Maria's Pass. Because of its strategic importance, the Blackfeet strove to keep its location secret, especially from railroad engineers. They knew the railroad would bring more people, thus increasing pressure on their already declining reservation. However, in 1889, railroad surveyors, with the help of a Blackfeet guide called Coonsah, discovered the pass, paving the way for a new railroad route to Seattle and the west coast.

I followed the train towards Whitefish, passing a village called Hungry Horse, named after two logging horses called Tex and Jerry. These two independent souls thought that hauling logs was beneath their dignity, so they escaped, but had the bad luck to run into severe weather. To the amazement of all, they survived, but were so darned hungry when they were found again that the place was named after them.

On arrival in Bigfork, I called once more into Creative and Native where Jill and her husband greeted me like a long-lost friend. Jill noticed my necklace and when I marvelled about Eva's generosity, she said that Native people didn't have the same attachment to possessions that we have. She had just followed her inner voice. Jill said that 'give away celebrations' were sacred events within Native culture. They can be held on behalf of a deceased person, to honour someone, or, as in my case, they can be no more than a chance event. There is something in it for the giver as well. If the gift has a personal or sentimental value, it is a sign of a giving heart. It builds spiritual strength and suggests that the act of giving will return to them in a different form when they need it. Jill looked at the embedded stones in my necklace and wondered what they might represent. As I had no idea, she rang the chief of the Blackfeet. When she finished on the phone she said, 'That's a nice piece you've got there. It symbolises the promise by the father to the Native people that the Great Big Dipper will shine again in their lives. There are seven stones for the Big Dipper and a stone for the Great Spirit and one for the North Star. Keep looking at the piece and it will come together for you at the right time.'

I rambled around the shop and my attention was drawn to a piece of art full of circles and vivid colours. Jill said that the circle is a common symbol in Native life and art. Native people see the circle every time they look at nature, be it a bird's nest or the shape of wind-swept grass. Native people sit, dance, smoke and live in a circle and the round door of their tepee opens onto the rising sun. The circle is also a symbol for the movement through life from childhood to old age. She quoted a saying attributed to Swift Rabbit, a medicine man of the Blackfeet nation: 'If we lead a good life, we'll again find the wonderment, the acceptance and the resilience of a happy child.'

Einstein wrote that if we headed off into space and kept going in a straight line we would end up back where we started. Truly, life is a circle and straight lines aren't what they seem. When I left, Jill's parting words were, 'Keep smiling and enjoying; remember money and things are man-made, we live with what we have and are rich because we have the Great Spirit to look up at.'

I arrived back in Whitefish and, having bade farewell to Crusty, I arrived at the railway station for the 10.40 p.m. train to Seattle, often called the 'Iron Goat' because of the difficulty of the route through the Cascade Mountains in Oregon.

§

In late July 1898, word came to Micí from his friend Jim Anthony that there was loads of gold in the Klondike and that he should get his ass up there quick before it would all be gone. His message said that 'they were making a good bit.' When an Irish man says something like that, it means he's making a fortune. He also told them to take the gentleman's route to the Klondike. This involved taking a boat from Seattle to St Michael at the mouth of the Yukon in the Bering Sea and from there going by paddle boat to Dawson City. He warned them to avoid the route via the treacherous Chilkoot Pass. This inspired Mící and ten other colleagues to pack their few belongings and begin their journey from Butte to Dawson City via Seattle. All these guys understood what 'a good bit' meant.

Mící spent his last night preparing for his trip to the coast. He had none of the certainties that I had and might not have gone if he had realised what was in front of him.

When Mící came from Pennsylvania to Montana, he had paid for his train ticket, but now he and his friends wanted a free ride. They crept into Butte railway station. When a mile-long freight train stopped there, they slunk quietly along until they found an open goods carriage. They climbed in, locked the door behind them and travelled in relative comfort until they reached Missoula where they had to change trains.

§

The Iron Goat rolled into the station on time. We shunted forward and I was off on the last leg of my journey across America.

When we reached the first station at Spokane, the train ground to a prolonged stop. Curiosity aroused, I went out onto the platform and talked to the conductor. A short, sandy-haired man was also asking the reason for the delay. The conductor explained that, 'a man of senior years', as he elegantly put it, had died in a sleeper carriage and they had to break through a locked door to reach him. This news produced a sudden, passionate response from the sandy-haired man.

He dropped to his knees and began striking his breast, saying in a fervent, tremulous voice, 'Oh God, oh God.' He rose moments later and with tears in his eyes said to the conductor, 'I'm sorry man, oh my God I'm so sorry', and formally shook hands with him.

The conductor accepted his condolences with measured calm. Shaking his head he said, 'We see many things on this train, and sometimes it isn't a natural death.'

'Oh my God', the sandy-haired man repeated, his eyes even wider.

I returned to my seat beside a middle-aged woman who was gently snoring. In the seat opposite, a young woman's feet jutted out into the aisle as she sprawled asleep on her partner's lap, under a mountain of coats. During the night we passed through the Cascade Tunnel, which was built in 1929. At eight miles, it's the longest railway tunnel in the US.

When I awoke, the grey light of the early dawn had appeared in the rearview window of the carriage, framing ghostly silhouettes of massive mountains. I joined a small, elderly man to stare at the view of the snow-capped Cascade Mountains disappearing behind us. He was from Pennsylvania and had been a boat builder all his life. I suspected he was a good one because he had patient eyes and a strong hand. He enjoyed gazing at the countryside, especially as this was the first long trip he and his wife had taken in forty years. They had worked hard to rear their family and were now going to visit a son in Seattle. The man would have loved to give up work but was fearful, like many Americans, that if he did, he would lose his health insurance entitlements.

At this stage, we were leaving the land of jagged mountains, rushing white streams, clear skies, cottonwood, grizzly bear, eagle and raven and entering a flat land with mixed crops, grey rainy skies, Hereford cows, small airfields, towns, houses, maple trees, traffic, lumber yards and roads. We were leaving a wilderness of story and mystery and coming into a land of planned usage.

A forest of gently waving white masts was the first indication that we had arrived at the sea again. The marina at Everett was jam-packed with yachts bobbing and swaying unevenly to the beat of the ocean. The Iron Goat now turned south and galloped alongside Puget Sound on a narrow strip of land between cliff and shore. I could see the slight swell of the sea slapping on the seashore. Seven big birds flew flat and low across the water, six landed together, leaving just one to fly on farther. Where the heck was it going on its solitary journey, and why? A man with a poodle stood on a small expanse of beach no more than ten metres long. Both were gazing across the bay at a trawler steaming in mid-channel under a white cloud of gulls. We were entering Seattle, the second biggest port after San Francisco on the west coast.

This railway had taken me across America. The journey had been a mixture of friendly people and spectacular landscape. Paul Theroux said travelling by train is conducive to melancholia. He felt this because he was sitting behind glass, inoculated from the world, seeing bits of lives as they pass by. It did not affect me in this way. When I looked out of the window and saw bits of lives and bits of scenery, I was filled with curiosity and wonder. There is something freeing about travelling by train, as everyone is equal and each person's story is interesting. The trappings of the outside world disappear and only the journey and the stories exist.

Later I was to meet Marie, an environmentalist, who argued, 'we should nationalise the railways', as she felt that investment in high-speed rail travel for passengers and business users between cities would help build a sustainable economy. I wondered how popular nationalisation might be in the US.

'We've done it before, we can do it again.'

I was surprised at this answer, but Marie told me that the US government nationalised the railways twice, once during the First World War, and again in the 1970s when they went bankrupt. They were refinanced and quickly re-privatised.

Like Rome, Seattle is built on steep hills. After leaving the station, I wandered around, getting a feel for a surprisingly homely city. There were, however, large numbers of homeless people on the streets. They were mostly men, but one of the most striking images I saw was a six-year-old girl, with scared eyes, sitting in a pram full of alcohol, being pushed by two haggard and unkempt parents.

I found accommodation near the Space Needle, which, at over six hundred feet high, is visible for miles in every direction and is a useful homing device.

People often compare Seattle and Ireland because they have the same natural colours of grey and green; grey reflecting the water-laden skies and green the foliage. Seattle sits at 47 degrees latitude and Ireland somewhat higher between 53 and 55 degrees. Both are open to the oceans, with prevailing winds sweeping in from the water. Seattle only has 35 inches of rainfall per year, but it falls in continuous dribs and drabs, giving the city lots of gloomy skies, drizzly days and a mild climate. This, however, makes it a great place for growing things. This climate produced the magnificent conifer trees, especially the Douglas fir that filled this landscape before the white man came. This greenness was the main reason that a city developed in this otherwise unsuitable spot, with its tidal flats and steep hillsides with gradients of up to 49 degrees. Trees, cut initially for the San Francisco market, provided the source of wealth from which the city of Seattle developed. The steep terrain had one advantage as, after felling, it was easy to 'skid' the trees down a mountain path to the sea. The path down which the trees were skidded later became Pioneer Square, a place where ne'er do wells hung out, giving rise to the phrase 'Skid Row'.

It was in a downtown art gallery that I met Kathy, a five-foot, fair-haired dynamo from South Africa. Kathy had travelled the world but had settled in Seattle.

'Have you ever couch-surfed?' she asked brightly.

'Yeah, I do that a lot, usually watching sport.'

She laughed a surprisingly hearty laugh for such a small woman. I realised I must have cracked a joke unknown to myself.

'I have two couch-surfers coming in tonight. I'm expecting a call from them later.'

I nodded my head knowingly, saying little. Gradually, I learned that couch-surfing is an online community where people get free accommodation anywhere they go in the world.

As I left she said, 'I'm meeting the Italian couple in an Irish pub later. Why don't you come along too?' As an extra inducement she said, 'There's a table quiz on there. We could form a team.'

Later, in the Fadó bar, I had the privilege of naming the quiz team for Kathy and her two Italian visitors.

'Something Irish?' she suggested.

'Amarach.'

'What does that mean?'

'Tomorrow.'

'How do you spell it?'

When I spelled it, she said, 'You better write it.'

We were into the thick of it, but the first six questions were all about American football and it was downhill after that. We had the honour of finishing last. Our team blamed parochialism in Seattle. The neighbouring team jeered us. Defeated, I walked the few miles back up the hill towards the beacon of the Space Needle. I found it ok, but had to walk around it twice to figure out the direction to my motel. No wonder we came last.

On a muted grey morning I sat beside the totem pole near the modernised Pioneer Square. I had arrived too early for the 'Underground Tour of the City', which I had been told gave a good insight into the origins of Seattle. It was Saturday morning and the street was quiet. A pigeon picked amongst the scattered confetti of yellow leaves on the ground and a young man in a T-shirt ambled by with both hands in his pockets. Two caped policemen on horses clip-clopped slowly up the tree-lined street. One of them nodded as he passed. A man in a brown coat and denim jeans looked closely at the carvings on the sixty-foot totem pole. At the top, a raven with a moon in its beak was bringing light back into the world. The history of this totem pole goes back to 1899 when the Seattle Authority sponsored a 'goodwill' tour of Alaskan ports aboard the steamer *City of Seattle*, in other words, a junket for politicians and other 'leading citizens'. Some of these leading citizens saw a totem pole in an Alaskan Tlingit village and they stole it, thinking that it would be a grand ornament in the middle of Seattle.

A tall, lean man with a twinkle in his eye called everybody to attention for the Underground Tour. He told us it was his intention to tell us the story of Pioneer Square and to introduce us to the founding fathers of Seattle, who he said 'were all scoundrels in their own way'. The three founding heroes in his story were Arthur Denny, Doc Maynard and Henry Yessler. It was they who thought it would be distinctive to call the new city Seattle, after a local Native American chief. Chief Seattle was initially hostile to the idea, as he feared that the use of his name after his death would lead to an eternity of unrest. However, when offered a yearly payment for this discomfort, he reluctantly acquiesced. The chief had the last laugh however, as Seattle was an English version of his name. His real name in his own language was See-athl. People love to be able to define the moment when a place was founded and named, because then we can have heroes and sacred places. Yet people have lived in the vicinity of Seattle for at least four thousand years. They too had a name for this spot. They called it 'Little Crossing-Over Place'.

The next morning, on my way to the Klondike Museum, I stopped at a café for a leisurely breakfast. Sixties music and pictures of modern art created a vibrant ambience. I sat near to a young, stylishly dressed couple. Three friends sat at another table, each with an Apple laptop open in front of them. They exchanged the occasional fleeting word but spent the rest of the time engrossed in their solitary screens. An agitated African-American man came in and bought a cup of coffee and a muffin. He was in his sixties and wore a purple hat, a leather jacket and a pair of shiny tracksuit bottoms, ripped to the knee. He sat down at a table and occasionally his face and body twisted into contortions, which would be followed by an involuntary shout. It was as if his body were possessed by a cruel energy.

The Klondike Museum celebrates the link between Seattle and the Klondike. When the gold rush was at its height, cartoons of the time depicted the Klondike King and Seattle Queen in entwined union. The Queen survived and flourished whereas the King faded away after a brief, spectacular sparkling.

§

Micí walked into Seattle because he and his friends had found a crate of whiskey in the freight carriage on the journey from Missoula. The inevitable party drew the attention of the conductor and the stowaways jumped from the train for fear of arrest. When, a few days later, they straggled into Seattle, they found a city bursting to the seams with people preparing for the arduous trek to the Klondike. It was late in the summer of 1898 and all the hotels and guesthouses were jam-packed with prospectors, so much so that Micí had difficulty finding a place to stay. The city throbbed with excitement, speculation and trade. As Micí said himself, 'People from the four corners of the world were on the streets and more coming every day ... servants from the cities, cowboys from Texas, shopkeepers, outlaws, gamblers and other tricksters.'

Advertisements for the many outfitters and suppliers confronted him. Each miner was required to purchase two thousand pounds weight of supplies, as the Canadian government demanded that they must take with them sufficient goods to survive independently for one year. The merchants of Seattle had struck pay dirt. The suppliers, outfitters and markets were choked with miners buying everything from sleds, stoves and rip saws to evaporated potatoes. Micí and his friends were fortunate, as friends had established a valuable claim in the Klondike. They didn't buy many supplies, trusting to the providence of friendship.

Walking up the street, news vendors with peaked caps standing on street corners would have titillated Micí with the latest news from the Klondike. Indeed, there was little other news in the newspapers since the *Seattle Post-Intelligencer* first announced the Klondike gold strike on 17 July 1897. The newspaper got the scoop by chartering a tug to meet the SS *Portland* in Puget Sound, which was rumoured to be full of gold returning from the north. Upon receiving confirmation of the rumour, the reporter Beriah Brown raced back to port.

The following morning, the headline ran, 'GOLD! GOLD! GOLD! GOLD! STACKS OF YELLOW METAL'.

The very next day, the steamer *Ai-Ki* left Seattle for the Yukon full of stampeders and three hundred and fifty tons of supplies. Cities along the western seaboard had difficulty keeping employees as gold fever struck. Nearly all of the fire department in the nearby town of Tacoma resigned. People deserted from the army and, to cap it all, the mayor of Seattle, W.D. Wood, left too. The town was full of frenzy. One returning miner called Hunter Fitzhugh said, 'I'm besieged by dozens of people who call to talk about the trail … on all subjects as snow shoes, moccasins and camp fires … they're all going crazy.'

It is estimated that altogether, one hundred thousand stampeders set out to the Klondike. Only forty thousand ever arrived and of this forty thousand perhaps five hundred made enough to call themselves rich. An even smaller proportion managed to hang onto whatever wealth they had accumulated. More money was spent getting to the Yukon than was ever taken out of it.

All of this activity represented a boom for the city of Seattle, which became the main gateway to Alaska and the Yukon. This didn't happen by accident. It was brought about by the actions of the chamber of commerce and journalists who energetically marketed Seattle as the commercial gateway to the gold rush. One of the key decisions was hiring Erastus Brainerd as a publicist for the city. He got stuck into the job with gusto, placing ads nationwide in newspapers, promoting Seattle as 'the only place to outfit for the Klondike'. He printed 120,000 copies of a 'Special Klondike Edition' which he sent all over the country to mayors, libraries, railroad employees and postmasters. He lobbied Washington successfully for an assay office, reasoning that if miners could change their gold into cash, Seattle would benefit accordingly.

Marketing itself as the supply, transport, infrastructure and manufacturing gateway to the Klondike, the city went head to head with other powerful centres such as San Francisco, Tacoma and Vancouver, but Seattle emerged pre-eminent. The *National Magazine of Boston* said, 'Seattle is the Gateway to Alaska, you may get there by way of other west coast cities, but you'll be as a man using a side door.'

Seattle's momentum has continued until the present day, with the recruitment of Boeing and the development of the city as an information technology hub, with Microsoft as a key tenant. A positive culture, once created, can span generations.

What motivated this surge of people north towards a place few of them had ever heard of? As one American politician of more recent vintage said when explaining people's behaviour, 'It's the economy, stupid.' So it was then too. The 1890s in America have often been described as the 'decade of misery', when millions were forced to work for dimes a day, if they could find work at all. Agriculture went into sharp decline, farms went bankrupt and people often lived by their wits alone. Vast corporations owned by people like Andrew Carnegie and John Rockefeller became wealthy beyond imagination through the consolidation and takeover of businesses, which were then merged and downsized. This produced waves of protest as people vainly fought to save their jobs and their way of life. Society was on the verge of disintegration because of the disparities in wealth and power. Race relations became more troubled and the process of segregating blacks from whites gathered new pace. In the midst of this misery and cooped-up vitality, the Klondike Gold Rush provided an outlet.

Many professionals and relatively well-paid industrial workers also abandoned everything to join the stampede. As Micí said, some of them had never held anything heavier than a spoon in their hands. For these people, it was the oppressive nature of their work that seemed to gall them. That, and the fact that no matter how hard you worked, meant there was little chance of making any real money. That feeling of imprisonment is captured in the letters of miners.

Hunter Fitzhugh wrote, 'to be sure I long for home and civilisation with a longing that's me doom, but if I was in the States, I would be under the hand and eye of a boss.'

Another miner, Bill Ballou, wrote home describing all the activities he was involved in. He learned how to build a cabin, build a boat, hunt, fish, cook, sharpen tools, cut ice and a thousand other tasks. Civilisation had emasculated many people, made them feel inadequate in the world. On this venture, they had to dig deep and discover what they could do. It was about the search for freedom and independence, about adventure and testing your limits.

Of course the Klondike adventure was also a stampede and a stampede is surrounded by exhilaration and flowing energy. We're like the geese and the caribou. We tend to migrate together in flocks across the land, responding to some mysterious call. There's an excitement and a comfort in such a migration, and a feeling that adversity can be best overcome through banding together. The glistening gold beckons and casts an ancient enchantment that snares people's dreams.

§

It was Halloween night and I strolled around town, tasting the atmosphere. Downtown was like an exotic cocktail laced with sensuous wickedness. The dark side of the human personality was being celebrated with total abandon. It seeped out of doorways and poured down the streets in colourful waves of bobbing gaiety, seeming to converge on a club where a large group of black-suited bouncers lay in wait. Nearly everyone seemed to be in a costume that evoked horror, lust and wildness. Werewolves, vampires, skeletons, daleks, spidermen, zombies, Cleopatra and Hitler were among characters on the street. George Bush arrived with fangs and blood dripping down his chin. I stood outside the club watching the spectacle.

It got particularly interesting when a group of placard-waving religious fundamentalists arrived with soapboxes and loudspeakers and started to shout at revellers, 'Repent, repent. You are on the road to perdition. Repent and embrace the Lord!'

I started to laugh, which drew a wondering query from a young woman dressed as Pocahontas standing beside me, 'Why are you laughing?'

'It's funny', I replied pointing to a heated argument between one of the fundamentalists and two gay men dressed as angels. The fundamentalist was accusing them of wickedness.

She laughed too and said, 'I love your accent.'

'Yours is nice too', I plamassed, 'is it a Seattle accent?'

'Yeah, I'm native Seattle, not like all those other transplants that live here.' Pocahontas, waiting on friends to go into the club, declared in a slightly high voice, 'I love to let myself go free.'

'I'm sure Halloween is good for that.'

'It sure is. After the club tonight we'll go down to the park to a rave. I'll take some "E". It'll keep me going all night, though I'll regret it tomorrow because I won't be able to sleep.'

She added an afterthought. 'You should come too.'

I smiled in response, thinking that fish can only survive for a short time out of water. I asked her what she did.

'I'm studying psychology.'

'Is university expensive here?' I asked, looking up at her in her high heels. There are limits to authenticity in costumes.

'Yeah, it is, but I make more than enough money as an exotic dancer to pay for it.'

The casualness of the remark threw me for a moment. 'It must be difficult studying days and working nights', I said, trying to be equally casual.

'Naah, I like the work, it's fun; I'm in control and the money is good. In a few years I'll be able to buy my own apartment.'

'I think I'll take up that job too.'

She laughed full-heartedly at this suggestion. I didn't know whether to be pleased or insulted! Shortly afterwards her two friends came and she waved goodbye.

Standing idly outside the club, people must have thought that I fitted the stereotype of a ticket tout, as a few stopped to ask me for tickets. One of these was a brown-haired woman who was remarkable for the fact that she wasn't wearing fancy dress.

After a brief conversation I said impulsively, 'Let me help you find a ticket.'

'Ok', she said, 'but I don't want to pay much more than the cover charge.'

'How much is that?'

'Twenty dollars.'

With that, we stood at opposite sides of the door and started shouting, 'Any tickets for sale?'

Almost immediately a strongly built man sidled over. 'Want a ticket, man?'

'How much?'

'Eighty dollars.'

'It's too expensive.'

'You won't get cheaper. Demand for this club is mad. It won't last long.'

He was proved wrong when Wonder Woman came up and offered a ticket.

'How much?' I asked.

'The cover price.'

As I left, one of the fundamentalists offered me a card with a religious message. I refused, saying truthfully that I got one earlier. He climbed on to his soapbox and shouted into his microphone, pointing at me, 'That's what they all say. They all make excuses to avoid the Lord's words. You can't escape … repent your sins, the time is nigh.'

At that moment three men with horns, tails and short skirts arrived with placards and another microphone and started shouting mockingly, 'All ye lost souls, repent, repent.'

At this all hell broke loose as a few of the fundamentalist Christians became apoplectic at this ridicule, and a battle of the microphones ensued. With this din reverberating in my ears, I escaped.

To celebrate my final day in Seattle, I planned to go to Bellingham, ninety miles from Seattle. Kathy, the girl I had met on my first day in town, had suggested that it would be interesting, as many fishing boats left from there for Alaska. The following day, I was flying home to Ireland for a few months before continuing my journey in Alaska. When I got to the fishing port, one black-haired captain with a deeply scarred face offered to give me a berth the following March. He was a bit vague however about where I might land on arrival.

I looked out across the bay. If I had stood there in mid-August 1898, I would have seen boat after boat steaming north, each one low in the water with a heavy load of supplies and people. Each deck was crammed with men attired in hat, coat and moustache, each with his eyes on the sea and a shimmer of excitement and expectation running through him. Micí Mac Gabhann was on one of these boats, indistinguishable in the crowd. He too was looking north with eager eyes, in the hope of reaching St Michael at the mouth of the Yukon River. He had paid twenty dollars to secure his cramped berth, equivalent to five hundred dollars in today's money. It was nearly all he possessed.

He'd thrown the dice. It was impossible to turn back.

14

Anchorage, Alaska

Alaska. The word is like a sharp, clear bell ringing in the mountain air. It has always appealed to my sense of wonder and curiosity. I imagined that journeying there would be like the experience of a polar bear cub as it first pokes its nose out of its den into the awakening landscape of spring. It pauses at the entrance, pulled both ways. Eventually the cub comes tumbling out (often after a push) into a thrilling and unpredictable existence. Its senses absorb every detail: the crunch of snow underfoot, the feel of the wind on its round, whiskery face, the fresh scents of the landscape and the gurgling of a river, newly unleashed from the clutch of cold ice, surging forth towards the sea. The pulse of the young cub accelerates. Its body stretches full length as its mind responds to new notes in this melody of ice and creation.

The word Alaska is derived from two words, the Aleut word 'Alyeska' and the Inupiaq word 'Alakshak'. Both mean 'the great land'. Indeed, Alaska is a great land. Twice the size of Texas, it contains one-sixth of the landmass of the US.

It is two thousand, five hundred miles from east to west and one thousand, four hundred miles from north to south. It spans 43 degrees of longitude and 21 degrees of latitude and is filled with huge mountain ranges, long rivers, flowing glaciers and primordial forests. In this wilderness, there are animals that have never seen or heard a human being. It's the home of caribou, moose, bear, salmon and bald eagle. Whales, dolphins, seals, walrus and otter feed in its abundant waters. Yet it has a population of only six hundred and twenty-seven thousand people, of which one hundred thousand are Native. Half the population lives in Anchorage, with the remainder clustered around small towns and villages throughout the state.

The Russians must still be kicking themselves for selling Alaska to the Americans in 1867 for only seven million dollars.

Late in the evening, I sailed through baggage and arrivals, then quickly found a taxi. The straggly, red-haired taxi driver, who wore long, seventies-era side locks, looked at me with mock horror when I told him where I was staying.

'What's it like?' I asked him.

'There are better motels. We don't usually pick up people from that one. All sorts hang out there. A lot are on something and there's always the prospect of trouble with people like that. It has one consolation', he added, smiling.

'What's that?'

'There's a strip club right across the road from it, but I wouldn't go near it if I were you.'

'It might be easier to get into than out of?'

'Exactly.'

He dropped me off near the reception of a typical horseshoe-shaped motel. I entered the small, dowdy reception and eventually a heavily built young man wearing a turban came to the desk. I was surprised that after a few wordless minutes he actually found my internet booking. When I got to my room, however, I couldn't open the bathroom door. He came and resolved this predicament with a wire hanger, instructing me where to poke it in case of further problems. I distrusted such high technology and adopted the low-tech solution of leaving the door open.

At 10.00 p.m., the long Alaskan day still had four hours to go before sunset. I decided to walk downtown to look for a cheaper, more central motel for the following few nights. It would stretch my limbs after thirty hours of travel.

When I asked for directions, the receptionist looked at me as if I was crazy and told me it would take forty minutes to get downtown. In the courtyard of the motel, I was assailed by the sound of women shouting in a dimly lit doorway across the road.

A middle-aged man entering the motel exclaimed, 'Listen to that racket.'

'What's going on over there?'

'That's the local whorehouse. Mustn't be much action inside tonight.' The shouting intensified. 'Sounds like there's trouble in the camp', was his parting shot.

A tough-looking security guard from the strip joint stood at the edge of the sidewalk. He was dark, stocky, sullen and scarred and I certainly wouldn't like to confront him in any dark passageway.

There wasn't much traffic on the long, straight road into town. Light aircraft were landing and taking off from a small airfield. The taller buildings of downtown beckoned in the distance but, like a mirage, they seemed to recede with each footstep. The long journey caught up on me. I trudged on, passing vacant lots, small businesses and garages full of gleaming cars. The only person I met was a cyclist who didn't return my greeting. I reached the edge of downtown and spotted a small motel. I went in and was greeted by a tall man with tattoos and a long beard who was fixing a bicycle behind the reception desk. We talked about cycling and this mutual interest, he claimed, prompted him to offer what he described as the best deal for a motel room in all of Anchorage. It was considerably cheaper than the previous motel, but I still thought I might find somewhere even less expensive. He laughed and told me that I wouldn't. To prove him wrong, I went next door to enquire at the four-star Sheraton Hotel.

'It's $265', the receptionist said.

'For a week?'

'No, for a night', she laughed.

§

It took over a month for Micí's steamer to cover the three thousand miles to St Michael, Alaska. The vessel went north along the coast until it reached the Aleutian Islands, then into the Bering Sea, that formidable stretch of water between Alaska and Russia. During the journey, Micí was wrapped in a shroud of misery brought on by seasickness. He was totally oblivious to the world through which he passed. He didn't notice the fabulous sea cliffs, the mountain ranges, the innumerable islands or the fabulous seascape of Alaska with glaciers flowing into the sea. He was in one of the richest wildlife habitats on earth and never mentioned seeing any humpback whale, grey whale, sea otter, walrus, elephant seal – nothing.

Well, that isn't totally true, he did see something. He observed in detail the many wrecks of boats that had sunk on the journey north. The Bering Sea is a wild and treacherous place and many gold rush boats were not up to the task. The old sailors lament was apt: 'Many brave hearts are asleep in the deep, so beware, beware.'

Mící unwrapped the shroud of misery when he saw St Michael, which sits strategically amidst the many mouths of the Yukon River. It was mid-September 1898 and theirs was one of a hundred boats which had arrived, all on the same quest.

Initially developed by the Russians, St Michael was a supply centre for trade on the Yukon River. The surrounding countryside is flat tundra. Travellers have said that you could go mad there, because in summer, the sea, land and sky merge into one grey, all-encompassing world. Mící and his friends waited anxiously for a week until they boarded a stern wheeler called *Susie*, bound for Dawson City, two thousand miles upriver. It was late in the year and a chill was beginning to invade the land. Mící had to pass through Fort Yukon, an Athabaskan village on the northernmost reach of the Yukon River, north of the Arctic Circle.

My plan was to reconnect with Mící's journey there. The only access to Fort Yukon in the present day is by a small mail plane from deep in the Alaskan interior.

In Anchorage, the early morning sun created a warm shaft of colour on the face of the mountains. A few empty beer bottles littered the pavement as I left the motel. I pulled my luggage three miles to the new one, and found that the receptionist there was an Eskimo man, and not my cyclist acquaintance.

I explained the arrangement agreed the previous night, but he curtly enquired, 'Did you make a reservation at that price?'

'Well, no', was my tentative reply.

He told me that the price changed on a daily basis, and that it would be ten dollars more than I had been quoted. I wasn't too pleased and tried to haggle but the man was not for budging. Realising that the other guests in the lobby had paid this price, I asked him if it would be ok to leave my case in the luggage room for a while. When I got him there alone, I asked if I might get a better rate later. He nodded.

Downtown Anchorage was busy, with locals sitting out in the sunshine and tourists like myself looking half lost. On a green area beside the sidewalk, I saw a barrel-chested, fit-looking man in his sixties flogging books. Interested, I stopped to talk. He told me that he had taken part in the first Iditarod dog-sled race in 1973 and had subsequently written a book about it. The 1,050 mile route from Anchorage to Nome had taken him thirty days to complete. In those days, 'it was the real deal.' Contestants were spread out over a wide area and you were totally alone in the wilderness.

'Nowadays', he claimed, 'a stockbroker from Boston or a teacher from Idaho is a typical contestant.' With a tinge of regret he continued, 'They can't compare with guys brought up in the wilderness long ago. They knew how to survive when things went wrong. The Iditarod is safer now because more people are doing it and if something does go wrong, there's always assistance nearby. The equipment is better, the dog teams are all well-trained and contestants are in continuous contact. One of the biggest problems now is that with GPS, wives are ringing in, worried if their husbands haven't moved for a few minutes.'

Hopes rising, I enquired, 'Could anyone do the Iditarod?'

'Well perhaps not everyone!' he said, hedging his bets.

He loved dogs, and told me that in the past, people could not have survived without them in Alaska and the Yukon. Provisions were always a problem as most of these areas were cut off for eight months of the year. Without dog-sled teams, it would have been virtually impossible to take in supplies. During the Klondike Gold Rush, the miners tried to use all sorts of animals, including horses and oxen, to carry equipment and supplies. Neither were suitable. Horses tended to slip and break their legs and oxen were too heavy to cross the difficult terrain. Dogs became valuable commodities and even pet dogs were likely to be stolen, shipped off to the Arctic and sold to eager miners.

He said that the greatest nuisance facing travellers in the wilderness wasn't bears or crazed moose, but mosquitoes.

'You can't get away from them pesky insects in the summer. They're everywhere in their millions and the only thing that works against them is pure DEET. Nothing else works and I've tried all the remedies. You'll be rubbing yourself and killing hundreds at a time but more and more of them keep coming.'

He suddenly laughed and asked, 'Do you know how to get revenge against mosquitoes?'

'No.'

'You need someone with you to do it properly. First, roll up your sleeve, and put your arm out in front of you, palm up.'

'Am I supposed to lure them in and catch them?'

'They don't need a lure. No, you wait until one lands on your arm and starts to suck your blood. Mosquitoes are transparent when sucking. You'll see the blood going in. When it has started sucking, tighten your fist so its hairs are trapped on your skin and it cannot escape. Put your other hand around your wrist and get your friend to put his hands around your arm, on the other side of the mosquito. Then if both of you squeeze and push towards the mosquito, it'll explode. Bam!' he said, throwing both arms in the air, laughing.

I could see from that story what people get up to on long nights in the wilderness.

By this stage there was a queue of people waiting to buy his book. I moved on further up the street and went into an Irish shop called Suzi's. I don't know why I went into an Irish shop; it wasn't because I was going to buy anything. When I entered, a petite woman greeted me in a friendly way. Her name was Shasta and she wore a Hanna Donegal tweed cap.

'Would you like a cup of tea?' she asked.

'I would never refuse one.'

With that she brought me into the 'scullery' behind the shop and boiled the kettle.

'Now you've got to show me how to make a proper cup of Irish tea', she said.

'I can, provided you've got one thing', I replied.

'What's that?'

'We need to have loose tea. I hate those tea bags; they destroy the art form.'

'Well it's your lucky day. I have loose tea here. We sell Barry's Tea in the shop. Explain this art form then', she laughed.

'Well, tea is a fragile combination of a number of things', I pontificated, 'the amount and quality of tea, the temperature of your teapot and the quality of your water, which should only be added when boiling. You have to get the right combination of these things to get the perfect pot of tea.'

'Well let's get started then', she said.

'Where's the teapot?'

'Oh, you need one of those?' Shasta went off rummaging and returned with a small tin teapot. 'Will this do?'

'Well, I'm guessing it'll have to', I laughed.

I gave her precise instructions on what to do. When she had completed them to my satisfaction, I told her to let the tea 'draw' for at least five minutes. I asked her, 'Have you a tea cosy?'

There was no tea cosy, but we improvised with a few woollen cloths placed over the pot.

Shasta was a blow-in from Washington state. She had two children in their twenties who were travelling and exploring the world. She was taking the opportunity to do a bit of exploring of her own, to write a book, learn the banjo and work two jobs. I was exhausted thinking about it.

'It's time for the tea', I said and told her, 'the last thing you have to learn is how to pour it properly.'

Shasta went to serve a customer and I was sitting back with the cup of tea in my hand when an energetic grey-haired woman came into the scullery. It was Suzi, the owner of the business, who was busy organising an Irish Street Music Festival for that weekend. She was in a panic trying to source beds in friends' houses for musicians from various parts of the US and Canada. She probably needed a loafer in her scullery like a hole in the head.

'It's going to be a real fun party', she said.

I spent the rest of the afternoon wandering around the streets of Anchorage. I drank coffee in a street-side café and admired the abundance of magnificent flowers in the flowerbeds and hanging baskets. The blooms in Alaska are up to 30 per cent larger than normal. This is caused by the increased amount of nitrogen in the air, due to the melting of glacial ice. The connections between things in our world are indeed enthralling and surprising.

Later that evening, a smattering of Irish music hit me as I entered McGinley's pub. It was packed. The musicians, gathered in one corner, were tuning their instruments. I squeezed into a space at the counter and ordered a steak and a beer from a waitress attired in green.

I met Norman, a heavily built, retired Canadian businessman battling manfully with a triple-decker sandwich. He emphasised the separation of Alaska from the rest of the US.

'When you order something online which claims to have free postage, there's usually a darned clause in there, in very small writing which says, "only in the contiguous United States". We are like a different country here. We have to pay for everything.'

He told me that Alaska was going through a property and speculation boom even though the rest of the country was in recession.

Later he asked, 'Do you want to go to a local bar?'

'Yeah, sure.'

We walked for about five minutes along quiet streets and entered a
bar throbbing with energy and bursting at the seams. There were all
sorts there: young and old with varieties of tattoos, leather gear, tank
tops, piercings and the ubiquitous baseball caps. When we some-
how got a seat at the counter, Norman said, 'Tourists don't come in
here. They take one look inside the door and avoid it because they
think it's too rough. It's not rough at all. Alaskans can be loud and
look scary.'

A frail, hawk-eyed man with a sturdy stick sat down beside us. He
ran an art gallery and, on hearing where I was from, announced, 'I've
got the thing for you.' He took a packet of photographs of Alaskan
wildlife from his pocket. 'You might be interested in buying these as
a keepsake of Alaska.'

They were photographs of wolves, bears and moose and I quite
liked them. He must have sensed an opportunity. 'I'll give them to
you at a special price, eighteen dollars for you, though they're usually
thirty.'

'Too much for me', I replied.

He nodded regretfully.

When we got on to politics he announced, 'Sarah Palin should run
for presidency the next time … we need to get rid of that fu***r Obama
in there …. I don't trust him. Palin has a 90 per cent approval rating
here in Alaska. Did you know that?'

'I didn't know it was that high.'

'She'd sort out Afghanistan …. They're evil bastards over there,
they torture every prisoner.' He then went on to describe in graphic
detail the torture meted out to prisoners, and concluded, 'Our troops
should never be captured or surrender to these guys. They should kill
themselves first.'

The night descended into a contentious but safer debate on the
merits of Scotch, Irish and Bourbon whiskey. Each had to be sampled,
though that brought no resolution to the matter.

The next morning, I was pleased to find that the Anchorage
museum was hosting a special exhibition on gold, featuring three
hundred beautiful golden objects from around the world. Arranged

around the exhibition space, covered totally in gold leaf, were gold bars and an Apollo space helmet. There was also a gold Buddha, gold daggers, skulls, necklaces, gold coins from ancient Lydia, mummy ornaments from Peru and a large ornamental gold chest plate from Panama.

Gold is a strange substance. It seems to hold all the good and bad of the world within it. People have killed, lied, suffered and stolen for it and at the same time it adorns some of our most sacred objects and buildings. For the Andean tribes, gold was known as 'the sweat of the sun'. It's an evocative concept and is closer to reality than we realise. According to current scientific thinking, gold originated in dying stars and became part of the core of our newly developing world. However, gold doesn't remain at the core. It arises from those hot molten depths and drips onto the earth's skin. It does this when rainwater seeps down through the earth's pores into the depths, where it combines with hot magma. There, it forms a vapour into which gold dissolves and the combination rises towards the Earth's surface. As it does so, it cools and the gold becomes solid again, filling cracks and crevices in the rock. Over time, wind and water erode the rock, resulting in flecks and gold nuggets being washed down rivers, streams and creeks where they settle into placer deposits, to be hunted by the keen eyes of the prospector.

The Andean peoples were wise in that they recognised that all things are connected in this universe. A dying sun in a far-off galaxy is part of what we are.

One of the things I learned at the exhibition was how rare gold actually is. In nature, only one atom in a billion is gold and if you collected all the gold that has ever been discovered, it would fit into sixty tractor-trailer loads. This was surprising to me, having been brought up on tales of vast golden treasures. I thought for sure that those Spanish conquistadors had moved mountains of the stuff back to Spain from South America. The fact that all the gold in history could be contained within a twenty-metre cube got me thinking that there must be a lot more out there, still waiting to be found!

A little gold can go a long way, as one of its great attributes is its malleability. One ounce of gold can be hammered thin enough to cover a ninety-seven square foot wall. Traditional artists can beat gold between pieces of leather until it's nearly invisible; gold leaf can be seven millionths of an inch thick.

In my mind's eye, I like to visualise gold leaf with the light of the sun shining through it; a sun praying to its ancestors, recognising that one day too it will create gold.

After visiting the museum, I put my nose into the Irish music festival. Suzi's shop was doing a bomb, as were the stalls on the street, which were selling a variety of Irish crafts and music. On stage, a plaintive flute complained about some deeply felt loss, which the fiddles caressed and magnified. It was strange that the first street music I encountered in Alaska was Irish. Maybe this music is a homing device for a portion of the Irish race compelled to restlessly wander this earth. Perhaps we should adopt, as our symbol, that little three-ounce bird with long slender wings called the Arctic tern. This 'bird of the sun' might be small in stature, but it travels from the Arctic to the Antarctic and back again, following its instinct on a forty-five-thousand-mile migration that's unsurpassed in nature. As it can live for up to thirty years, it clocks up one and a half million miles on its travels, equivalent to three return trips to the moon. The tern is a true wanderer on this earth.

Jet-lagged, I departed towards my motel for an early night.

The next morning in the lobby, I was disappointed to find only stodgy muffins and lukewarm coffee for breakfast. A strongly built, fit-looking man in his late forties greeted me cheerily as I poured the coffee. 'Make sure you leave some for me.'

'I don't think there's going to be a huge demand', I replied.

He laughed, mockingly stroking his beard between thumb and index finger as he looked at the food on display. 'I wonder what I'll have this morning.'

His name was Doyle and he owned a refrigeration business, which he operated all around Alaska.

'A refrigeration business in Alaska? That's a bit like taking coals to Newcastle.'

Doyle had been a pilot. He told me the story about the first plane he bought. A priest accompanied him to collect it and as Doyle had no piloting experience, he had assumed that the priest would fly it back. When they got to the plane however, the priest told him, 'It's your plane, you fly it.'

'I never looked back after that', he said, 'I flew for years, for work and for fun. I used to pack my eight children into it. At one airport, my plane became known as the cartoon plane because when it landed, they were always amazed at the amount of children that climbed out of it.'

'It must be a great feeling to pilot a plane.'

'They aren't difficult to fly. You can pick it up quick and they don't cost much more than a pick-up. I used to love going up early in the morning when the air was still and you could see everything in the soft light.'

'Do you fly much now?'

'I don't have a plane now. It went in my last divorce.'

After breakfast, I went by minibus to the attractively designed Native Heritage Centre located a few miles outside Anchorage. I needed a grounding in Native culture and by all accounts this was the best place to get it. The main building housed a theatre, a café, a gathering place, artists' workshops, an exhibition hall and a shop. We trooped inside and I attended a short introductory talk given by a broad-shouldered man with jet-black hair. He compared the centre to the first warm breeze of spring bringing new life to the bud. This bud, germinated by the elders of their tribes, grew into a place of education for Native and non-Native peoples on Native culture. Its purpose was to help Native people reclaim their heritage, pride, knowledge, language and culture, which had been undermined since 1741 by a succession of Russian and American regimes. Following his introductory talk, he recommended we should walk around Lake Tiulana at the rear of the centre as it had five authentic Native buildings representing the different tribal cultures in Alaska.

Pointing to a large map on the wall, he explained that these tribes broke down into five major groupings based on cultural similarities or geographic proximity. This was news to me as I had always associated Alaska with Eskimos, which were undifferentiated in my head in terms of cultural identity. I had an image of Asian-looking people, living in extreme conditions, surviving on their wits and skills, and wrapped in huge layers of fur skins, building igloos to keep out the cold.

Now I found out that the most northerly grouping of Eskimos were the Inupiaq. The symbol for this group was a drum, and throat singing is central to their culture. To the south were the Yup'ik and Cup'ik. Their symbol was the eye of awareness that exists in all things, including rocks and bones. Further south, including the peninsula, the islands and the area around Anchorage, were the Unangax and

Alutiiq, and their symbol was a hunter in a kayak. These constituted the tribes that had an Eskimo heritage. I was surprised to find that the two other groupings had an Indian heritage. The first of these were the Tlingit. They inhabited that strange area of Alaska that juts out onto the bottom of the Yukon Territory in Canada and which contains Juneau, the marginalised capital of Alaska. The final grouping, the Athabaskans, inhabited the interior of Alaska. This group are related to the Apache and Navaho in New Mexico and Arizona. To finish off any preconceptions I had, I found out that Alaskan Eskimo tribes rarely built igloos. That was the tradition in Canada and Greenland.

Teenagers who had been trained during the year as guides staffed the village houses. In front of the Inupiaq house, two huge whale jaw-bones were arranged in an upright, semi-circular arch. These are a real symbol of the Arctic, and the design has a practical purpose, as in heavy snow it lets travellers know where safety dwells. This symbol has also been brought to worldwide attention, as McDonalds used it as the inspiration in the design of its arches logo. These Inupiaq houses are built partially underground for winter living and have two entrances: one from ground level, which also acts as a source of lighting and smoke ventilation, and the other a tunnel below the living area that traps the cold air and prevents it from entering the interior of the house. This lower tunnel is the main entrance.

I thought I would enter by the top entrance, which was like a small tunnel or slide. I tried to walk down on my hunkers, but as I arrived near the bottom I lost my balance and stumbled into a long, rectangular room bedecked with all sorts of fur blankets and mats. All around the sides of the room were benches, and sitting inconspicuously in a corner, trying her best not to laugh too loudly, was a teenage girl. I regained my dignity, smiled at the girl and started to look around the room. After a few minutes, I touched one of the furs and the girl said, 'polar bear'. I touched another fur and she said, 'caribou', and then 'beaver', and so on. A group of people came in the main entrance and she didn't say anything for a while. The people looked around the house and I don't think they even noticed her before moving on. When they left, she showed me other skins, hunting weapons and household implements. The people spent the majority of the winter in this room. The benches were used for both sleeping and sitting. She showed me the seal oil lamps that were used for light, heat and cooking. She used a minimum of words but at the same time she was observant as to what I was interested in. To communicate, it was necessary for me to take my time and let the information emerge. All the young guides in the centre had a gentleness and quietness about them, and a distinct lack of ego. This was particularly true of this young woman in the Inupiaq house. I later saw her off-duty, hanging out with her friends, with the white antlers of an iPod in her ears.

Later, back in Anchorage, I met a Yupik/Inupiaq artist called Jerry who was painting symbols onto caribou skins at his stall. He was in his late forties, had straight, black hair, a round, boyish face and a pair of eyes that could dance with the devil and get away with it. The wide gap in both his top and bottom teeth added to his aura of mischievousness. He was an alcoholic who had found peace in art.

As he put it himself, 'My energy had turned against myself but thankfully I'm in a different place now.'

The main root in his life had been his grandmother. Her example had helped pull him out of the dungeon of addiction. He told me that when she died, he made up a song for her based on the northern lights.

'Everyone thought it was great. We lived in Bethel then and Bethel doesn't often get the aurora. When they do, it's just a faint glimmer in the sky. The night of her burial was special as the aurora came out in all its glory. It was her way of telling us she was all right.'

He was working on a painting of a polar bear standing balanced on a small ice floe in the middle of the ocean. The face of a shaman was depicted on the stomach of the bear. This, he said, was to show the connection between the Yupik people and the polar bear. Both seemed to be in a precarious position.

He pointed to another painting of the black wolf and explained, 'The creation story of our people is bound up with the wolf, especially the black wolf, as we believe it carries the spirit of creation. When we hunt, if there's only one black wolf in a pack, we don't kill it. If there are two, we kill the smaller one. Bad fortune always comes to a person who kills a black wolf. Only a special person can do it and they have to make peace with its spirit afterwards. I remember when I was out hunting with a group of Inupiaq. It was a perfect day with not a cloud in sight. One of our members wanted to chase a black wolf and nothing would stop him. A little later, with no obvious warning, a blizzard broke and we could only see a few metres in front of us. The tracks of his snowmobile were completely wiped out. When we found him, his snowmobile had toppled over on top of him and he was at death's door.'

Now totally immersed in his stories, he pointed to another painting, of a seal that looked like a man. He said, 'This painting is based on a story of our people. When the men were out in their boats hunting seals, they suddenly saw a young man standing on a rock. The hunters were curious and drew near but as soon as they did the man turned into a seal and dived into the water. It was a sign to the people to go easy on the seal population, as they were suffering too much.'

At this stage I told him about our traditional beliefs. 'Our seals generally turn into women and come to live with a worthy man as his wife. If he ever mistreats her, she'll reclaim her skin and go back to the sea.'

'Our cultures have similarities', he said.

I saw him searching for a word. 'Leprechaun!' he announced with a flourish. 'I've heard of them. We have a small being like that too and when you meet it, you have to show respect. If you do that, your difficulties will disappear but if you don't, you'll be in a whole lot more shit that you were before', he laughed.

'We also have a bigger one too', he went on, 'which is about the size of a man. It always walks around, head bent, and with a hood that hides the face. When you approach him with respect and if it's the right time, he might lift his head. Guess what you see then?'

'I've no idea.'

'Your future.'

'I'm not sure I would want to meet him. What do you call these beings?'

He mentioned two names. Both sounded like double Dutch. I asked him to write them down and he shook his head, unsure of the spelling. Eventually, he wrote, 'Geenceeyuak and Echinhawk'.

A tall, strongly built, red-haired Inupiaq woman wearing sunglasses stopped to ask Jerry if he had seen her husband. Jerry shook his head. When the woman heard I was Irish, she laughed and said that one of her ancestors was Irish too.

She said, 'That line of our family always produced big people and they were the only ones the Athabaskans were afraid of.'

She added that her mother had brought her up with the knowledge of the eight-hundred-year occupation of Ireland and consequently she had always disliked the English as a young girl. However, she also hated the fact that she was from two oppressed peoples, and desperately wanted to be on the winning side. One of her only girlhood heroes was Niall of the Nine Hostages, because he was strong and was not a victim.

Moving to the present day, she said that she recently spoke at a conference in Washington on human rights and the environment. The conference had been opened by Mary Robinson, her modern-day Irish hero. With a wave, she left to continue her search for her husband.

15

Fairbanks

The following morning, when spears of light were beginning to crease the Alaskan sky, I stood at the train station contemplating the purchase of vending machine coffee.

'I'm not sure if this is what I need', I remarked to the tall man with a twinkle in his eye who stood beside me.

'Yeah, I don't fancy it too much either. I'll leave it and have breakfast on the train.'

John had retired a few years previously, and now spent his time travelling and studying wildlife. He was going with his son and daughter-in-law on a two-week hike in the north of Alaska around Arctic Village. Their supplies were going to be dropped by helicopter at strategic locations along their hiking route.

'What about polar bears?' I asked. I should have known the answer. This was Alaska. The hikers would have guns.

I was thrilled to be on the train to Fairbanks, and for some reason all the railway staff at Anchorage station seemed equally excited. Massing together on the platform, they waved as we pulled out of the station. One of the things to love about Americans is their unabashed enthusiasm. My enthusiasm being for coffee, I was one of the first to darken the restaurant door. The waitress, sitting engrossed in a book, viewed the advance of hungry hoards with a look of resignation. I ordered coffee and a full breakfast and as the coffee percolated into my innards, I relaxed. The waitress thawed a little and told me that she was a student, working and living on the railroad for the summer months. Two elderly couples sitting opposite me were deep in discussion. One of the women was describing in great detail a recent driving holiday across North Dakota and Minnesota. One of the men, not too impressed, exclaimed, 'The Great Plains are boring.'

The woman sharply replied, 'Boring is a lack of imagination.'

There followed much concentrated scraping of knives and forks on plates.

A softly spoken woman asked if she could sit beside me. She was in her forties, wore round, black glasses and carried a large camera, one of those with a powerful lens that would make it unsafe to pee on the moon.

Greta was open and friendly. A professional photographer, she was on her way to take photographs in Denali National Park, which has Mount McKinley as its centrepiece. She was a real jack-in-the-box. Every time she saw something interesting out of the corner of her eye, she hopped up to take a photograph. She had a unique capacity to be fully engaged in a conversation and take photographs at the same time. A pattern developed. Every time she hopped up, I followed suit, trying to catch the same image with my insignificant, matchbox camera. Of course, I was always that moment too late. Greta took photographs of imposing mountain ranges, never-ending forest and tundra, and angry rivers pulsing through valleys, while I took photographs of the train's window frames. Once, when I hopped up to take a photograph at what I considered to be a particularly fetching scene, she remained seated. When I sat down again I said, 'You missed a good shot there.'

She laughed. The cheek of her!

Greta told me that she specialised in taking portraits, and had many Californian celebrities on her client list, including one prominent and muscular politician. However, the winds of change were blowing through Greta's photographic world and she now had to supplement her income through teaching. The recession, digital cameras and scanners had reduced her business to a part-time enterprise.

An announcement on the public address system informed us that we were entering the Matanuska Valley. It contains some of the richest agricultural land in Alaska. As part of the 'New Deal', President Franklin D. Roosevelt's attempt to drag the US out of the Great Depression of the 1930s, he authorised 'America's only ever colony'. Two hundred and ten families, drawn mainly from the severely hit states of Minnesota and Wisconsin, were transplanted to the Matanuska Valley. Each family, most of whom were of Scandinavian origin, was given forty acres, a house, equipment and livestock. When the initiative was first announced, the cross-country trek from the Midwest to Alaska created great media interest. It was to become a triumphal march.

One of the new farmers, Wayne Bouwens from Wisconsin, said, 'What impressed me was the train; we'd a long dining car and porters standing around in white uniforms. In Seattle they'd a big party for us.'

In this instance, the New Deal was a big deal. The colonists made Matanuska Valley their home in May 1935 and the area became famous for giant fruit and vegetables. It currently provides 61 per cent of Alaskan agricultural output.

After talking to Greta, I went to the glass-domed observation carriage and found myself embroiled in a lively debate about the benefits of salmon. Paula, a smartly-dressed woman in her forties, held her hands out to shoulder width in front of her. She said, 'I caught twenty-two king salmon and they were all this size or bigger. The biggest fish was 25 pounds and the total catch was 240 pounds. I freeze them all. For protein, I only eat king salmon.'

She said that she had given up eating meat and taken up eating wild salmon eighteen years previously. 'My energy is a lot better, my eyes are clear and I have a healthy cholesterol level.'

Barry and Diane, a couple in their sixties, told us about their proud accomplishment of catching a 'magnificent' haul of pink salmon on a fishing trip in Alaska. Their problem was what to do with all the fish they caught. At great expense, they had them frozen and flown back home to California. They were not overly pleased to discover that they could have bought the same quantity of pink salmon in California for half the price! Barry said that they were eating salmon for years. Pink salmon, they told me, doesn't compare in taste to other types of salmon. This was news to me, as I thought a salmon was a salmon. Apparently there are many types, including pink, sockeye, silver and dog, all with their own particular flavours. King salmon stood at the top of the hierarchy, and the best place in the world to catch king salmon is Alaska.

Paula revealed her secret mission. She was the human resources head honcho on the Alaskan railroad and travelled this route a few times a year to ensure that the experience of train travel was of a high standard.

'And the staff don't know who you are?' asked Diane.

'No, that would put too much pressure on them. Most of the staff are enthusiastic students. It's better to see the service warts and all.'

'That's wicked', said Diane.

I still wonder why all those staff were waving at the station!

We were now coming into Wasilla, the town where Sarah Palin lived. Paula informed us that Wasilla had grown in the last number of years, because it was a popular retirement location for people from all over Alaska.

'I wonder is Sarah at home?' Barry asked jokingly.

Paula told us about a writer friend of hers called Peg who was researching the story of an Irishwoman called Nellie Cashman, known as 'The Frontier Angel'. Nellie was born in Cork in 1845 and emigrated to the US as a young child to escape the Famine. She became an adventurer who wandered the west, from Baja in Mexico to Alaska, subsisting in all sorts of frontier camps in search of her bonanza. She was small, some said beautiful, but was 'tougher than two penny nails'. One of the most famous stories of her was about the time she heard that miners in Cassiar, Alaska were trapped by a huge storm and no help could get through. She hired sleds and men and bought food and medicines, then travelled by boat to Wrangell in Alaska. From there, she battled deep snows and foul weather until she reached the miners with the food and medicines necessary for survival.

She spent seven years in the Klondike, and knowing that you can't eat gold, she was one of the few who prepared properly for her trip. The motto she followed was, 'If you're going to the Klondike I'll tell you what to do; better take a ton of grub or better yet – take two!' In Dawson City, she opened a restaurant, a store and a refuge for miners, providing not only shelter and food for the destitute, but free cigars as well. Wherever she went, she combined a talent for making money with a most generous spirit and an open heart. In her older years, she still carried on at the same hectic pace. Incredibly, at age seventy-nine she crossed the frozen Alaskan wilderness on her own by dog team from Koyukuk to Seward, a total of 750 miles. She crossed ice fields, rivers, mountains and every natural hazard that the mighty Alaskan wilderness could throw at her. Robert Service, 'Bard of the Yukon', celebrated her exploits in verse and when, in 1994, the United States issued stamps commemorating 'Legends of the West', Nellie Cashman was among the sixteen people honoured.

Some of the others were Buffalo Bill, Wyatt Earp, Annie Oakley and Kit Carson.

Diane and Paula escaped from the baking sun in the observation carriage, leaving Barry and I to talk. Barry was a thoughtful man with fine features stretched a little too tight over his bones. He was a retired academic and had many views on the world. We talked for a long time about politics, the environment and the future for humanity.

'It seems that no matter what we do', he said, 'our children will have a lower standard of living than we had. Our culture has squandered the gifts we were given through greed and the search for power. Maybe the next generation will develop better ethics if given the opportunity.'

'Life is often a matter of luck', he went on, 'good luck usually comes from good choices, bad luck from bad choices, but random luck comes from no choice.'

Tears came into his eyes and he continued, 'My son was killed at the age of seventeen in an auto smash. We were unlucky. We had done nothing to deserve it. It was pure random fate; a lovely, intelligent, funny person, just wiped out.'

As emotion flooded through him, his skin stretched even tighter on his face.

'Something like that hits your belief in things', I said.

'Yes it does. What do you believe?'

'I don't know. I suppose I don't believe anything unless I experience it myself and even then I'm not sure. On the other hand, I don't disbelieve anything either.'

'Well, that's a scientific mind.'

I continued, 'I suppose I would like to believe that we're all connected in ways as we all share atoms. It's said that we all probably have some atoms from Hitler and from Jesus in our make-up and my atoms will become part of other people as well. I don't know if that has any meaning.'

'That's all true. Matter is continually forming, breaking up and reforming. It's a totally random thing and has no meaning to the individual. We're just part of evolution, a spark in the universe that dies away. I was reared a Catholic and flirted with joining the Benedictines in my early twenties. I've now turned one hundred and eighty degrees and I'm a complete atheist. When the switch is turned off, that's it, finito. I want to choose when I die.'

We stopped at Talkeetna, which sits at the confluence of three powerful rivers. It's also the town upon which Cicely in the television programme *Northern Exposure* was modelled. Talkeetna is a base for intrepid souls who wish to climb Mount McKinley, and for less intrepid souls who want to fly over it by air taxi. After leaving the small station, we headed north again and crossed an iron railway bridge far above a fierce river flowing through a ravine called Hurricane Gulch. The train on the bridge cast a dark shadow far below.

We stopped at Denali Park railway station and there was a mass exodus of those who wanted to explore the national park and the foothills of Mount McKinley. Down below me, I could see people on rafts navigating a strongly flowing river.

Barry asked Paula if plans existed to extend the railway in Alaska. Paula told him that they were hoping to bring it as far to Nome, but she was more enthusiastic about extending the railway past Nome and underneath the Bering Strait to Siberia. She felt that this would accelerate the development of the whole area, but that it would take a visionary to make it happen.

When I studied geography as a boy, I was always struck by the grand isolation of Alaska, perched precariously at the edge of the page, bordering onto an inaccessible and frozen Arctic Ocean. This, however, is a flat-earth view of the world because if you look at the Arctic Ocean on a globe or from outer space, you can immediately see that this expanse of sea is the Mediterranean of the north. It is enclosed by some of the most powerful nations on earth, including the US, Russia and Canada. Given that this is one of the few resource-rich areas left on this planet, becoming ever more accessible because of global warming, it is inevitable that it will move closer to the centre of global activity in the future.

This demand for greater development of the region is already gathering momentum.

Paula told me that oil companies are trying to buy more land for exploration, without developing what they already have.

'They're like Scrooges hoarding as much as they can, knowing that it will only increase in value as time goes on. Sarah Palin put a stop to this when she was Governor and told them they would have to develop what they had before more land became available.'

Barry said, 'Natural gas will be huge for Alaska in the future. It will make you rich.'

'Yes, and we can minimise the impact by using the same holes that are used for oil.'

I wanted to know what was the likely environmental impact of oil and gas exploration.

Paula said, 'We have to get a balance between preserving the caribou herd, one of the great sights in nature, and the development of gas in the future. The plan is to connect the gas pipeline with Chicago and distribute it to the rest of the country. The main challenge is coping with subsidence in the permafrost, but a new technology for burying the pipes safely has been developed. Four large machines, nearly the size of football pitches, have been developed to lay the line and drivers are being trained to handle them properly.'

The mind boggled at such immensity but, then again, we were in Alaska.

If you're going to develop the natural resources of an area, you need clear title to the land. A plan developed by oil companies for an eight-hundred-mile pipeline linking North Slope and Valdez in Prince William Sound provided the impetus for the government to make a settlement with the Native peoples in Alaska. In 1971, an agreement was reached whereby the Native people gave up their claim to 90 per cent of the lands across all of Alaska in return for forty-four million acres and funding of one billion dollars to support the development of thirteen regional corporations, tasked with the development of their communities on a for-profit basis. Each Native person was entitled to a share. Paula felt that when it came to dealing with government, the Native peoples of Alaska had learned from the mistakes made by the Native Americans in the 'lower forty-eight' states.

'These corporations have performed very well in economic terms and have made lots of money for Native peoples here. I know of Native women, now living in Anchorage, who get cheques of sixty thousand dollars each year as a dividend from their corporation. Because of this wealth, Native people now often send their children to European schools to get the best education possible.'

'Do they not think that they can get a good education here?'

'No.'

Barry interjected, 'They don't have to do a hand's turn for the rest of their lives. I wonder is that good for people?'

'It is a problem in some cases but the Native people have been innovative in developing new business. Each year, the forty best business people under the age of forty in Alaska are invited to receive awards. Fifty per cent of the attendees are Native people, despite the high level of competition from many overseas companies. A young Native man I know has set up a company to process the waste from fish as a dog food product and it has been a great success. The dogs love it.'

'There's an idea for you', she said, turning to me, 'you're surrounded by sea and fish. You could learn from his experience.'

§

I had heard in Anchorage that during the winter months the train company organises weekly trips to Fairbanks specifically to view the aurora borealis. Some indigenous people believed that they were made by the spirits of children who died at birth, dancing in the sky. I visualised myself sitting in this glass-topped observation car, viewing the white Alaskan wilderness by starlight on a cold, clear winter's night, with the aurora borealis streaming mysterious colours across the sky. I imagined the lonely spirits of children who never got a chance to savour this world, asking to be remembered by the glory of their dance. I thought of Barry and all those who had lost a light.

Thirteen hours after leaving Anchorage, we arrived in Fairbanks, the second largest city in Alaska, with the princely population of thirty-five thousand souls. We had covered the distance at an average speed of twenty-seven miles per hour. The train travels slowly because subsidence caused by permafrost affects the stability of the rail tracks. To me, this was no disadvantage whatsoever. To hurry on this route would be a crime. It was 9 p.m., but the sun was blazing. I checked into a motel in the centre of Fairbanks, opposite the Chena River.

§

'Well, sometimes I have to knock them down on the ground, go muzzle-to-muzzle with them and show them who's boss. You always have to be the dominant one. If I decide to go into the middle of fighting dogs, I can't turn back because if I do, I'll never be able to work with them again. They would have no respect for me.'

The fair-haired receptionist in the hotel also owned a dog-sledding business.

She continued, 'It's rare that I have to intervene physically. Just a shout and a look is usually enough. I have fun trying to figure them out. They're all different and they have moods like us. I have two dogs that were the best of friends for three years. They ran side by side in the sled, but one day they fought and the loser has held a grudge ever since. I now place her directly behind the winner in the sled. She can chase her all she wants, to try to get her own back, and the best thing is, the other will run faster to keep ahead.'

She told me that she had undertaken many long solo sledding trips through the wilderness, which prompted me to ask her how she trained the dogs for these trips.

'You have to build a dog's confidence in small ways first, especially if you expect them to endure long journeys in difficult situations. The more they understand about what they might face, the better. You have to make sure to choose the right lead dog, because if he sits down, they all will.'

I told her about Mící's walk from Fort Yukon to Dawson City and how difficult it was.

'If he had had dogs', she said, 'he'd have been there in no time.'

Ravenous with hunger, I went searching for food, even though it was 10 p.m. A little later, I rang a friend to tell him that I was sitting outside a restaurant in the middle of Alaska at ten at night, in my shirtsleeves, with a prime view over the Chena River. He thought I was having him on, and joked that all that ice might have seriously affected my brain. I sat back, ordered a pasta dish, and relaxed.

§

My thoughts returned to Mící on his journey upriver from St Michael. Recovered from seasickness, he could finally appreciate the wonders of the north. He saw bears, caribou and moose, which he described as big bullocks. He heard the call of wild geese and cranes singing sweetly as they flew south over the tundra. The 'Indian' fish wheels impressed him as a method of catching fish. Did he wonder if the technology had any application in the sea at Magheroarty? He watched Native people working in fish camps, and burying their dead with great respect in little four-foot houses in riverside cemeteries. He felt however that they mistreated their dogs, whose night-time wailing created a fearsome, haunting sound on the quiet river.

They felt as though they were on a long cruise; Micí had time to pity those poor stampeders, battling up the Chilkoot trail. Soon however, he was to taste hardship himself.

They steamed into Fort Yukon on a beautiful though cold October day and came to a full stop. To their dismay, the captain told them he couldn't take them any farther, as the river was running low because of early frost. They had a choice. They could pay for a return journey, or disembark. In reality, Micí and his friends had no choice because they didn't have sufficient money for the return journey. They were abandoned with neither money nor food three hundred inhospitable miles from Dawson City. With winter rapidly closing its fist upon the land, their situation was perilous.

§

I woke up grumpy. Unbelievable. How could anyone be grumpy on a trip in Alaska? Breakfast and a few friendly words restored my good mood. I caught a bus to the Museum of the North, located on a hillside just outside the city. It had been recommended to me as a 'must see'. On arrival, I was impressed by the design of the building, which, appropriately enough, took an ice crystal as its inspiration. Inside, the museum retained its fluid design, flowing with energy and light. An intimidating security guard confronted me. He stood eight foot nine inches in his socks, had a reddish complexion and weighed twelve hundred pounds. His name was Otto, and he was a Kodiak brown bear that had been shot, stuffed and mounted here as a prize exhibit. He might even be the most photographed bear in the world; much good it did him!

Otto guards the one and a half million exhibits which document all aspects of Alaskan life. I focused on an exhibit detailing the tragic story of the Aleuts during the Second World War. About ten thousand years ago, an Asian people settled on a remote chain of treeless islands that stretched like stepping-stones for a thousand miles, from the Alaskan Peninsula to the island of Attu in the Orient. They called themselves Unanga, which means 'We the People'. They later became known as the Aleuts. These people adapted superbly to the marine environment, and developed specialised technologies for hunting whales, seals and sea lions. Their whole existence was based on their knowledge of the sea and their skills in working with it to survive.

One of the defining features of the Aleutian Islands is fog. This is brought about by a clash of warm air flowing from Japan and cold Arctic air. The resultant fog, like Harry Potter's cloak, serves to shroud the islands from view for a large part of the year. This invisibility helped protect the Aleuts for generations. They first encountered outsiders when Russians arrived in the mid-eighteenth century. This was the first of a series of calamities that reduced the Aleutian population from an estimated twenty thousand souls to two thousand today.

The Second World War had the most profound effect on these people. When the Japanese occupied two remote American-owned Aleutian islands, the Americans, fearing attack through Alaska, forcibly cleared the Aleut people from the islands and interred them in disused canneries on mainland Alaska. This had a devastating effect on their culture. Imagine having a continuous history of living in one spot beside the sea for ten thousand years and to be removed to internment camps with no basic amenities, not even clean water. The Aleuts had no concept of how to live this new life and many died. Some of the Aleutian women organised a petition. It simply stated, 'We the people of this place want a better place to live. This is no place for a living creature.'

Because of the deaths of many elders, within whom the knowledge, skills and spiritual direction of the people resided, their culture disintegrated. A demoralised people returned to their homes years later. When they arrived, they found their houses destroyed and the wild herds of animals, their source of food, decimated by bored, trigger-happy soldiers. Restitution followed but some things cannot be replaced.

A room, called, 'The Place Where You Go to Listen', created another lasting impression. The idea for this room came from an old legend which told the story of how an Inupiaq woman went to a sacred spot called Naalagiagvik, near to the village Kaktovik on the Arctic Ocean. There, the Universe spoke to her and she listened intently with her whole being. She heard the voice and song of birds, whales, the wind and the waves. She listened to the sound of snow falling, ice creaking, plants growing and all the animals moving. She tuned into the resonance of the seasons, times when life flared forth in abundance or went into brittle, icy rest. She was filled with the echo of the aurora, the sky and the deep earth gurgling. All of this came to her in an ever-changing song, the song of the universe, to which we're all attuned.

A composer and musician called John Luther Adams drew inspiration from this story and from the dramatic extremes of interior Alaska, light and dark, fire and ice. He celebrated the story of Naalagiagvik by combining music and technology to enable us to listen to the song of this extraordinary landscape. This isn't a work for mere mortals; one needs to be touched by the gods. He created a system where live data from seismological, metrological and geomagnetic stations all over Alaska feed into a computer on a continuous basis. Musical notes are assigned to each piece of data and these are then blended together to produce an ever-changing song. It is a symphony responding to the rhythms of sunlight and moonlight, the fury of storms and seismic activity, fluctuations in the earth's magnetic field, the movement of glaciers and the dance of the aurora in the sky. It took Adams years to complete the project.

An elderly man coming out of the room threw his hands into the air, proclaiming with disgust. 'That's all it is, noise.'

In dim light, soft streams of yellow luminosity flowed across five glass panels on a wall. Other colours – pale yellow, blue and green – flickered at the edges. The mood was peaceful. A couple sat on the bench in front of the panels talking loudly. I wished they would be quieter. I closed my eyes and tuned into the sound with all my senses. I became aware of the subtleties and changes within this music. Deep bass ripples of notes flowed through it; light notes came in rapid flurries, appearing and disappearing. An occasional bell echoed lightly at the very top of the scale like a light, announcing its presence, bouncing through the sky. Through it all, a constant background sound, something like a fridge mixed with a humpback whale, remained constant, varying only in intensity from time to time. As I sat there with my eyes closed, I became aware of people coming and going, their whispers merging with the sound. As a piece of art, this is a fascinating project. As a place to meditate, it's inferior to a quiet place beside the sea or a mountain lake. It stirred an ambition, sometime in the future, to find this place called Naalagiagvik, the place where you go to listen.

After the museum, I went to bed excited by the prospect of my first flight on a small plane to Fort Yukon. It was apt that I was flying out of Fairbanks, as the first ever bush flight in Alaska originated there.

Carl Ben Eielson flew out of Fairbanks on 3 July 1923 to deliver 160 pounds of mail to a village called McGrath. He used an open-cockpit De Havilland DH4 biplane and had to dress for the weather. He wore two pairs of woollen socks, a pair of caribou-skin sock moccasins that reached to his knees, a suit of long underwear, khaki breaches, trousers made of Hudson Bay duffel, a heavy shirt, a sweater, a martin-skin cap, goggles and a reindeer-skin parka with wolverine-fur hood, wool gloves and fur mittens. He was guided back into Fairbanks by a bonfire but, despite that, he managed to hit a tree and broke a ski on the plane. I hoped it wasn't an omen.

16

Fort Yukon

Two smiling, middle-aged women greeted me at the small reception counter. One of them, a tall, thin, black-haired woman, took my rucksack and weighed it. She asked my weight, apologising, 'We have to weigh everything because we have to balance the weight on the aeroplane.'

I had visions of my small rucksack making the aeroplane wobble in the air. However, I was pleased when my bag was returned with a label on it which said 'Fort Yukon'. It provided official confirmation that my destination was an Athabaskan village, ten miles on the far side of the Arctic Circle.

She warned me, 'We might not be flying today because of the smoke.'

Where's the rain when you need it? I thought, but what could I expect? I was in an area that experienced two thousand lightning strikes per day, producing the highest incidence of natural fires in Alaska. She must have seen dismay in my eyes as she added, 'We expect the smoke from that big fire in the east to clear a little later. It might be enough to let us fly. In the meantime, make yourself a cup of coffee in the kitchen. It's mainly for pilots, but they won't mind.'

I accepted her offer gratefully and another man with the same addiction joined me. Steve was a blonde-haired, strongly built man with muscular arms bursting out of the sleeves of his T-shirt. We took our coffees outside and sat on a wall. He worked at repairing communication and satellite transmitters on mountaintops and in remote locations like Fort Yukon. The way Steve described his job, it was like lighthouse keepers of yore, stationed on islands and remote headlands for months on end. With his work completed, he was often marooned by fierce storms on top of Alaskan mountains for weeks at a time. He had the use of a small hut for survival, until a company helicopter came and collected him.

'What's it like when you get off the mountain?'

'I tell my wife to say nothing to me for a few days.'

'I imagine how you'd get if you lived in the wilderness for a long time on your own.'

'Lots of guys come to Alaska to live on their own in the wilderness for one reason or other. They gradually go mad. Often, they kill themselves. There are four or five such deaths in Alaska each year.'

I asked him if he had he travelled much.

'Europe and Africa', he said.

'Where in Africa?'

'Mostly in the Congo.'

'What was it like there?'

'Mad. Guns everywhere. It's dangerous and you need to be able to protect yourself. The whole place has fallen apart. None of the different groups there can agree with each other.'

I thought to myself that they were getting ample assistance in their trouble-making from neighbouring countries like Uganda and Rwanda, as well as superpowers like the US and China, all interested in plundering their resources.

He changed the subject and told me that he loved to make things with his hands. He described with great passion how he made a simple device to conduct heat into a house while at the same time allowing the cold air to escape. It was all beyond my understanding, but it seemed like a good idea for Alaska. While rolling a cigarette, he described his other projects. He had hooked up the power systems for both computer games and television to a jogging machine in his house. If either his sons or his wife wanted to watch television or play computer games, they would have to exercise on the jogging machine first. That invention mightn't be too popular! Emboldened, he told me tales of how he had disarmed armed robbers and 'sorted out' men who were bothering his wife. This kind of talk put me on edge, so I stood up to get a better view of the sky.

'That smoke seems to be getting thicker', I said.

Shortly afterwards, however, a flight to another village was called and six passengers departed. Besides myself and Steve, there was only one other passenger for Fort Yukon, an elderly man with a long, white beard who walked slowly with a carved walking stick. He told us he had lived and worked in different parts of the world, but now he was living his 'last years' in Fort Yukon because he had found peace there.

The receptionist announced, 'The pilot is ready to go to Fort Yukon now.'

I jumped up, eager to be on my way, stepping on the heels of the receptionist as she led us out of the terminal. We walked through a forest of small planes of all shapes and sizes, until she pointed to what seemed to be the smallest plane in the airport. She then gave us ear-plugs and told us to wait there until the pilot arrived. A few moments later, a tall, overweight man in a sparkling white shirt turned up. He had a slightly vulnerable, boyish appearance.

'Are y'all going to Fort Yukon?' he asked.

In reply, he got an assortment of grunts and nods.

He unlocked the side door of the plane and motioned us to enter. I was first up the steps. Three of the six seats on the left were piled high with boxes of supplies. I sat directly behind the pilot, eager to obtain the best view. Steve and the old man, clearly old hands at flying in small planes, lumbered in after me. The smoke was still thick. In fact, it appeared thicker than when the flight was in doubt. I presumed however that the pilot knew something that I didn't. He turned the key and the engine grumbled into life. I expected the plane to move, but the pilot began a scrupulous sequence of turning on and off switches on the dashboard. He retested each switch at least twice. I wasn't sure whether to be relieved or worried by all of this testing. He taxied to the top of the runway but, when he got there, he started test-ing switches again. I thought to myself that I would have been to Fort Yukon and back, walking, by this stage. He revved up the engine to full throttle, and then I realised the value of the earplugs. He pointed the airplane down the runway and, gathering speed, we passed row upon row of small planes before he pulled a lever and we rose into the sky. Well, we rose into a grey, mushy cloak of cloud and smoke with virtually no visibility ahead. I looked around at my fellow pas-sengers. Both were totally unconcerned. Steve was sound asleep. I wondered were any other planes up there, imagining what would happen if one should appear suddenly out of the murk.

I was disappointed by this seemingly endless smoke and cloud, because I had been looking forward to viewing the White Mountain Range which lay between Fairbanks and Fort Yukon. As we flew over the invisible mountains, turbulence caused the plane to shake and my nerves to rattle. In these situations, small planes seem fragile, with precarious reality staring you full-square in the face. I was aware of everything from the reactions of the pilot to the straining of the bolts holding the wings in place.

Suddenly, we were clear of the murk and a vista of flat land opened up all around us, as far as the eye could see. It was a land of water and forest. Water predominated; there were huge lakes, hundreds of streams and small rivers everywhere. These weren't real lakes, just melted snow that had nowhere to seep because of the permafrost underneath. From the air, you could see where evaporation caused by the summer sun had reduced their size, creating a marshland within the watermark. It appeared to be an impenetrable wilderness.

This low-lying area between the White Mountains and the Brook Mountains, sculpted by water and scoured by ice, is known as the Yukon Flats. It is a 110 million acre wetland, five times the size of Ireland, a migration route for birds and a place of refuge for them in times of drought. I was told that in the spring, it's one of the great sights of nature to see clouds of swans, geese, duck and loon arrive in the Flats, transforming it from a land of snow and ice into one of the greatest waterfowl breeding areas in the world. This is bird nirvana, for part of the year anyway. It's also an area where moose, caribou, wolves, frogs, black bear and grizzly bear roam. And, of course, mosquitoes.

Later, I spotted a cobra-like river in the distance. This was my first glimpse of the Yukon, one of the mightiest rivers in the world. As we got nearer, it became clear that this river cast all shackles aside when it entered the plain. It spread out into a myriad of channels up to twenty miles wide, creating innumerable islands and sand bars of all shapes and sizes. A boat without map and compass would surely get lost there.

Buildings finally came into view; it was Fort Yukon. As we got closer I made out large, white, circular storage tanks, a labyrinth of gravel roads and wooden houses set in among trees. The plane flew over the village once and then set itself up to land on a long gravel strip beside the town. We landed smoothly and taxied to a prefabricated building.

When we disembarked, five pick-up trucks arrived in a flurry of dust; one for each of the other passengers, one for the pilot and two for loading supplies. Everyone was busy except me. The drivers stripped all the supplies from the plane and vamoosed as quickly as they could. I stood alone at the side of the runway. In front of me was the terminal building and beside it were two open gates leading onto a gravel road. I went into the airport building and asked the only occupant, a thin woman wearing a baseball cap, for directions to the town. She pointed wordlessly to the right. I later realised that she could have pointed to the left and been equally correct.

I wandered along a road verged by dense birch, willow, small bushes and long grasses. I could hear sounds from an as yet unseen town; children shouting, birds chirping, dogs barking and lots of hammering. The temperature was 95 degrees Fahrenheit, which certainly rendered the fleece in my rucksack redundant. I passed a large tank, with a sign that said, 'Crowley, Fort Yukon, Alaska'. In secondary school my best friend was DJ Crowley from Cork; these Cork men get everywhere!

Beyond the Crowley tank, I caught a glimpse of blue water. Quickening my footsteps, I reached the banks of the Yukon River, or in reality the confluence of the Yukon and Porcupine Rivers. I stood looking at the river for about fifteen minutes, letting it soak into me.

Perhaps this was the spot where Mící and his three friends were ejected from the paddle steamer, with just the clothes on their backs and a small basket of food, still three hundred miles from Dawson City. I imagined how this spot might have appeared then. The intense winter cold tightened its grip as Mící arrived into Fort Yukon. Biting winds and sharp, early frosts would have turned the ground crinkly white, and the leaves would have been gone from the trees. The forests would have been silent, as most songbirds had departed for warmer climes and the lumbering bear, sated with salmon and berries, would have crawled into its winter den. Hiding from hungry eyes, the Arctic hare and fox would have transformed from brown to white. The ice would have turned the land to rock, and would have crept onto the river.

In the August sunshine, my view was totally different. The channel beside the town was perhaps a half-mile wide and its blue grey water flowed slowly and tranquilly past. The far bank of this channel was heavily forested with black spruce and aspen, as was an island that lay in between. The river appeared shallow, with a wide foreshore of hard-baked mud, silt and gravel, upon which white skeletons of trees and other debris were deposited. The sharp whine of an engine pierced the air. A small, open skiff with two men on board powered up the channel, leaving a spreading line of white wake behind. I went out onto the foreshore and stood on a large log. I was aware of the heat on my head and back, the slight breeze on my face and the whisper of the river. I felt that by looking at this place I was taking it inside me. I can look at the same place on television, in photographs or on a computer but they are only shadows that cannot be inhabited.

A vehicle stopped behind me. A door opened and slammed shut. I turned around and saw a man walking towards me from his pick up. He was of sturdy build, had black hair, a round, jovial face and was gap-toothed. He shouted, 'Coastal patrol, where's your permit?'

For a second I wondered if he was serious. Had I breached some local law by wandering onto the shore?

'So you want all my fish?'

'Sure do. Hand them over straight away.'

'A man can get away with nothing nowadays.'

'That's the truth', he said, bursting into hearty laughter. 'What takes you to Fort Yukon?'

I told him my story, and said that I wanted to see the place and talk to a few people. He laughed and said, 'The bar opens at two o'clock. You'll have lots of people to talk to there. I'll be there too. There's always a few, hanging around, waiting for it to open from early morning.'

'Reminds me of Ireland', I said.

He rummaged in his pocket and brought out some small stones with stripes of colour through them.

'Have you a daughter?' he asked.

'Yes.'

'I found these stones in the river; they're agate and have been washed by the silt. Take one for your daughter. Have you any more children?'

'Yes, I've a son and another daughter.'

'Well then you'd better takes ones for them too. They'll remind you all of here', he said, pressing a group of polished stones into my hand. Joviality kept bubbling out of him as he talked.

'My father is the Episcopalian minister in town. He's in Fairbanks today but will be back tomorrow. How long are you staying?'

'I'm leaving on the last flight today.'

'Pity. He would have liked to have met you.' With a cheery wave, he was off up a track in a cloud of dust.

I began to get a feel for the town of Fort Yukon. Like most American towns, it was laid out on a geometric grid. Houses were made of logs or were prefabricated buildings, usually with tin roofs. They had plenty of space around them into which assortments of objects were collected: quad bikes, trucks, bits of trucks, oil barrels, boats, small sheds, dog kennels and log piles. Each house had its own particular character.

As I walked along the street, a voice called out, 'Hello, do you want a map of the village?'

I turned around to see a thin, black-haired man, standing in the doorway of a prefabricated house, waving at me to come over. A dark blue bus was parked beside the house with 'Fort Yukon Transit System' printed on its side.

'Step on inside', he said.

Just then, a car pulled up. Four middle-aged people – two men and two women – tumbled out in a tangle of grocery bags. The black-haired man greeted them with a joke and we all went into the house together. The small living room was suddenly full. I stood with the owner beside the stove and the others started to make sandwiches. Well, the women did. The two men wandered off outside.

The dark-haired man turned to me and offered his hand, 'Richard Carroll'.

I introduced myself and added, 'This is a real coincidence; I'm married to a woman called Carroll in Ireland.'

'We might be connected', he laughed.

He explained to me that he and half the village were descended from an Irish explorer and hunter called James Carroll, who opened a store in Fort Yukon at the beginning of the twentieth century. This wasn't long after Mící had passed through. Carroll married a Native woman and they had twelve children, of whom all but one survived to adulthood, hence the multitude of Carrolls in the village.

One of the women asked Richard if he would like a sandwich to take on the trip. He nodded. The four people were going on a boat trip up the Porcupine River, with Richard as pilot and guide. He asked me why I visited Fort Yukon and after listening to my story about Mící, he immediately started talking about the nineteenth century as if it was yesterday.

'I heard about two boats getting stuck here in the fall of 1897. Most of the men wintered in Fort Yukon before going on to Dawson in the spring. He might have been one of those men.'

'No, he came in the fall of 1898 and walked most of the way to Dawson along with three other men. The river was beginning to ice up at the time.'

'I've not heard of that boat. It would have been better had they stayed here and travelled in the spring. It wasn't an easy journey in winter without dogs.'

I told him that they were ill-prepared for such extremes and journeyed on the generosity of others, receiving food, a rowing boat, sleds, warm clothes and axes from miners fleeing the winter hardship and potential food shortages in Dawson. These miners warned them that all the gold claims had already been staked and not to go there. Mici and his friends continued on, in the belief that their friends in Dawson would be able to assist them. Having received the gift of a rowing boat, they presumed they could row all the way.

Being a boatman himself, Richard was interested in the boat journey. I recounted how Mici, along with his three friends, tried to row the skiff against the current towards Dawson City. They hadn't realised how powerful the current would be. The only way they could make any headway was by rowing and poling close to the bank where the current was weakest. Progress was slow. The greatest problem they faced was fallen trees. If they couldn't cut through them, their only means of progress was to row to the opposite bank, a manoeuvre which could see them swept a mile back downriver. Once there, they would have to battle their way back up the channel, hugging the bank, until they encountered a similar impenetrable obstacle on the other side, forcing them to row across the river again. In this way, they zigzagged along, making progress towards Circle, the next town on the route.

Cold weather closed in on them when they neared Circle, wrapping the river in an icy embrace. It froze the area closest to the banks first, forcing the men to abandon the boat. Mici and his friends then travelled on foot, pulling sleds behind them. One of their number contracted frostbite. If it wasn't for the intervention of a Native woman who had a traditional cure, he might have died. Then, while over-nighting in a cabin, Mici became ill with frostbite in both of his legs. When he couldn't move the following morning, his companions abandoned him. Fear for their own survival and lust for gold surpassed their compassion for a colleague. Micí, fearing death, sought salvation in prayer. Eventually, his limbs recovered and he was able to set off, pulling his sled over mountains towards the Klondike, catching up with the men who abandoned him. You can imagine their faces when who appears over the horizon but the bould Micí.

Richard took my email address and told me that he would search for any local information on Micí's boat and on traditional cures for frostbite. When a young boy went past bouncing a basketball, he told me that basketball was popular in the town because of the influence of the army base, there to protect the 'DEW line' radar base near the town.

I said goodbye to Richard and continued towards the town's only store. The small street was busy with quad bikes and pick-ups buzzing hither and thither carrying all sorts of bits and bobs. A few young children cycled past an elevated log food cache. I said hello to a woman standing outside a church.

She replied, 'You're doing a lot of walking!'

A man sat relaxing outside his log cabin. Wood smoke rose out of the chimney and even in the heat the image provided comfort. I got a jolt when I recognised the skin of a grizzly adorning a tree outside another house. It had been camouflaged in the tracery of the tree.

When I arrived at the shop, a few young people were standing outside, tossing a basketball from one to the other. Inside, I loaded up on starch, water and some fruit. This was the first piece of fruit I had found since I came to Alaska, and I had to come inside the Arctic Circle to find it. There were no corner shops in Anchorage or Fairbanks. If I wanted fruit, I would have to go to superstores on the outskirts of the cities. When I came out of the shop, a tall, lean man on a quad bike pulled up beside me and asked where I was from. He had faraway eyes and didn't talk much during our conversation except for a few monosyllables. He then asked, 'Do you want a ride anywhere?'

I declined, telling him that I enjoyed walking.

On the way to eat my food beside the river, I saw a scraggly piece of paper with a scrawled message on a community notice board, '$15 reward for the return of folding table and chairs.' There was a telephone number below it. How could anyone keep a table and chairs concealed in a small place like Fort Yukon? It has a population of only five hundred. Someone was bound to spot them!

I continued along the riverbank until I reached forest. I followed a narrow path through spruce trees until I came to an opening, where two small motorboats were moored beside a fish wheel mounted on floating logs. I was pleased to see a fish wheel, as Mici observed Native peoples using them on his journey up the Yukon. It works like a windmill, using the power of the river current to drive netted buckets that scoop fish from the river. The fish then drop into a container tank, before the bucket swings around into the water once more. It only works because the water is murky and the fish cannot see where they're going. I sat on a fallen log and ate my lunch accompanied by the sound and sight of assorted vicious insects hovering around me, taking lumps out of any bit of flesh they could get their wee teeth or nippers around.

As I walked back along the riverbank, two men got out of a boat. One was a lanky, fit-looking man with long, grey black hair. Time had bent his frame into a slight stoop. The other man was small, straight and thin, with bright eyes that shone out of his head. When the tall man heard I was Irish he said, 'It was the Irish and Scots who introduced fiddle music to Fort Yukon. It has become part of our music now. We have some of the best fiddle players in Alaska here.'

His voice was mellifluous. It intonated in a slow melody, like a gentle air on a fiddle.

His friend reminded him, 'You've a plane to catch; don't forget.'

He nodded in response but ignored the impending deadline. He told me that their jobs entailed monitoring the environment in six Native villages along the Yukon River. They were all cooperating to clean up the environment.

'We should be able to drink the water from the river', he said.

This meant that all hazardous waste such as old oil barrels, obsolete electrical equipment, lead paint, asbestos and old vehicles had to be identified and collected.

'How do you get rid of all this stuff?' I asked.

'We ship it out. The scheme is working good.'

I asked them about the possibility of getting to Dawson City by boat. They looked at each other and shook their heads.

'No, there are no boats to Dawson now', said the taller man, 'most of the traffic in the river is local, between the villages here or to the fishing camps.'

'What sort of fish can you catch?'

'All types; salmon, trout, grayling, but my favourite is the white fish. As a child though we loved to eat smoked salmon eyes. When our parents smoked the fish at fish camp, we would take any opportunity to feast on those eyes. We were easily caught though as the eyes made our mouths black.'

After chuckling at the memory, he continued, 'I also shoot moose for meat. You can lure a moose by rubbing bones, but the easiest way, using a boat, is to spot one crossing a river and shoot it as it comes out on the bank. This is a great place to live. We've got good food and clean air. But it can get cold in the winter.'

'How cold?'

'It can get to minus sixty. When it's that cold, you're better off indoors beside a good fire. Such cold weather isn't good for the lungs. When you breathe, it sounds like corn flakes being eaten.'

The smaller man nudged the taller man, again pointing to his watch, 'You'll miss the plane if you don't go now.'

The taller man said reluctantly, 'I'm going to a meeting in Fairbanks to discuss the river.'

They both said goodbye and hurried off along the path.

I decided to follow the riverside track that went twenty-eight miles out of Fort Yukon into the wilderness. Some large houses were under construction at the edge of town. This was suburbia, where the richer people lived. I walked five miles along this path, bounded by slough, wild bush, spruce trees and shrub, which brought me to a building that looked like a giant golf ball in the sky. I took this to be the radar station. There was an assortment of concrete buildings around it, probably living quarters and administration buildings. I couldn't see any sign of life in the immediate vicinity, but I'm sure someone somewhere was watching. Large signs told me not to go any further unless I had specific permission. Conscious that I was a guest in the village, I didn't progress far past the signs. I saw a few large hangars with empty oil barrels lying inside. The rest of the hangar space was empty. Perhaps it's used during the winter months for vehicles and machinery, or perhaps they're for hiding UFOs, recorded as a matter of public record over Fort Yukon!

At one stage on the walk back into the town, I became aware of two men on quad bikes stopped about one hundred yards behind me. One of them was the man with the faraway eyes. They seemed to be watching me. I got uneasy so, once around a corner, I hid in the trees.

A few moments later, the quads passed on by. After a few minutes, I resumed my trek, until I heard the quads coming back up the road again. Letting my imagination get the better of me, I scooted off down a small adjacent path. Eventually I found myself back in town, standing in Burke Street.

I thought that the tribal council building might be a good source of information on life in Fort Yukon. The building seemed to be empty, but I finally found a young woman in an office. When I asked whether anyone could tell me about the town's history, a look of panic came over her face. She obviously hadn't the foggiest notion what to do with me.

Suddenly, her face brightened. 'The radio station. Talk to John or Vicky there. They know all about history.'

She showed me the way to the radio station, a large, white wooden building across the street. When I went in, a receptionist greeted me. She said, 'Wait in the waiting room. John and Vicky are finishing up on air. You can talk to them when they come out.'

I sat on a wooden bench in the spacious room and seeing a notice board I clunked my way over to have a look. One poster in particular caught my attention. 'The buffalo were wiped out but you can save the Car(ibou).' Clever, I thought.

A door opened and John and Vicky emerged from the studio. I introduced myself. Vicky had a shock of wavy hair while John was younger, with a stubble beard. Vicky said she would have liked to stay and chat but she had a sick child she had to get home to. She asked me if I was staying until tomorrow.

'No, I'm flying back this evening.'

'Pity, I would have liked to do an interview on the show tomorrow. People would like to hear about Ireland.'

John said that he would take me to see the beadwork in the Episcopalian church, but first asked me to wait a few minutes while he went to the store. While waiting, a well-dressed man came out of an office and sat beside me. He had an air of serenity about him. I introduced myself and pointed to the caribou poster, 'I like that poster. It gets its point across.'

He nodded and said, 'The caribou are important to us. Our tribe, the Gwich'in, have a special connection to them. Our creation story tells how people and caribou were once one. When we were separated, people kept part of the caribou heart and caribou kept part of the human heart. They're part of our culture. Our songs and dances speak to them. It's said in the story that whatever happens to them, happens to us as well. They help provide us with food and clothing. We need to protect them.'

'Are they in danger?'

'Oil and gas development is the biggest risk both here in the Flats and north of us in the Arctic Refuge.'

'I read that oil companies claim that oil development will have no impact on the caribou.'

'That's not true. It interferes with their calving and migration routes because the caribou will avoid human development. It means that they spend less time feeding and so their health disimproves. If there's disturbance in their traditional calving grounds, they'll abandon traditional sites and search for quieter ones. These aren't as good as the old sites, so the herd declines. Some of our people regard the calving grounds of the caribou as sacred.'

'What's going to happen?'

'Gonna be a big fight, I guess.'

'Are oil companies going to drill soon on the Yukon Flats?'

'At this stage they're only interested in getting more land. They want to hoard the resources so they can make fortunes in the future. If they put roads though, it would be a disaster.'

'In what way?'

'It would bring more hunters using snowmobiles. Snowmobiles can run animals for long distances in cold weather.'

'Does global warming affect the caribou?'

'Yeah, some of the herds are affected. As the level of the rivers rise, the caribou can no longer cross. They get cut off from part of their territory', he said regretfully. 'There's a shadow over the caribou and our way of life is under threat.'

John returned and we headed off to the Episcopalian church. He wheeled a bicycle en route to his second job in a day-care centre at the other side of town. He had embraced the American dream, having at least two poorly paying jobs.

He said, 'I leave the house every day at eight in the morning and I don't get back until nine in the evening. I also care for an elderly relative at home. It's midnight before I get to bed.'

'Do you get a break at all?'

'Well I live a little outside the village. It's quiet and away from the noise at night. When I have time off work I like to hang out there.' He paused and added, 'I might go to Anchorage for a week in September.'

'You have a street called Burke Street. I have neighbours in Ireland called Burke.'

'Yeah, it's called after Doctor Burke. He ran the hospital in Fort Yukon at one time.'

Dr Grafton Burke came to Fort Yukon in 1908 as a medical Episcopalian missionary. He stayed, married Clara and reared two children. His unwavering commitment to work made him the most popular man in the territory, a status undermined when he became a Justice of the Peace in Fort Yukon. He tried to rid the town of the twin scourges, hooch and what he called 'low down whites', whose only intention, in his mind, was to debauch Native women. He was not successful. Cutting his losses, he went back to full-time medicine and found that his popularity shot up in response.

John took a shortcut through a narrow path in the trees to St Stevens Episcopalian Church. I admired the bell above the porch. I felt an urge to ring it.

John said, in a near whisper, 'It's better for you to be seen going into the church with me even though it's open to everybody.'

Inside, the church was simple, with plain wooden benches and a picture of Christ behind the altar. 'This was made by local women', said John, showing me a highly ornamental braided cloth made of buckskin. 'It takes a long time to complete a cloth like this and get all the designs perfect.'

It had Christian and Native symbols made from beads. In the centre, a circle of white beads spelled out 'IHS'. Once I had glanced at it, John was for leaving. I thanked him for his time, we shook hands, and off he whizzed on his bicycle.

On the way back to the airport, I passed the only gas station in town. It was 1950s style. Two pumps beside a gravel track.

In the airport waiting room, I daydreamed about the caribou, imagining myself living in a tent in springtime as the tundra burst into life, with wild flowers blooming and squadrons of squawking birds arriving from five continents to partake in its bounty. I imagined hearing the rumble of the caribou herd at dawn; the clatter of hooves in the distance, the calling of the mothers and calves, the bellow of a lost calf, the plaintive call of a searching mother and the distinctive clicking of the caribou's ankle joints as they move. Rushing out of the tent, I would watch them as they pulsed across the plain, tightly packed together to protect against mosquitoes and black flies, their antlers bobbing up and down like masts in a harbour rocked by ocean waves.

One of the couples I met earlier with Richard came in and sat beside me. Ed was recently retired, which explained the grin as wide as the Grand Canyon. Peggy was part Native and had come to search for her roots.

Ed told me about the boat trip. 'Fishing was simple, we dropped our lines in the water and we caught fish straight away. We cooked a few on the river bank and they were beautiful.'

'Better than sandwiches?' I teased.

'Much better', laughed Peggy, 'we went on to see a new education centre on the river which aims to pass on the skills of the elders to younger people. When we arrived, twelve pupils were learning how to cut fish.'

'We joined in', said Ed.

'Did you learn much?'

'Yeah', Ed laughed, 'not to slice off my fingers as well.'

On board the plane, I ended up sitting beside a young woman from the village, a lookalike for Marion Jones, the athlete. She was studying to be a nurse and wanted to work on an Apache reservation in Arizona. The Athabaskan and Apache peoples belong to the same tribe; connections still exist. She was going to Fairbanks to attend the World Eskimo and Indian Olympic Games (WEIO).

'They're traditional Native games that take place every year', she told me. 'We've games like the blanket toss, high kick and greased pole walk.'

'Sounds fun.'

'You might like to try them', she grinned.

I wanted to find out more, but at that moment the pilot's door opened and a grizzled man with a roguish eye hopped into his seat. His long, grey hair was tied up in a ponytail, on which a blue baseball cap was perched, skewways. He didn't test switches. He just turned on the engine, we put in our earplugs and we were in the air. The view was clear on the return journey. Again, I marvelled at the expanse of the Yukon Flats, but this time I could view the rounded contours of the White Mountains, which looked from the air like little piglets lying side-by-side, suckling a sow. As we neared Fairbanks, I saw what once was a mountain, but all that remained was an enormous scar of excavated earth. This was Fort Knox, the largest open-pit gold mine in Alaska, covering 3,800 acres. To produce an ounce of gold, they have to process thirty-three tons of rock. That's an awful lot of digging. At peak production, they produce $250,000 worth of gold per day.

When I returned to the motel, I did an unusual thing. I had a bath and wallowed sumptuously, feeling the fatigue leave my arms and legs. I inhaled the humid air and relaxed. When I dragged my heavy legs out of the bath, I decided to shave, as it would save me the bother in the morning. I wiped the steamed-up mirror with a towel but the humidity was stubborn and clung grimly to the surface. I shaved my face by feel, then went to bed and slept like a log.

17

Fairbanks to Dawson

'We are going to Dawson City tomorrow, are you interested?'

I had made phone contact with the only transport provider between Fairbanks and Dawson City.

'When will you be going next after that?' I asked.

'We go twice a week; we'll be going again in four days time', the sharp voice replied.

'I'd better go tomorrow then.'

'Is that definite?'

'Yes.'

'I'll collect you at five o'clock in the morning.'

Having one day left in Fairbanks, I wanted to see the WEIO. The games were the brainchild of two pilots, Bud Hagberg and Frank Whaley, who were passionate about preserving and promoting Native Alaskan peoples' traditional games. These 'Olympic' games built on the tradition where Native villages regularly met to compete with each other in contests that required strength, balance, agility and endurance, attributes necessary for survival in a harsh wilderness. The first games were held in 1961 and Fairbanks has hosted them every year since. The names of the events intrigued me: knuckle hop, blanket toss, Alaskan high kick, greased pole walk, ear pull and muktuk eating contest, to name but a few.

That evening, I walked the three miles from Fairbanks along the Chena River to the venue. *Hink a hink honk, hink a hink honk*; a squadron of Canada geese flew low over the bushes and small trees on the riverbank. Their calls and the whish of their wings filled the air and brought a feeling of exhilaration; freedom on the wing. When I arrived at the sports arena, a buzz of activity greeted me as a crowd of people congregated around the door. I bought my ticket and went in. The venue was a purpose-built sports arena with tiered seats for up to seven thousand spectators. I passed numerous stalls at the back of the arena selling crafts and fast food, telling fortunes and giving out health information. Avoiding all of them, I found a seat high in the stands and watched dancers in full-feathered regalia flowing through the arena to the beat of drums, while the spectators enthusiastically stamped and clapped. To my surprise, I spotted the girl I'd been sitting beside on the plane from Fort Yukon walking amongst the competitors on the arena floor. She was the reigning Miss WEIO queen.

The night's programme promised events such as high kick, knuckle hop and blanket toss, all interspersed with traditional dances. I soon realised however that the order of events as detailed on the programme had little meaning. Time was as it is supposed to be, elastic; it stretched to accommodate events. This was no place for an impatient mind so I surrendered to the evening's rhythm. A typical announcement ran along these lines: 'We're looking for one of the competitors for the blanket toss; we'll have a dance whilst we wait.' A dance involved people of all ages, shapes and abilities from a small village having fun together.

A girl of about five or six and her mother were sitting directly behind me. The mother said, 'Darling, we'll go home soon.'

'Why?'

'Mommy is tired and has to get up for work tomorrow.'

'Why?'

'Because.'

It was time for the men's Alaskan high kick. In this competition, the contestants begin in a seated position under a small ball which is suspended in front of them. They grasp one foot with the opposite hand and then, using the free hand, they spring off the floor to kick the ball with the free foot, before landing in a balanced position. The ball is raised continuously until there's a winner. It's a game that requires great strength and agility.

The little girl asked, 'What are those men doing?'

'They're going to kick the ball.'

'Why?'

'The person who can kick the highest wins.'

'Why?'

'Because.'

'Why is he taking so long?'

'Because he has to get ready. He has to make sure he kicks the ball.'

'Why?'

'If he misses the ball, he'll be out of the game.'

The competition progressed until there was only one man left.

A young female announcer, with increasing excitement, said, 'The height is now 96 inches and Elijah Cabinboy will break the world record if he makes it. Please everyone give him your support.'

Elijah Cabinboy walked out and stood under the ball. Even on his tippy toes he could barely reach it. He sat down on the floor and looked up at the ball, visualising what he would do.

The mother, forgetting about going home, enthused to her daughter, 'See darling how far it is above him. If he kicks it, he'll have kicked higher than any other person ever has. He'll break the world record.'

Elijah Cabinboy placed the palm of his free hand on the floor. Then, with an explosion of energy, surging from palm to toe, his body turned upside down, straightened and stretched towards the target.

Cheers erupted. The mother jumped up, clapping.

'He did it, he did it, darling, he kicked it. He broke the world record. Did you see how high he jumped?'

The blanket toss grabbed the little girl's interest. People were invited from the audience to toss some poor unfortunate up to thirty feet into the air. To do this, they used a huge walrus-skin 'trampoline blanket', which had a rope looped all the way around its circumference. Forty volunteers gathered around, grabbed a bit of the rope and, with a coordinated heave, launched competitor after competitor into the sky. The competitor who combined height, grace in flight and acrobatics was declared the winner. The blanket toss was originally used by the Eskimo to spot game over the flat tundra horizon.

The little girl said, 'Mammy, can I do that?'

'Yes darling, you can do it when you're bigger.'

'Can I go down beside them to watch?'

'No darling, we'll watch them together from here.'

The knuckle hop required the contestants to take a press-up position, with only knuckles and toes touching the floor. The object of the game was to hop as far as they could along the floor in this position until they eventually collapsed in pain. The competitor who hopped farthest won.

The event felt like a bazaar of my youth, a real community gathering. People wandered around chatting, eating or going for a cigarette. Children played, toddlers laughing and cried, everyone took photographs of everyone else, teenagers preened, older people greeted and were greeted. Competitors helped each other, congratulating every success and commiserating with every failure. On completion of their event, they hugged and shook hands with the judges. The founding fathers of the games could only have been pleased.

On my walk back into town, I passed the little girl and her mother, still chatting away as they strolled along the banks of the Chena.

§

'Are you the Irishman going to Dawson?'

It was 4.45 a.m. The person standing opposite me was a small, thin, feisty woman in her sixties. She wore a visor and sunglasses and was obviously in a hurry. When I identified myself, she grabbed my suitcase and, despite my protestations, hauled it after her out the door. She salvaged my pride by allowing me to load it into the back of the minibus. Inside, a New Zealand couple in their fifties called Ed and Jane said 'Hi.' Both looked lean and fit. Paula, our driver, told us that we had to collect two Germans and then we would be on our way to Dawson. When we got to the motel to pick up the Germans, only one appeared. Heinz had a mountain-load of gear with him, all of which had to be shoved into the rear of the bus. He had an inflatable kayak, on which he hoped to voyage downriver from Dawson City to Circle. The only problem was that the person who was supposed to be going with him had chickened out at the airport in Fairbanks and returned to Germany on the next flight.

Paula told us that she had been a soldier in Texas and an investment broker on Wall Street. Desiring a more meaningful existence, she spent a year in divinity school and then made a new life in Alaska. She now worked with her husband driving people across Alaska and the Yukon. She loved living in Fairbanks.

'People think that it's all dark here in the wintertime but it ain't. We have the most beautiful soft light. When the sun is below the horizon in the morning, there's a reddish glow for three hours. The colour keeps on changing until the sun rises and showers our world with a soft, yellow light for a few hours. We then return to the red light again before darkness descends. It's really magical at times. It seems mellow, gentle and slow even though in the wrong circumstances it might kill you in an hour.'

'It mightn't be very pleasant then', said Ed.

'Freezing would be a nice way to die. You only feel anything when you start to thaw.'

Jane asked what happened to people who died during the winter.

'They just stick you in a big truck and bury you in the spring when the ground thaws.'

Having found a knowledgeable person on all things Alaska, Paula had to endure a series of questions on what it was like to live in Alaska, what Alaskans were like, how butterflies hibernate in Alaska and the size of the mountain ranges around Fairbanks. Some of her answers were quite cryptic.

'What do you think is the main disadvantage of living in Alaska?'

'The older you get, the worse a fur coat gets!'

Puzzled, someone asked, 'What do you mean?'

'The weight of it pulls old bones down.'

Not to be outdone in inane questions, I asked, 'Which is the most dangerous, the black bear or the grizzly?'

'Bears are wild animals. If they're hungry, you get ate.'

Well that put matters into perspective fairly quickly. I wondered how you would know whether a bear was hungry or not.

She then reassured me a little by saying, 'In the wild, they tend to keep their distance, except if you're on a bicycle.'

'On a bicycle?'

'Yes. One of the most dangerous places for bear attacks is a bicycle path. The bear gets curious about what those critters on two wheels are doing and investigates. The first few cyclists are usually safe enough until the bear figures out the situation; when it does, it often attacks.'

'They're like dogs', I said, 'they love to chase bicycles.' I thought to myself that the guy in Montana might have been right in thinking that bears were a mixture of dogs and pigs.

'Yeah, bears like to chase things', said Paula, 'that reminds me of a story of when I first came to Alaska. I didn't know it at the time, but bears love the smell of gas, or indeed any noxious odour. I was out filling the truck with gas when a big grizzly came into the shed. I turned around and he was there looking at me. I was scared witless and climbed up on top of the truck, screaming. The bear then started to climb after me and then I really started to holler. My husband came out and in a stern voice, he said, "Shoo! Get out of here bear!" And off it went. My husband said to me, "If you're going to live out here you gotta learn that bears love to chase small things that run and squeal."'

We passed a town called North Pole. Had we taken the wrong direction? No. Some bright spark decided that it would be a good idea to rip off Santa Claus. The town has a plethora of Christmas shops and receives hundreds of thousands of letters to Santa each year, all acknowledged for a fee. Additionally, lots of people request the town's postmark on their Christmas greeting cards, again for a fee. Not a bad little niche. The fact that the town is 1,600 miles from the real North Pole isn't that relevant!

Paula told us that North Pole had the highest number of churches per capita in the US. It was largely a dormitory town for the military and anyone involved 'in that sort of business' needed their religion. Shortly afterwards, we drove past the air base and saw a big bomber on a runway. It was a B52, a big, brooding, ugly lump of a thing carrying mayhem in its gut. Large signs warned us in bold red letters not to stop or take photographs.

We continued along the Richardson Highway, bounded on either side by predominantly black spruce forest which had been cut back ten metres from the road 'to keep us and the animals safe'. The black spruce is a small, stunted, columnar tree, native to the boreal forests of North America. Paula told us a bit about it.

'Black spruce will only grow as tall as their roots go down into the soil. That's usually three to ten feet in permafrost. Some trees could be hundreds of years old but never get any taller. However, if there's a hot summer and the permafrost melts or if earthquakes crush the ice underground, then the tree puts on a growth spurt, pushing its roots deeper into the earth. If permafrost forms again at the original level, it'll lift the tree right out of the ground. That's why if you drive around Alaska, you'll see drunken trees leaning against others. They've all been pushed out of the ground by the permafrost. They and the surrounding trees will all die.'

Jane asked about forest fires.

'Every summer we've lots of fires', said Paula, 'it's a healthy part of the system here and leads to regeneration. Fire can go down into the roots of the trees and stay dormant there until the following spring, when it can rekindle in a different spot. Usually the fires are slow-moving because there's virtually no wind and the animals just graze, keeping ahead of the fire as it advances.'

'Probably kills all those mosquitoes?'

Paula laughed. 'I've no idea. The fires are toughest on birds. Their heart beat can increase to more than one hundred and sixty times the normal rate. If they can't make a quick escape, they fall out of the sky.'

The conversation turned to the Native people.

Paula explained, 'The Native people of the interior are Athabaskan, and of all Native peoples, the Athabaskan were the poorest. It was always a real struggle to get enough to survive in the interior. Because they had to put all their energy into survival, it meant that religion or art didn't develop to the same extent as with other tribal groups. Then colonisation came and really stole their soul. In their villages, the unemployment rate is very high and welfare payments and payments from the corporations means that the men have no meaningful role to play in family life anymore. Alcohol, drug abuse, physical abuse, sexual abuse and suicide are the result. The suicide rate amongst the Native peoples is twice as high as the rest of the Alaskan population and four times higher than in the US as a whole. Child abuse is prevalent in some villages. Some elders have their heads in the sand in relation to this, but the truth is now beginning to emerge. Once it starts coming it'll become a torrent.'

Jane said that the tribal people she had met seemed to have a good level of education. 'Surely that provides a good base for the future?'

'Their average graduation age is 36. It usually takes them a number of efforts before they're successful.'

'Why is that?'

'Mostly cultural reasons. In villages, people move between houses and share everything. Your food is my food. This idea doesn't work too well in college dormitories. Native people are often accused of stealing but in fact they just have a different way of looking at food and possessions. There are also language difficulties. Because Native people take longer pauses between sentences, many teachers and others assume they've finished speaking, but in fact they're only starting to make their point. They're then labelled as stupid. So for a Native person to graduate they have to overcome significant difficulties.'

We stopped near the Delta River to view the oil pipeline that runs from Prudhoe Bay on the Arctic all the way through Alaska to the frost-free port of Valdez. The pipeline zigzagged its way across the landscape and the river. It's designed to withstand earthquakes and subsidence and is also impervious to fires and gunshots. Many experts regard it as one of the great engineering achievements, but others believe that this pipeline pierces the heart of Alaska and that the concrete slabs supporting it are the footprints of a monster. Environmentalists believe that the spell of the North is ruptured and the idea of total freedom in nature has disappeared.

Paula and I went to stand beside Heinz at the river. Paula explained that the fast-flowing river originated from a glacier and that if you fell into it, you would have very little chance of survival, even if you were a good swimmer.

'Why is that?' Heinz asked, probably thinking of his proposed kayak voyage down the Yukon.

'When you fall into a river like this, the water is so cold that the shock of entry drives the breath out of the body and you sink like a stone. The body doesn't rise like it does in a normal river and may never be found. Because glacial rivers are silty, there's no prospect of seeing the body. The Athabaskans search for people by prodding the river bottom with long poles. When they hit something soft, it might be the body.'

Back on the bus, Paula told us we would meet her husband Dan in Chicken, and that he would take up the rest of the way to Dawson.

'Chicken?'

'Yeah, it's our first stop on the "Top of the World Highway". I suppose you're wondering how any place could be called Chicken?'

'We sure are', said Jane.

'This was once a prosperous gold mining area and quite a few people had claims hereabouts, but they never named the area. One day they all got together and said that the place needed a name. They decided to call it after a common bird called the Ptarmigan. However, they couldn't agree on the correct pronunciation, so when one guy said, "just call it Chicken", they all agreed and got back to drinking.'

Modern-day Chicken consists of three buildings: a café, a house and a saloon. It has a summer population of seventeen people and a winter population of one. Outside the saloon, a sign read, 'I got laid in Chicken, Alaska.' Well, maybe not in winter! We all went into the café and I ordered a buffalo burger, which had more burger than buffalo. When the inevitable call of nature came, I found the bathroom, otherwise known as 'the chicken coop', which stood just outside the café.

This was a thin wooden structure which sat directly over an open septic tank, dug deep into the ground. When the tank was full, you just had to dig another deep hole and move the coop. As we finished eating, Paula's husband arrived with his group of passengers and the swap was arranged. Dan was a large, solid-looking man in his seventies with a deep voice. He looked like the type who would tell a bear to 'shoo'.

Leaving Chicken, we took the 'Top of the World Highway' to Dawson City. This road began as a pack trail out of Dawson during the gold rush and connected often-transient mining communities. Though classed as a highway, it still felt like a pack trail. It was a rough ride over gravel, frost heaves, washboards, giant potholes and dirt, and it jolted the living daylights out of us. However, the road was aptly named because you felt on top of the world there. Most of it was above the tree line and wove its way along a series of mountaintops. The mountains seemed to go on forever; countless ranges were visible in the distance. River valleys snaked their way through the landscape, creating character and mystery. You could wander there for months and not see a soul.

Dan told us that outfitters guide hunters into this area. If hunters shoot a moose or a caribou, they have to pay up to $1,500 to process the meat and ship it out to the lower forty-eight, or even to Canada.

'It makes for expensive meat', said Jane.

'Some don't even bother to take it with them, in which case the outfitters keep it. The advantage for me is that I often get boxes of meat for nothing.'

He told us about potlatches he'd attended in Native villages. He recounted a recent event when a person from Beaver, a village on the Yukon River, died in Fairbanks.

'They don't fly the body home. The tradition is that they take the body up the river and then carry it into the village where the people meet it. The person's house is then emptied of furniture and a meal is prepared. You can't refuse the food, whether you like it or not. It's usually moose meat with lots of vegetables and it's cooked until it's complete mush and nearly inedible. Potlatches last for three or four days and involve giving away some of the dead person's belongings as gifts.'

We halted at a green shed near the crest of a bare, rocky mountain. This was the joint Canadian and United States border post, the most northerly and isolated border post in the Americas. They only recently begun sharing a building, having previously inhabited two separate huts. It was a beautiful, sunny evening but in poor weather this would be a bleak location. A pleasant customs official stamped my passport with the image of a miner panning for gold. I was pleased that my arrival in Canada was marked in this way. The border post is open from nine in the morning to nine at night. Miss the time and you would have to wait until the next day.

It was still seventy miles to Dawson but the road improved and our speed picked up. We met a cyclist after about thirty miles. I wondered if he would make the border crossing in time.

Dan finally pulled in at a vantage point overlooking Dawson, which sat at the confluence of the Yukon and Klondike Rivers. The town nestled between the rivers and Moose Skin Mountain, a site measuring two miles long and one mile deep. The evening was still and the forested mountain and town were perfectly reflected in the blue water. The Yukon River was totally different in character to the sprawling monster at Fort Yukon, being constrained by the surrounding hillsides into a deep, flowing channel about half a mile wide. The town now had a population of one thousand eight hundred people, compared to about forty thousand in Micí's time.

Our road descended steeply to the swiftly flowing river where we were met by a ferry. It was late evening when we crossed the river and landed in Dawson.

18

Dawson City

Mící would have first viewed Dawson City from a similar vantage spot. It must have been with great relief that he gazed at the town lying below him, a little pinprick in the midst of a vast wilderness of mountain, forest, rivers and lakes. Two years previously, all that existed in Dawson was a handful of prospectors living in tents, but the gold strike at nearby Bonanza Creek changed all that. Mící encountered a town containing five hundred log cabins, hotels, saloons, stores, warehouses, sawmills, churches, schools, St Mary's Hospital and a barracks with thirty Mounties over which a British flag flew. The structure of the town had been established in a very short time. You would think this would be a classless society, but even at this early stage, professional people, business people, miners, unemployed people and tribal people all had their own localities. Some less fortunate were banished to Lousetown, situated outside the town limits.

When Mící walked down the hillside and across the frozen river into Dawson City, it was two weeks shy of Christmas 1898. It was five months since he had left Seattle and it had taken all of his resourcefulness to survive. Smoke coiled into the air from dwellings, leaving a sweet, welcoming smell hanging in the cold, crisp air. People were everywhere, on wooden sidewalks and in saloons. Mící remarked that every second establishment was a saloon, or maybe he was just thirsty. Dogs were either lying in the street or working in teams of two to ten, yelping as they pulled sleds which rasped along the rutted snow. Nothing was cheap. Flour was twenty dollars a sack, it was one dollar to post a letter and fur robes were four hundred dollars. Drinking water was scarce and 'entrepreneurs' took barrels of the stuff from wells in the hills to sell in the town. It was probably the most expensive place on earth.

The currency wasn't dollars but gold dust. Every miner had his gold poke with him to pay for goods. It was valued at sixteen dollars an ounce. For a meal or a drink, you poured gold dust out on to scales, which was scrupulously measured. It was fashionable for many waiters and bar attendants to have long fingernails and greased hair. The long nails were a great way of collecting any stray gold dust and if your hair was sufficiently greased, storage was achieved by rubbing hands through your hair. At the end of the night, 'tips' could be collected by washing your hair in a basin.

Mící's luck was with him, for who did he bump into on the street only his cousin Jim Anthony. Jim and Mící had left Magheroarty together and it was Jim who sent him the message to come to the Klondike. They remained connected all through their journeys, a testimony to the power of friendship. Mící didn't recognise Jim at first, as his face was smeared with grease and ash to protect him from the cold. He knew him only by his distinctive laugh. To celebrate their reunion, they went out on the town. Jim treated him to a meal and then they went drinking and gambling, before finally finishing up watching the dancing girls in the Monte Carlo Club. A dance cost one dollar, but Mící claimed he kept his hands in his pocket all night to make sure the few coins he owned stayed there.

Jim, being part of the first wave of miners to reach Dawson, was fortunate to strike it lucky. These miners had travelled light and trusted to providence. Those who took time to make adequate plans to survive in the harsh northern environment arrived too late; all of the valuable mining plots had been taken. Jim, having made his fortune, was leaving the Klondike and offered Mící his place on the mining claim. The next day Mící left Dawson and walked thirty-five miles to All Gold Creek where hard work and fortune awaited.

When we arrived in town, Dan asked us where we were staying. I was the only one who hadn't booked in advance. A slightly alarmed look came into Dan's eye and Jane exclaimed, 'It's a really busy weekend in Dawson. The music festival is on.'

'You might find somewhere', said Dan reassuringly.

I could have kicked myself, because I had read how popular the music festival in Dawson was before I left. It's the one time of the year that the town strains at the seams as the population expands from 1,800 souls to bursting point, perhaps as many as in the old mining days. As we drove along Front Street, young people were hanging out, as were several long-haired geriatrics. I accompanied Ed and Jane to their hotel and asked the busy receptionist for a room.

She shook her head. 'No, we were booked out for this weekend months ago and I'm not sure there's anywhere else in town either. Hold on, I'll try a few places.'

Two hours later, benefiting from a late cancellation, I found the last available bed in town.

After I cleaned up, I went to see the river. Music throbbed in the air and people filled the streets. I passed along Front Street, a colourful collection of stores, pubs, restaurants and ice cream parlours, with names such as Sourdough's Restaurant, Klondike Cream and Candy, and Dawson Trading Post. In an attractive park between Front Street and the river, people sat and relaxed, cooking, playing music and throwing Frisbee. I climbed a grassy bank overlooking the river. This bank doubled as flood control and riverside walk, where couples strolled in the evening sunshine. A large paddleboat was moored at a wharf and a red and white ferry, grey smoke billowing from its funnel, ploughed across the river. This ferry provides the only direct connection with the Top of the World Highway, but only operates from mid-May to October. A man on a jet ski buzzed around on the river below me, like a frantic dog trying to catch his tail. The inevitable happened and he fell off. The jet ski floated away and for a moment I thought they were parted forever. After a frantic swim, he caught it, but wasn't able to remount. I had visions of him disappearing around the river bend. I ran towards the wharf because I thought there might be help available there. However, other eyes had been watching. A small lifeboat pulled out of the ferry dock, went to his aid and reunited him with his jet ski. Pride prodded him to perform a few subdued stunts before he returned, chastened, to the riverbank.

Hunger pulled me through blue swing doors into a large saloon. I surveyed the scene. All but one bar seat was taken and two waitresses, dressed in black, were taking orders from people seated at tables. Two large fans swung lazily from the ceiling and cowboy hats dangled on tips of moose horns mounted on the wall. I sat down at the bar. A large, burly man sat at the piano. He had long, grey, unkempt hair with specks of black through it. Mischief flickered in his eyes. He announced in a strong, gritty voice that he was going to sing some 'Yukon songs'. Then his large, awkward-looking hands transformed into surprisingly nimble fingers, coaxing a sweet tune from the piano.

Warm-up over, he began to sing, but immediately stopped, holding up his hands, 'I won't insult you with that, I need lubrication.'

He picked up his glass from the piano top and knocked two shots of liquor straight back. This did the trick and, duly fortified, he successfully belted out tune after tune in that melodious, gritty voice.

I met an old-timer called Ken at the counter. He was stooped with years and had a white beard and grey eyes set deep into the creases of his face. He leaned over and asked, 'Did anyone tell you yet about the turkeys that walked from the Pacific Ocean across the mountains to Dawson during the gold rush?'

A guy called Irwin, astonished at the exorbitant price of poultry in Dawson, made a fortune by buying hundreds of turkeys in Seattle, which he shipped to Dyea in southern Alaska and herded over the mountains to Dawson. For his trouble, he sold them for $20 each, equivalent to $600 dollars in today's money.

Ken was only getting started. He told me that there were many fires in the early days in Dawson. In one such fire, a hotel was burned down and an embarrassed roulette wheel operator and a dancer, who were in bed together, escaped with just a sheet for cover. This was reported extensively in the local press. A love rival mailed a number of copies of the newspaper, one at a time, to the roulette wheel operator's wife, who was living in the 'lower forty-eight'. The roulette dealer got an unexpected shock when his wife landed, suitcase in hand, on his doorstep.

When leaving, I joked that I might try my hand at prospecting in All Gold Creek and asked Ken what were the chances of getting a gleam in my pan.

'That dawg don't hunt no more', he said, 'it's all big-time boys now with their diggers and trucks. There ain't any easy gold left.'

The next morning I stretched my limbs and sniffed the crisp morning air, pulling it deep into my lungs. The town was between breaths, resting after the night's frantic festival activity. Three sandal-wearing twenty-somethings sat on the sidewalk deep in discussion. A busy little café on Front Street supplied breakfast to early birds, most of whom were of the older vintage. I come from a village called Moutcharles, so after breakfast I went to see the Monte Carlo Gold and Gift Store on Front Street. It was closed. The pink and blue exterior was slightly shabby and a range of faded pictures of Yukon animals and landscapes filled the windowpanes.

The Monte Carlo, once a far glitzier place, was founded by Swiftwater Bill Gates and Jack Smith. Swiftwater Bill, a small, dapper man with a huge black moustache, arrived in Dawson in 1896. He didn't intend to get his hands dirty. His life was full of triumphs and disasters, but after each setback he always picked himself off the floor and set forth on the next venture. He was a gambler, an entrepreneur and a lover of women, and he combined the three in one package when he helped found the Monte Carlo Club in 1898. Smith, however, was the man with the money, and everyone thought he was mad when he financed Swiftwater Bill to go to San Francisco to acquire furnishings for the club. No one believed that he would return. However, some months later, those same doubters were surprised when word came that Bill was nearing Dawson with a cargo. Thousands gathered on the riverbank with heightening curiosity to await his return. When his small flotilla, comprising a canoe and two barges, came around the bend in the river, Bill was standing in the prow of the canoe, dressed to the nines. He wore a silk hat and his long, black moustache swept over his shoulders. He held his arms out wide, milking acclaim from the assembled audience. Seated behind him on a keg of whiskey was a beautiful woman dressed in red. The barges contained not only all the new furniture for the Monte Carlo club, but also barrels of whiskey and, to cap it all, thirty showgirls. At this sight, a massive roar erupted from the masses and Swiftwater Bill became a legend.

I had two special places to see in Dawson. The first was Bonanza Creek, where gold was first found on the Klondike, and the second, All Gold Creek, where Mící unearthed his fortune. I needed transport and thought that a bicycle would solve my problem. A young man, looking forlornly at the engine of his broken-down jeep, guided me to a bicycle shop at the quiet end of town. Seeing the shop sign through some bushes, I climbed a small, winding path around rocks to a shed behind a dwelling house. The door was open and a neat array of bicycles was arranged in rows outside. I called out, and finally a lean, black-haired man in his thirties appeared. His small, round glasses gave him a studious look. His hands were black with bicycle oil but he had clean overalls. I told him about my plans for cycling around Dawson. He shook his head regretfully and said that all his bicycles were booked.

'Come back in thirty minutes and I'll see if I can repair an old one for you', he said. 'Would you be happy with that?'

True to his word, he had a sturdy bicycle ready for me on my return. I asked for directions to both Bonanza Creek and All Gold Creek; All Gold Creek was 35 miles away so I concentrated on Bonanza Creek for the first day's expedition. I hopped on the bicycle and tore off down the winding path towards the dirt street, expecting an enjoyable day. I was definitely not expecting the massive blow that my pride took when I crashed in a tangled heap of bike and legs on a sharp, gravelly bend. I gingerly picked myself up and my first reaction was to cast a mortified look around to see if anyone was watching. Reassured that the disgrace was a private moment, I checked the bicycle and myself for any possible malfunction. After such an ignominious beginning, things could only get better.

I cycled out along Front Street towards the Klondike Highway. The road changed from dirt to tar. I crossed a narrow metal bridge spanning the Klondike River and, following the sign for Bonanza Creek, I turned right past a store onto a wide, gravel road. There was evidence of mining everywhere. Long, worm-shaped tailings littered the valleys and the route. A labyrinth of gravel tracks and roads curving through the wooded hillsides added to the feeling that this was a vast quarry. Still, there was a kind of magic in the air that belied this ugliness.

The road was challenging as it wound higher into hills, but the day was sunny with a nice breeze. I caught up with a couple of other cyclists, a friendly pair in their early sixties from California called Jim and Carol. Carol said that they lived right on the beach and sometimes they wondered why they should go on holidays at all. She had had enough of cycling up hills by that stage and expressed great relief when we reached Claim 33, a working gold mine. When we dismounted, Jim told me that he was an expert in spiders and surfboards. My ears pricked up when I heard about spiders and I let him know that I had heard about the hobo spider earlier in my trip.

'Well, I've another one for your collection', he said.

'What is it?'

'It's called the violin spider. It's one of the three deadliest spiders in the US.'

'What would happen if it bit me?'

'If you get bitten on your leg or arm, you might lose your limb. The symptoms don't show themselves for about a week and then it's too late.'

Claim 33 was still an active gold mine, but, recognising that other 'mining' opportunities existed, the enterprise had diversified into a souvenir store and offered, for a fee of course, to train people how to pan for gold. Inside, Ann, a woman with a shock of curly red hair, greeted us with a smile that spread freckles across her face. Carol asked about gold panning and Ann bounced to the other end of the store to get a few gold pans, giving one to each of us to hold and feel. I thought to myself that it would make a decent container for apple pie. The pan was half filled with muck and gravel containing a few specks of gold, which we had to find. Ann told us that she was managing the place while trying to buy it from the family of the previous, deceased owner.

The purchase of the mine seemed complicated because, she said with a tint of annoyance, 'A delay of even a day between the offer of sale and purchase would mean ownership of the mine reverting to the First Nation. It isn't fair at all. The First Nation get too much for nothing.'

But the cloud vanished when she brought us outside to learn how to make a fortune in the creeks. The trick in gold panning is to wash dirt and gravel out of your pan while at the same time leaving gold in the crease at the bottom. The theory is that because gold is heavy, it will sink, while the swirling water washes the gravel away. At first, I feared that I would wash all my valuable gold back into the earth, but I soon got the hang of it. Delight surged through me when I spotted tiny flecks of gold and I immediately understood how you could get hooked on this particular bait. I said goodbye to Jim and Carol and left to find the Discovery Claim, further up the creek, where gold was first found on the Klondike.

On the way, I stopped at 'Number Four Gold Dredge' site. It was the largest wooden-hulled dredge ever built and is now a historic monument managed by the Canadian parks service. The arrival of dredges, about ten years after the gold rush commenced, marked the beginning of an era when big business replaced stampeders and individual prospectors. These dredges, like giant slugs, ate up ground as they moved along, using a continuous ladder of buckets that stripped river and creek valleys bare. When the dredge finished processing the material for gold, it excavated the waste behind it into worm-shaped piles of barren gravel. When the big boys move in, the small boys move out, and it was no different in gold mining. Companies such as the Yukon Gold Mining Company flooded valleys, bought out the claims of individual prospectors and eliminated any obstacles that confronted them. It's rumoured that the bones of more than one stubborn miner form part of the gravel piles along the Klondike Valley.

A man called Joe Boyle, who started off in the Klondike as a bouncer in the Monte Carlo Club, owned this gold dredge. He had a remarkable and adventurous life and became exceedingly rich in the Klondike. Afterwards, he enlisted for action in the First World War and had many adventures, which included fixing the Russian train system, negotiating a peace treaty between Russia and Romania, saving starving Romanians, organising daring rescues of Romanian dignitaries and negotiating at the Treaty of Versailles. For his efforts, he was decorated by Russia, England, Romania and Canada, and became the Queen of Romania's lover.

As I got off my bike, two hearty, middle-aged women sitting on plastic chairs outside a prefab office greeted me. Dressed in the Canadian national parks uniform, their job was to manage this historic site for the summer months. At this moment, that involved enjoying a coffee and a large slice of cake. I commented on the number of swallows I'd seen flying about and, in response, one of the women pointed out the swallows' nests high on the dredge keel.

'It's a full-time job keeping the place clean with all those swallows', she said. 'In the old days swallows were the miner's friend and they built lots of artificial nests to encourage them to visit their site.'

'Were miners superstitious?'

'No. Swallows eat lots of mosquitoes. Mosquitoes were a real scourge for miners.'

I cycled on another few miles until I came to the Discovery Claim. I dismounted and, plagued by mosquitoes, I walked down to the small, two-metre-wide stream surrounded by bushes and trees. It was here on 16 August 1896 that Shaaw Tíaa, otherwise known as Kate Carmack, spotted a gold nugget glistening amongst other stones. Kate, a First Nations woman, was the common-law wife of the prospector and trapper George Carmack, with whom she had a daughter. Imagine her exhilaration as she dashed back to camp to announce the find to her husband, her brother Skookum Jim and her cousin Takum Charlie. The group immediately raced down to the creek with their picks and pans, and found more gold nuggets. They were rich. Of the hundreds of people prospecting in the area at the time, it is ironic that three of the four who made the discovery were from the First Nations. Native people generally couldn't understand why white people lusted for gold; the local chief raged against prospecting not because the white man mined gold, but because he trapped animals.

The three men rushed to register their claims and the Klondike Gold Rush began. Soon, every inch of this creek was pegged and then the panning and digging started in earnest.

No one considered putting Kate Carmack's name on a claim. First Nation men had little status, but a First Nation woman had none. George Carmack, Skookum Jim and Takum Charlie became rich and two years later George, Kate and their child took their newfound wealth to the outside world. George revelled in recognition and rode around Seattle in a carriage with a big sign on it, proclaiming him the 'Discoverer of the Klondike'. This was Kate or Shaaw Tíaa's first venture outside her Native support system and she did not adapt well to the change. Problems arose between Kate and George and, as a solution, he sent her and his daughter to live with his sister. He returned to Dawson to revel in more acclaim, and there he fell in love with a brothel owner called Marguerite Laimee and decided to marry her. Kate was only a minor inconvenience. He planned to get custody of his child and send Kate back to her tribe in the Yukon. Kate sued him for divorce and claimed half his fortune. She, however, could establish no rights whatsoever. She lost access to her child and was left penniless. Her brother Skookum Jim built a cabin for her and she died there in the 1920s. If Shaaw Tíaa could relive that moment on the creek, when she spotted the gold nugget, would she pick it up again?

As I cycled back into Dawson, ominous black clouds closed in from the surrounding mountaintops, casting an oppressive hood over the town. A flash of lightning lit the scene, followed almost immediately by a heavy peel of thunder which rolled across the parchment sky. A few large, languid raindrops fell on my bald patch. As the sky inhaled before the sneeze, I abandoned the bike and raced to the nearest possible shelter, the elegant Dawson Museum. I got in just as another fork of lightning struck, followed by a deep bass rumble of thunder which shook the building. Rain began drumming furiously on the roof of the museum. A problem arose inside. Closing time energised staff to attempt to empty the building of wary stragglers looking out at the downpour. This group, like a stubborn donkey, made a silent, collective decision to dig their heels in. The staff reluctantly relented.

I wandered around looking at the pictures. One, an iconic Klondike photograph, was of a black line of men climbing a steep, snowy Chilkoot pass. This ant-like line of men were bent over, heads down, hauling supplies up over the snowy 45 degree pass. Each person had to make many journeys to carry the required 'ton of gear' and you couldn't afford to lose your place on the line. What made this photograph arresting was that while everyone else laboriously climbed, one man, perched on a thin bag, sledded precariously down the precipitous pass, in a mad rush to start all over again.

The thunderstorm petered out and we all emerged to clear air and puddles of water everywhere. I dried the seat of my bicycle and cycled around the town. I inveigled my way into Diamond Tooth Gertie's for free to have a look at the cancan dancing, roulette wheels and poker tables. This establishment commemorated the activities of one of Dawson's most famous madams, Gertrude Lovejoy, who distinguished herself by lodging a diamond between her two front teeth. The cancan dancers were hauling some poor unfortunate onstage to join in the dancing. Fearing capture, I beat a hasty retreat.

Later, I walked around the town, poking my nose into festival venues. I bought a hot dog from a stall and ended up in a pub teeming with people. All age groups intermingled and swayed to the rhythmic sounds of an eclectic band comprising an Elvis look-a-like singer, a guitarist dressed as a toff, a female fiddle player with a long flowery dress and hippy jewellery, and an African-American drummer with a white shirt. They enjoyed their music, belting out old Elvis and Chuck Berry songs. I moved around and got into conversation with a group of people, one of whom was Daisy Maguire, the manager of a local hotel. As she talked, her body and blonde hair flowed to the music. After a few minutes, a man in his seventies wearing a bandana joined us. He introduced himself as Jeff. He announced that he had bought five new gold claims. He had prospected all his life, but was still waiting on the big one. Like many prospectors before him, gold wasn't the only item on the agenda as his eyes kept drifting to Daisy, still shifting to the beat. For some reason, he asked me, 'Would you mind if I asked her to dance?'

Not waiting for a reply, he whisked Daisy out onto the floor. The last I saw of them was the bandanna and the blonde head bopping away on the floor. Only the resilient risk-taker finds gold!

The next morning I carried my bike out of my room to go looking for All Gold Creek, the place where Micí mined for gold. The bike was solid and chunky, not built for speed. It was, however, ideal for gravel roads. I stocked up on supplies and cycled off towards the Klondike Highway. I passed a store and an RV park and wondered if this was the spot where an Irishwoman called Belinda Mulrooney built her store in 1897. Belinda, like most of the women stampeders, was a very resourceful person. She first heard of the gold rush in Alaska and immediately invested her life's earnings in hot water bottles. She knew that Irish mammies spoiled their sons and she suspected that other nationalities were not much different. A cosy bed is a sanctuary in tough times. She ferried her cargo into Dawson on a raft manned by two First Nation people and, when she disembarked, threw her last coin into the Yukon River, swearing that she'd never need such small change again. She sold the hot water bottles at a 600 per cent profit, which funded her new store near Bonanza Creek. All the other traders built their businesses in Dawson but she decided to locate her store closer to the mining creeks. Most people laughed at her but with the aid of a few hired men and her mule called Gerry she built her premises. The rich and influential flocked to her bar and all of life's intrigues were played out there. It was a place where you could have a drink and a laugh and hatch a deal. It all made Belinda Mulrooney a very rich woman.

The first twenty miles cycling along the Klondike Highway felt like a mini version of hell; slightly uphill, against the breeze, through mile after mile of swampy boreal forest with a blister on my foot. To top it all, when I went into the undergrowth to pee, I was attacked by hairy-looking mosquitoes. One look at them and I fled. I passed the cut-off point for the Dempster Highway, reputedly one of the most beautiful highways in the world, which crosses a desolate Arctic and mountain landscape. This gravel road follows an old dog sled route and extends 450 miles across the Arctic Circle, north to a small town called Inuvik. In the winter, the road continues a further 120 miles to the north coast of Canada, using the frozen Mackenzie River delta as an ice highway.

Ravenous, I stopped under a cliff face to eat a sandwich. To my consternation, part of it fell onto the ground; at that particular moment I couldn't conceive of a greater disaster. A raven flew out of the cliff face above me and into the forest. Almost immediately, a raucous,

wailing noise arose that continued for a few minutes as some genu-
ine disaster unfolded in the undergrowth. Prompted by a mosquito
lodged up my back, I hopped on my bicycle, followed my directions,
and after ten further miles found All Gold Creek. When I was certain I
was in the right place, I got off the bike and laughed out loud. Walking
down to the small creek, I washed my face, then cycled up the gravel
track beside the creek and thought how different it must have looked
in Micí's time, when every spare inch of ground was claimed.

If I had happened on this place on a winter's night during the gold
rush, I might have thought I had come to a thermal spring. Smoke,
sparks and flames would have streamed out of hundreds of holes in
the ground. On closer examination, I would have seen the outlines of
log cabins illuminated by fires but shrouded in smoke. With the first
murky, morning light, hundreds of miners would emerge and disappear like spectres down these holes, which could be twenty-five or
thirty feet deep, to shovel muck and gravel into large buckets, which
were then winched to the surface. This 'pay-dirt' had been thawed by
the previous night's fire and, when extracted from the hole, was collected in a large heap for processing at the beginning of spring. Every
evening, when the miners were finished sending their raw material
to the surface, they would light another fire in the hole, making sure
that they 'scooted up' the birch ladder as fast as possible before it
took hold. These fires were the only way the miners could make the
iron-like permafrost soft enough to dig through. Other methods were
explored. Micí and his friends for instance had tried to blow up the
ground with explosives, but to no avail.

Springtime was bounty time. Released from its icy grip, the water
started running and the miners built small dams and sluice boxes
to wash their gravel for gold. When they separated the gold, they
roasted it on a pan, turning it continually over a hot fire until it was
completely dry. Micí described how he enjoyed the final part of the
process, blowing any remaining sand and soil off the gold before stor-
ing it in a little box. The satisfaction must have been mighty. When
spring gave way to the short, hot summer, it was no longer possible to
work in the mines, because when the ground thawed the holes filled
with water. They used this time to cut and stack wood for winter fires.
When the ground froze again, they loaded up sleds with logs and slid
down the mountain as if on a sleigh. It sounds like fun, but it was
dangerous and many miners were killed in this way.

The availability of food was always a problem in the Klondike. In 1897, the first year of the gold rush, as stampeders raced to this remote Arctic region in search of one valuable commodity, they ignored making provision for an even more valuable one – food. These miners, travelling light, got to Dawson first, but those who carried adequate provisions were now stuck, far to the south of Dawson, at the top of Chilkoot or Dyea Pass. They would have to wait for spring to arrive to continue their journey. In the autumn of 1897, there was panic in Dawson because of food shortages, and when ice tentacles moved onto the river it must have felt like the closing of a prison door. Some minds turned to mutiny; perhaps the warehouses should be raided and distributed amongst those in need? The Mounties, on high alert, managed to keep the peace. Fear of starvation dominated the discussion and, in a panic, hundreds of miners, abandoning hopes of riches, left in a flotilla of small rowing and passenger boats to head for the outside world.

The man who delivered the mail to Whitehorse by dog sled put on a special rescue offer. He charged men a thousand dollars to walk behind the sled but he charged women fifteen hundred, as he assumed they would want a seat. Eventually, however, a few supply boats got through to Dawson, alleviating the situation to the extent that although people might go hungry, they wouldn't starve.

Even after Micí arrived, food shortages were common and prices were extortionate. At the best of times, there were few vegetables. This caused scurvy. Miners' teeth fell out and many bled and suffered intense pains. Death wasn't uncommon and Micí recounted that during wintertime he saw bodies of miners, 'in a habit of frost', draped on cabin roofs to await burial when the thaw arrived. Their camp suffered no illness of that nature, as Micí believed that eating sourdough bread helped maintain their good health.

I hopped on the bicycle and headed back the way I'd come. It was much easier with the wind and the gentle gradient assisting me. I cycled over to the service station at the end of the Dempster Highway. Service stations on this highway are few and far apart and travellers have to make sure they have adequate provisions. I stocked up with a giant-sized Kit-Kat and sat outside the store as a convoy of motorbikers pulled in to refuel for their journey.

Back in Dawson, I went to see the cabins of Jack London and Robert Service, two of the authors who shaped the public perception of the

North American Arctic. Jack London is renowned because of his writings on nature in the north, but he was also a radical socialist who marched on Washington to protest against the treatment of workers by big business during the recession. When I returned the bicycle, the owner said that I should apply for the author in residence position in Dawson. An author can come and live in the Pierre Berton (author of *The Last Great Gold Rush*) cabin for three months. He felt that if I did that, I would get a real feel for life in Dawson. He left me with the sobering assessment that he didn't like travel writers, as they only skimmed the surface of places and people's lives, offering little insight.

Micí was a shrewd man. His head wasn't easily turned and he didn't allow his money to be dissipated foolishly. Many prospectors made lots of money and lost it as quickly. Other prospectors avidly followed the news of the next big strike and were forever rushing off in the expectation of easy wealth. He used to quote the old saying to anyone who would listen, 'Wherever the world is heading, head the other way.' Micí had to work hard on his claim; the returns weren't spectacular but they were steady. By the end of 1901, he had accumulated enough and it was time for him to leave the Klondike. He planned for what was probably the first holiday of his life with his friend Jim Anthony, who had settled in Seattle. He would visit San Francisco before heading home to Ireland. When winter settled upon the land, he went to Whitehorse, now the gatehouse town into and out of the Klondike. Having learned a lot about survival in the Arctic, he travelled by sled dog and wind raft on the icy river.

19

Dawson to Whitehorse

Dan collected me for the early morning trip to Whitehorse. An Austrian couple sitting hand in hand in the back of the people carrier were the only other passengers. Dan asked me to sit up front with him. I felt it was an honour bestowed, a little bit like a passenger on a stagecoach of old who got to sit beside the driver on top. Dan had an inscrutable face, but a feeling of solidity and competence emanated from him. As we drove along the highway, I proudly pointed out All Gold Creek. He looked suitably impressed that I cycled there, though I presumed it was small beer to a man who chased away bears.

Dan told me that two friends of his father's came to Dawson City in 1898 to operate a dog sled, and later a stagecoach service. This was a winter business, as all mail and supplies were carried by river in summer. They lugged mail, passengers and supplies between Dawson and Whitehorse, a six-day journey, following traditional First Nation trails. Horses wore protectors over their chests and nostrils to keep out the cold. They, at least, were moving, but the drivers, called skinners, though wrapped in racoon coats, resorted to all sorts of tactics to keep warm on their exposed perch. Their favourite tactic, according to Dan, was drinking rum. Passengers huddled together under mounds of blankets as they jolted along over rough countryside. For this pleasure, they paid $125 each; food and board were extra.

We later stopped at the ruins of the Montague roadhouse, a typical stop on the overland trail for both stagecoach and dog sled teams. I walked around the building and was surprised by its size and solidity. Huge trunks of trees formed the walls. These two-storey log roadhouses were situated about twenty-two miles apart all along the route. They provided food and board for the passengers and stables for the horses, while the horses themselves were changed at each roadhouse.

Later, Dan said, 'Nomadism and my family go together. My father was always on the move, working on cattle drives between Texas and Montana.'

'That's tough work.'

'Sure was. Long, hot and dusty, and not much pay at the end of it. My father always said that the most difficult part was when the steers stampeded after getting the scent of water. There was damn all the cowboy could do to stop them, except to try to guide them in the safest possible direction. They would gallop their horses at the head of the stampede and try to keep turning the cattle so that they ran in a circle until they finally tired and stopped. Sometimes it worked and sometimes not. When my father got tired of that, he went to herd sheep for French families who lived near Billings.'

'French families in Montana! I never associated the French with sheep.'

'They were French Basques. Many of them settled in Wyoming and around Billings in Montana. Another ancestor used to carry goods into Mexico, and now here I am, ferrying passengers around Alaska and the Yukon. None of our family liked restrictions or rules.'

'Is that why you came to Alaska, or was it to find gold?' I laughed.

He quoted a poem by Robert Service, 'It's not the gold I'm wanting, It's the finding of it.'

We stopped at a vantage point overlooking the Tintina Trench, a wide rift valley stretching over a landscape of forest and wetlands to the barrier of high mountains in the distance. This six-hundred-mile natural corridor provides a migration highway for low-flying birds such as the Sandhill crane, whose migration, Dan assured us, was the most spectacular sight. The Sandhill crane is a large bird with a distinctive bugling sound that can spiral high into the air. Every September, in the space of a few weeks, up to a quarter of a million of them migrate along this valley. Mící had mentioned the beautiful call of these birds on his journey up the Yukon River.

As we approached Whitehorse, Dan asked, 'Where are you staying?'

I looked at him and shrugged.

He chuckled and said, 'You're not the planning type. I know a place on the outskirts of town. It's cheap and cheerful.'

He dropped me off outside a motel that had an Indian restaurant on one side and a laundromat on the other. Inside, two small armchairs cluttered up a dreary, narrow lobby. I checked in, and later talked to the receptionist, an Indian man in his late twenties whose strong frame carried some puppy fat.

'When I came here three years ago', he said, 'it was my first time outside India. I moved from forty degrees above to forty below.'

'That was some change!'

'It wasn't the biggest change.'

'What was?'

'Getting used to the social conditions. In my country, men, women, boys and girls are very separate, but here all is together. I still feel self-conscious when meeting people socially.'

Just then a customer pushed through the door and the receptionist said, 'Hi Norm.'

Norm was a wiry man of about sixty, sporting a beard at least three days old. He flashed a wad of cash and asked, 'Have you a double room for two nights?'

'You have to fill the form, Norm.'

'All this bloody paperwork! I've been out in the wilderness, trapping for five and a half months and I need some entertainment', said Norm, throwing gnarled hands in the air. Then turning to me he asked, 'Where are you from?'

'Ireland.'

'You should watch the film made about me by a French guy. It's called *The Last Trapper*.'

'What's it about?'

'It's about me surviving in the wild, trapping and hunting for food in the Yukon wilderness. It took two years to make and I starred as myself. You should rent it out on DVD.'

'What about the money, Norman?' the receptionist interjected, more interested in material matters than some yarn about living in the wilderness.

Norman counted out one hundred Canadian dollars with a flourish.

'It's one hundred and three dollars and ninety-five cents, Norm, and we require fifty dollars deposit as you're paying in cash.'

Norman looked at him askance but handed over an extra fifty-five dollars. He got a key, but no change.

Norman said, 'I hope this is a room for two, with a great big bed.'

'It is Norm.'

'I've no time to check it now. I have a woman waiting for me in the taxi. We're going to a bar and will be back late.'

The next morning I walked into town. The fast-flowing Yukon River was about a quarter of a mile wide, with tundra extending from the far bank to a distant mountain range. A small tourist train chugged along beside the river, ferrying tourists a few miles out of town.

Whitehorse has wide, attractive streets and holds thirty thousand of the fifty thousand Yukon souls. The vast Yukon area has nearly as many volcanoes as people! Whitehorse is the capital and exists because of a happy combination of river, rapids and the Klondike Gold Rush. In the spring of 1898, a flotilla of seven thousand self-constructed boats, full of stampeders in a rush to reach Dawson, approached these rapids. Many capsized. The stampeders needed a place to dry off and some decided that they would be better employed piloting boats through the rapids, for a fee of course. Whitehorse grew rapidly and became a transport hub for the Klondike.

That afternoon, I went to the MacBride Museum of Yukon History. A fair-haired young woman who had spent a summer in County Wexford greeted me at reception and told me with earnest eyes that she wanted to go back and live there.

'And leave this beautiful spot?'

'Well, Ireland is beautiful, the people are awesome and … it's near Europe.'

How could I argue with that? She gave me a map of the museum and, while I was nosing around, I came upon a reconstruction of Sam Magee's cabin. The cabin contained two beds in the corner, a plain table and chairs, some pots and pans hanging on the wall and a food cabinet with tins of ingredients, all warmed by a big pot-bellied stove. Sam Magee was a road builder and prospector who lived in this cabin with his wife and two children in the early 1900s. There was nothing unusual about Sam but through a quirk of fate his name has been enshrined for posterity by the poetry of Robert Service, 'The Bard of the Yukon'.

In 1896, Robert Service, a small 22-year-old with bright blue eyes, left Scotland and travelled across Canada on a train with a copy of Robert Louis Stevenson's book *The Amateur Emigrant* tucked under his oxter. He had dreams of being a cowboy, and getting into character for the train journey, Service dressed up as Buffalo Bill. During the trip he paced up and down the carriages, acting the part, oblivious to any outside comment. The poet in him was enthralled by the dramatic Canadian landscapes.

When he arrived in Western Canada, the dream of being a cowboy faded as he realised that it involved hard, physical, monotonous work. He preferred to be free to roam this magnificent wilderness. He had to survive however, so finding a job that maximised holidays and minimised work was the ideal solution. He thus ended up working in a bank in Whitehorse, where he spent some of the most enjoyable moments of his life. He described himself at that time as 'bursting with sheer delight'. He had a secure job, a good social life, was a volunteer in the church (he believed in church but not religion) and had enough time to feed his soul, wandering in the wilderness. He began writing and took the advice of the famous journalist Stroller White, who encouraged him to 'Give us something about our own bit of earth.' He accomplished this with great success and a stream of poems ensued. His characters included Dangerous Dan McGrew, Sam Magee, the Lady Known as Lou and the Ragtime Kid. Unusually for a poet, fame, money and success found him. He documented the seamier sides of life, with lots of graphic language and cuss words. Vice was more interesting than virtue.

There was one man with a grievance against Service in Whitehorse. The poet, searching for a rhyme for Tennessee, asked permission of Sam Magee to use his name. Sam readily agreed. After all, it was just a 'wee poem' that no one was going to read! *The Cremation of Sam Magee* became one of the iconic poems of the Yukon and catapulted Magee into unwanted fame, making him the butt of many cremation jokes in the community. He brooded, before coming up with a plan to take revenge. He invited Service (in a seemingly friendly way) to go with him downriver on a log raft. Once out on the river, Magee pointed the raft at Miles Canyon and whilst they bounced down the foaming rapids, Magee is reputed to have threatened Service by saying, 'You cremated me once and for that I'm going to show you a watery grave.' They survived, but honour was salvaged. Magee had a good story to tell.

The next morning at breakfast, I read in a local newspaper about a remarkable grandmother called Josephine Mandamin, a First Nation Anishanabe elder from the Thunder Bay area of Canada who had undertaken a symbolic walk around all the Great Lakes carrying a bucket of water. The lakes and nearby rivers are so polluted that they are nearing irreversible collapse. It is a problem of considerable import given that thirty-five million people depend on them for drinking water. Josephine Mandamin was moved by the spirits in 2003 to do something about it, so she got her bucket and started walking. She had completed seventeen thousand kilometres at that stage and had inspired other like-minded grandmothers to join her for portions of the journey. The pail of water was symbolic for Josephine as women are the carriers of life. Moreover, as a child, she carried many buckets of fresh water from wells and streams. Her message was simple. 'The water is sick ... people need to speak for water, to love water.' At every tributary entering the Great Lakes, she stopped and offered prayers and thanks. She exhorted all people to honour water at least once a year. Water is alive, water can feel and water can hear.

I walked out of town to the dam that had tamed the Whitehorse Rapids. On the far side of the dam, where the river had been calmed into a reservoir, a number of small seaplanes were parked. I watched as one of these planes sped across the reservoir and dragged itself into the sky, disappearing in the direction of a distant mountain range. Returning from the dam, I crossed a small bridge onto a wooded island, a nature reserve. A couple, stuck together like limpets, were sitting on a seat. What was strange however was the sight of a black bra draped over an overhanging branch on the path in front of me. As I ducked to avoid it, the woman laughed gently. The sound of her happy laugh stayed with me as I walked around the island. On the way back into town, I sat down on a riverside seat near to where the sternwheeler called the SS *Klondike* stands, stranded in the park, as a dry land museum to the times when these great boats delivered people and goods up and down the Yukon River. The fact that it is now earning an income from tourists is due to the carelessness of a river pilot, who managed to beach the boat near this spot. Rather than repair it, the authorities dragged it out of the river to get it out of the way.

Whilst gazing at the river, the hair stood straight up on my head as I spotted a naked man being swept down river in the middle of the fast-flowing current. His bald head looked towards the shore while he did an ineffectual breaststroke. In the matter of a few short, shock-filled moments, he was swept away down the river. I jumped up, and to my relief I saw a policeman and policewoman walking along the bank. Obviously, they hadn't spotted him.

I raced up and said, 'Quick, quick, there's a man being swept downstream in the middle of the river.'

The policeman looked down the river for a brief moment. He turned, shaking his head, and said, 'He'll not last long if he stays in there.'

With that, my report was summarily dismissed. It was their turn to ask me a question. 'Have you seen a man with a large black dog hanging around the river bank here?'

Slightly taken aback, I muttered, 'No.'

'Well let us know if you see him.'

I went back to my bench hoping that the man in the water was some sort of athlete and had managed to survive. Perhaps it was his daily ritual.

To recover, I went into a bar and stood, wondering where to sit and where I might find a menu.

A weak voice called out, 'You look a bit lost there.'

A heavy-set man with a grey, stubbled face sat on a stool leaning against the bar counter and a side wall with a beer in front of him. He was in his seventies with rounded, stooped shoulders and was wearing blue overalls with braces over a red and white check shirt.

'The story of my life', I replied.

He pointed at the stool beside him, 'Come join me; I could do with the company.'

John Wilson lived with his wife in Nova Scotia, though he hailed from a family of fourteen in Alaska.

'That was a busy house', I said.

'My mother did the switching; my father, he just wanted peace. He left my mother at it. He worked hard to provide for us all on a few acres. We had our own cows, hens, vegetables and caught our own fish. The children came every two years on the button.'

He paused, shook his head and continued, 'The eldest now is ninety-two. He's such a dandy, all dressed up to the nines, not like me', he said, pointing to his own braces. 'They all have big families too, just like our parents.'

'What about you? Have you a family?'

'We were only able to have one, a daughter. She's married and living near to us. She isn't lucky enough to have a child.'

He paused again and announced, 'I was zapped. I worked in the air force on radar for many years. We suspected that it wasn't good for us. They tell you it's safe, but you can't tell me that it doesn't affect you. They never listened to us, just kept fobbing us off with words.'

'Well, people come second when security issues are at stake.'

'They sure do. My wife and I went on a trip to Egypt recently. We went to a special place in the desert and asked someone to take a photograph of us. I told the group who came with us that our daughter had been conceived on that very spot many years previously and we'd returned to celebrate it.'

Shaking his head he said, 'I was so eager that night that I stuck it in the sand a few times by mistake, but eventually I got it spot on and that was the only luck we had. We were blessed that night. Goddamn those radar stations.'

'Well it was great to have one child. I was an only child too.'

'Yes, we were lucky.'

The evening paused into silence, which I interrupted. 'What are you doing in Whitehorse?'

'I'm coming back from a trip. It had always been an ambition of mine to stand on Little Diomede Island in the Bering Sea. It's the most westerly point in the US.'

When he saw my perplexed look, he said, 'It's beside Big Diomede Island.'

'Right.'

'Big Diomede is owned by Russia and is its most easterly point.'

'Ah, ok', I said, pretending enlightenment.

'My son-in-law took time off work to come and help me. They don't think I should be travelling on my own to these places anymore.' He laughed and continued,

'We got as far as Wales, which is close to Nome. You can take a helicopter trip to the island. But as soon as we reached Wales, the fog set in and didn't shift for all the weeks we spent there. Day after day, I would wake up hoping to get to Little Diomede only to be greeted by more fog. It was impossible to get out there by air or sea. I asked a helicopter pilot to fly us over the island, so at least we could say we saw it. I offered him five hundred dollars extra for the flight, but he refused to do it because of regulations. If he wanted to, he could have done it, no problem. We were stuck in a little room and couldn't move around much because of the weather. My son-in-law had to go back to work so we had to abandon our efforts. The whole journey cost me nearly twenty thousand dollars.'

'That's expensive. Is it a big place?'

'No. If there are one hundred people living there, that's the height of it. It's an Eskimo village. There's no easy way to Wales.'

I could well believe him. When I looked up Wales, Alaska, I saw that it was on the very tip of the land mass. If Little Diomede is the most westerly part of the US, Wales is the most westerly place on the US mainland, exposed on its perch to the onslaught of the elements. The population of Wales is precarious. It was nearly wiped out by the flu epidemic in 1918 and has never recovered. According to John, a demoralised people live there.

He told me that he had travelled around the world by freighter.

'By freighter? Were you working?'

'No, I just go on my holidays by freighter. You can book a room on board and eat with the crew. My last trip was on a Polish ship to Europe. It cost fifty dollars a day, which included food and a luxurious room. It had a great shower, not like those fiddly things in motels. We stopped in Valencia as the crew wanted to let off steam, and they invited me along too. I had eighty dollars with me and we ended up in a club which was full of really beautiful Romanian women. All the men had a good time.'

'What about you?'

'There are some advantages to being old. They all spent a fortune. I spent all of my eighty dollars on a few bottles of coke so you can imagine what they spent.'

'So where next?'

'I haven't told my wife yet, but I intend to fly to Columbia and get a freighter to the southern tip of the Americas. From there I'll go to Antarctica. It's the only continent I haven't been on.'

'Does your wife ever go with you?'

'No, she has no interest in travelling. Her passion is her garden and spending as much time with our daughter as possible.'

'Would you like another drink?' I asked him.

Much later, back at my motel, the receptionist I had met on my first night in Whitehorse confided that he worked fourteen hours every day and twenty-four hours on a Friday. On Friday, he had to spread his time between three businesses: the hotel, the Laundromat and the restaurant.

'What do you do for rest?'

'Well I try to grab a little sleep on the couch during the night if it's quiet.'

'It must take a lot out of you.'

'Yes it does, but the owner recognises that it isn't good for me. She allows me to take thirty minutes off for a shower.

A rugged man came into the lobby with four hunting dogs. The receptionist hopped up and sold him and the four dogs a room for the night.

When he came back out, I asked him, 'Do you charge extra for the dogs?'

'No, we allow dogs if they're clean. Sometimes it isn't dogs you have to worry about. In the winter, social services pay us to take in vagrants because of the cold. The place is full all winter.'

Because Micí had rowed a boat on the Yukon River, I wanted to experience the same thing. I thought however that, unlike Micí, I would go with the flow of the river. I hired a kayak and equipment for two days and asked to be dropped above Miles Canyon. I wanted to kayak through the canyon that had spelt death to some during the gold rush.

I was pushed out into the flow of the river by one of the staff and was initially surprised by the speed of the river. For a moment, I felt out of control but after a moment I regained composure. After about an hour's kayaking, I reached Miles Canyon, accompanied by two canoes lashed together with a crew of five seasoned Australians. Two steep cliffs of basalt rock bound the river at this point, but a dam had tamed the flow and it was relatively safe. I spotted the white head of a bald eagle perched on a branch high on a cliff-top tree and swallows nesting in small holes in the cliff face. A crowd of people waved from a footbridge over the river.

I parted from my temporary travelling companions and passed through Whitehorse, the river carrying me swiftly onwards. Soon, Whitehorse was behind me but, for a while, the sound of traffic on the Alaska Highway kept me in touch with human civilisation. Then it went quiet. The only sound was the kayak slipping through the water and the light splashes of my paddle in the river. I arrived in a small lake where the current slowed right down. On one side, there were high cliffs with trees on the rim. On the other bank, the forest seemed to grow right into the river. An eagle soared overhead and I craned my neck to follow its graceful form floating on the breeze. A smaller bird followed it, shrieking in either anger or despair.

I wasn't sure exactly where I was or where I was going. I had a map, but felt totally disoriented, as one bend in a river seemed much the same as another and I could recognise no distinctive features. The river had many channels, with spruce and birch blanketing the hills and mountains for as far as the eye could see. An anxiety grabbed me. I was so small in the face of such immense nature. I kept reassuring myself that if I followed the flow of the river I would end up in some small settlement somewhere. I told myself that it was silly to worry, and subsided into the moment. I stopped on the riverbank for a few hours, had something to eat and lay down on a large stone. A dense shrubbery of aspen surrounded me. I walked a little way through it but didn't venture far because I had visions of my kayak disappearing. What was likely to happen in the middle of nowhere?

Later, I decided to camp on a small island in the middle of the river, calculating that big, hairy visitors would be less likely to disturb me there. Having secured my kayak, I found a place for my tent and, having lit a small fire, I was prepared for the night. I had some dry food and wandered around the small island. The closest I came to seeing any wildlife was when I found a beaver's lodge and spotted a woodpecker hole in a tree. As I sat by the fire, a vast silence lay over the land. The river rippled on by but nothing else stirred, not even a breath of wind. Underneath the stillness, energy vibrated, creating a slight sizzle; the hum of the universe. At one stage I heard a loud crack not too far from my camp. I sat motionless for a moment, my ears straining. Again, everything was silent. I threw small pieces of wood into the river and watched them being swept away. A line of geese flew over; the vibration from their honking filled my senses.

During the night, as I lay in my tent, I could feel the river gently breathing, pushing its formlessness against the solidity of the land. I listened to its voice mumbling, grumbling, complaining and whispering as it flowed past all obstacles on its way to its ocean home. At times, it sounded like people talking. I filled the emptiness with multitudes from my imagination.

The next morning, a breeze brought clouds of ash smoke from some distant fire. It sucked all the colour out of the landscape, leaving everything shrouded in a creamy grey hue. As I loaded my kayak, my feeling was of exquisite menace, a sense of vulnerability at being alone in such a vast wilderness, combined with a deep thrill. There is an attraction about being alone. The relationship is primal and raw. It strips away our veneer and reduces everything to its essentials.

The paddling was similar to the previous day and curve followed curve on the river. Far too soon, I reached the agreed rendezvous spot at the entrance to Lake Laberge where a young college student waited for me. He hoisted my kayak effortlessly onto the top of the jeep and we headed back to Whitehorse.

20

Whitehorse to Anchorage

It was 5:30 in the morning and I felt uneasy. I was looking for the bus station for the twice-weekly service to Anchorage and I couldn't see anything that resembled even a bus stop. Scolding myself for my lack of planning, I re-checked the address. It seemed the correct street; perhaps it was the wrong day? I pulled my case along the sidewalk looking for a re-assuring clue. It came in the shape of two people pulling cases, each coming from a different direction, converging on a small, blue, wooden house on a street corner. This house became a magnet. The cawing of crows and the sound of cases rattling across rutted sidewalks scattered the silence. We three passengers arrived together and were reassured by a sign on the wooden fence which said 'Alaskan Direct Buslines'.

My fellow passengers were Sally, a red-haired Englishwoman in her late twenties, and Hiro, a small middle-aged Japanese man with short hair and a beard. He left his case beside the fence and walked around, taking photographs of anything that looked out of the ordinary. Sally knocked on the door. After a slight delay, a young Asian woman answered and waved us into a small living room. The room was neatly decorated with a mixture of oriental art and flowers, while a large, incongruous desk, overflowing with paper, filled one corner. The three of us sat down into the sofa and the woman told us to wait a few minutes, then disappeared into another room. Thrown together, we talked and laughed about anything and everything. A grandfather clock ticked in any silence that arose.

The kitchen door opened. Our bus driver, a big man in his late thirties with a slight stoop and a laconic, tired expression, came in and said, 'How can people be so good-humoured in the mornings? It's too early.'

'The journey is only sixteen hours. No wonder we're in good humour', was Sally's riposte.

Dave let that statement sit for a moment while he gingerly positioned himself behind the desk and took out a hard-backed book.

'I've something to tell you before we start the paperwork.' He rubbed his back before continuing, 'the air conditioning unit is broken on the minibus. We'll have to open the windows on the journey to keep cool.' He waited a moment. 'Is that all right then?'

We shifted and looked at each other, but as we didn't have many options we nodded glumly.

Dave had been out fishing the previous day and his grouchiness could have been due to the fact that his back had got sunburned on what was the hottest day of that summer.

'Did you catch any fish?'

'Caught nothing, though they were jumping.'

His misery couldn't have been more complete. Well maybe it could, because he had to write our details into a ledger. His mood improved a little when I paid my fee. When he asked Hiro for his information, Hiro sat bolt upright and smilingly held up his index finger, as if he'd just had a good idea. With a flourish, he brought a roll of adhesive labels out of his pocket. His name and details were printed on each one. He peeled a label off and proffered it proudly to the driver.

'I'm from Japan', he said.

The driver took the label with a bewildered look. 'My wife is Japanese too', he said, and shouted, 'Ami, come here for a minute.'

Ami reappeared and she and Hiro dutifully had a brief conversation in Japanese before it ran out of steam.

Suddenly, the front door opened with a rattle and a big man, a healthy seventy, poked a baseball-capped head around the door. The most prominent features on that face were a bulbous red nose, an extravagant moustache, plain black glasses and roguish eyes.

'Do you remember me?' he said, addressing Dave as he walked into the room. 'We had a great time on that last trip. My brother and I are looking forward to going with you again.'

Dave did not respond with the same level of enthusiasm. It was as if he were waking up to heavy metal music after drinking whiskey all night.

'What's your name?' he said wearily. 'We get many passengers.'

The man answered with a name that certainly wasn't Smith or Jones, and which I couldn't pronounce.

'What sort of name is that?' asked Dave.

'Ukrainian, and there's a woman from Switzerland wanting to be picked up at our hotel as well. Can you do that?'

'Yep, sure.'

Thirty minutes later, we were on the road, having collected our passengers. The other Ukrainian was nearly an exact replica of his brother except that he was smaller, thinner and older. He wore the same design of black glasses and they sat together, like roosters on a perch, with big grins on their faces and twinkles in their eyes. Of course they weren't from Ukraine at all but were retired farmers of Ukrainian extraction living in Alberta, Canada. The trim, middle-aged Swiss woman was an avid hiker, fond of extolling the beauty of Switzerland. Ami sat beside Dave in the front of the minibus. She rode shotgun on all his long journeys.

On passing a place called Champagne, Dave pointed to a grave-yard on a hillside with small houses on it. 'Native people have built houses here for their dead that are a lot better than what they're living in themselves. They're kept spotless. Now they've put a guard on the cemetery for fear of vandalism.'

'Is that a traditional way of dealing with death?' I asked.

'Well, I think before the white man came they used to cremate the bodies and put the ashes in a skin bag in a tree. The missioners brought the idea of burial with them, except this is the Yukon and bodies don't go into the earth too easy.'

'How did the place get the name of Champagne?'

'Are you going to be asking me difficult questions all the way to Alaska?'

He eventually told me that during the gold rush, a group of cow-boys, driving a herd of cattle to Dawson City, stopped here and celebrated completing the most difficult part of the journey by open-ing a bottle of champagne.

'Just one?' I asked.

Views of magnificent mountains accompanied us all the way to Haines Junction where Dave, to great acclaim, announced that we were going to stop for breakfast and 'the best coffee in the Yukon'.

Afterwards, he pointed to layers of snow-capped mountains in the distance and told us that this was Kluane National Park, regarded as one of the prime wilderness areas in the world. The park, at twenty-two thousand square miles, is half the size of Switzerland and, within these majestic surrounds, twenty peaks soar to in excess of sixteen thousand feet. Moreover, one among their number, Mount Logan, is the most massive mountain on the planet. At 19,520 feet, it is lower than Mount Everest or even Mount McKinley, but its total mass is greater, because it has a broad base that begins near sea level. The park has vast ice fields and its largest glacier, as it retreats, releases as much water as the Amazon River. Dave told us that much of Kluane National Park is uncharted with unpredictable weather, as the mountains create their own climate. It's fitting that this imposing landscape should be home for the highest density of grizzly bears on earth. The name Kluane provides a clue as to why grizzlies feel at home there. In the local First Nation language, Kluane means, 'place of many fish'.

I was sitting beside Hiro for this portion of the journey. He was full of boyish energy and all of his sentences were accompanied by many hand and body actions, which sometimes made it dangerous for those sitting near him. He was a retired maths teacher and retirement had allowed him to travel around Australia on a motorbike. He illustrated this by grabbing imaginary motorbike handles and revving the engine.

'Many kangaloos', he said, as he enthusiastically mimicked weaving his way through them on the road. 'Long distances', he added, 'up in morning … ride for four hours, then break … then ride more and then get place to stay. Then beer … many beer, and then, many more beer. The next morning … UUUH!' he said, holding his head in mock agony. He then pretended to fall asleep. 'Very hard to stay awake on motobike. Suffer, suffer.' He shook his head at the memory.

He also had biked across Canada where, 'I wanted to see bear … very dangerous bear. I didn't see … very dangerous bear', he said, making claws with his hands.

'So you don't plan to take a motorbike to Alaska?'

'My wife … she no like it … she scared. So I agreed with her that I wouldn't use motobike.'

But every time Hiro saw a motorbike on the road he would excitedly point it out while grabbing imaginary handlebars. 'See, motobikes!'

We came to Kluane Lake, which stretched along the highway, providing an enthralling view for fifty miles. The lake was edged on the far side by the rugged Ruby Mountains, so called because their red rock provided a tinge of warm colour that contrasted with the icy blue of the lake. It was here that we first started to feel the lack of air conditioning. Open windows are fine but not on sections of road that are made of gravel and dust. We started to bake and Dave had to put up with an earful from the irascible Ukrainians.

'We have to pay to suffer on this bus.'

Dave thought that more coffee might relieve the suffering, so we stopped at a place near Soldiers Summit. 'This is the place where the Alaskan Highway was completed', he said. 'There's a monument commemorating this on the hill above us.'

Two regiments of American soldiers were involved in the construction of the road. One group set out from Dawson Creek in British Columbia and the other from Fairbanks in Alaska in 1942. They completed the fifteen-hundred-mile road in eight months. Some people consider this one of the greatest engineering achievements of the twentieth century, surpassing even the construction of the Panama Canal.

Dave told us that there was one problem: 'The two ends didn't meet.'

They were so intent on speed that they miscalculated the meeting point, and this necessitated the building of a large, unplanned curve on the road.

The Alaska Highway is really a vulnerable pathway through a vast, inhospitable wilderness that threatens to reclaim it at every opportunity. The road would probably not have been built at all but for the Japanese attack on Pearl Harbour, which created a fear within the political and military establishment that the United States was vulnerable to attack through Alaska. Two airbases in Anchorage and Fairbanks, that could only be re-supplied by sea or air, were all that stood between the enemy and the state. It was a matter of national security to construct a road that would ensure consistent supplies and quick mobility should the occasion demand. However, there was a problem. The only possible supply route was through Canada. Recognising this impediment, the US offered to build the road through the Yukon and the Canadians, not looking a gift horse in the mouth, accepted. Twelve thousand troops and seventeen thousand civilians punched a road through this wilderness of forest, mountain, ice, permafrost and raging rivers, enduring severe winter weather. All machinery had to run 24 hours a day, because they might not start again if turned off. According to Dave, the greatest enemy was the brief, hot summer sun. When they stripped a sod from the ground in summer, the sun melted the permafrost and the whole area turned into a quagmire that devoured men and machines. And of course there wasn't a moment's peace from the mosquitoes and black flies.

The last stop before the Alaskan border was a restaurant called Buckshot Betty's in Beaver Creek, so called, I was told, to encourage diners to pay up promptly! Dave told us that people had inhabited a nearby archaeological site fourteen thousand years ago, which was the oldest record of human habitation in North America. This is a long time in archaeological terms but a small blip in the life of the planet. Similarly, I felt like a minute ant travelling through this massive wilderness; my imprint was faint and fleeting.

Before we reached the border, Dave warned us that we might experience delays, as customs officials could be pernickety. When the American officer emerged from the customs hut, he shuffled uneasily around, commenting on the weather. He kept looking from our faces to our passports. We were a little bit puzzled by his behaviour but the reason became clear when he gave Sally my passport and I got Sally's. When I had my passport photograph taken seven years previously, I had long, fair, curly hair and no goatee beard. I don't know which of us was the most embarrassed.

Between the border and Tok, I ended up sitting beside the large Ukrainian man called Ivan, who told me, 'More Ukrainians live in Alberta than anywhere else in Canada. We are farmers and everyone in our community is Ukrainian.'

'Why did Ukrainians go there?'

'Because we're good farmers and land was available in Alberta.'

Many Ukrainians took up the offer from the government to buy one hundred and sixty acres of prime agricultural land for ten dollars. This was more land than most of them could ever imagine owning. According to Ivan, Ukraine, because of its rich land, had always been occupied by foreign powers. These occupations kept the people in poverty, thus leading to emigration, especially at the end of the nineteenth century.

'If I came across a Ukrainian town in the middle of Alberta', I asked him, 'how would I know that it was Ukrainian?'

He laughed and immediately said, 'Good food', but after a moment's thought, he added, 'the shape of the roofs on our churches.

They're onion domed. They would be the first thing you would see when you entered a town.'

'You're going on a holiday to Anchorage?' I asked.

'Yep, but the tourists are paying for our holiday.'

'How's that?'

'Well they hire RVs in Alberta and drive them to Anchorage. They don't want to take them back again. We collect them and drive them back, all expenses paid', he grinned.

We arrived in Tok. The town is like a long string of pump water, long streets with buildings spread out thinly. We stopped at Grumpy Grizz's restaurant to swap buses. We unloaded our luggage and stood waiting in the shade of a big container truck. I went to the diner for a coffee, leaving my case under the watchful eyes of my new colleagues.

I said to a gangly man behind the counter, 'It's a great day out there.'

'It is, but the leaves are starting to curl.'

I wondered what that meant but said, 'That heat would curl anything.'

'It's not the heat, it's a sign that we're heading towards winter.'

Time keeps marching onwards, especially in a climate where the summer is brilliant, but painfully brief. In such a place, people are more likely to be attuned to the signs of change. We were now in August and the light was beginning to walk away with a quickening pace. The bear knows that it's time to build a store of fat and the leaf knows that the summer days are going. I drank my coffee in a hurry, in case I missed the bus.

Our new bus driver, John, was a swarthy guy with tattoos and a baseball cap. His minibus might have had air conditioning, but we had picked up extra passengers in Tok and it was jammed full. I sat beside the window with Hiro in the middle seat beside me. On the other side of the seat, the large Ukrainian acted as a bookend. His ample frame wedged us in tighter than sardines in a tin. The road out of Tok is wide and has little traffic so I was perplexed when I saw a fully signposted cycling lane going for miles alongside the highway. Any cyclist I knew would be using the road in such circumstances, so I asked John the driver his opinion.

He laughed and said, 'I've never seen a cyclist using that lane.'

'So why build it?'

'The road is funded by the federal government. They can only get maximum funding if a cycle lane is included in the specification. A road out of New York is regarded in the same way as a road out of Tok.'

A little later, we thought our driver had gone mad, because while talking about his adventures skinning a porcupine, he veered off the road and headed up a gravel side road.

'I nearly forgot', he said.

The object of his forgetfulness was an old, grey-haired woman, sitting erect on a stone wall outside a small store in what appeared to be the middle of the forest. Beside her, she had a white cane and a big bag of supplies. John hopped out, opened the side door of the minibus and asked if people would mind squashing closer together for a few miles. I think a few sardines popped out of the can! He helped her aboard and we set off again.

When she heard where I was from, she said, 'I've a bit of Irish in me, probably explains a lot.'

She lived on her own in a small cabin, and she laughingly proclaimed, 'I hope to die there.'

John again veered off the road and dropped the woman onto a track leading to what presumably was her cabin. Once on familiar ground, she moved confidently along the track, disappearing into the forest with her supplies.

When John got back into the bus, he shook his head and said, 'Some woman that.' He told us that she squatted in the cabin with forty acres of forest. In Alaskan law, it was possible to claim the land if you showed that you had made improvements to it and had built a cabin with dimensions of twenty by twenty-six feet. He explained how a friend of his had overcome this requirement. He had sneakily built a small cabin with a big roof, thus fooling the authorities, who check everything by taking photographs from the air.

I asked John, 'How is the woman going to make improvements?'

He shrugged.

As the hours and the miles mounted, Hiro fell asleep. Of course, he fell asleep on my shoulder and started to snore with his mouth open. I definitely wasn't prepared for such an intimate moment. Hiro was a deep sleeper and no amount of 'involuntary' movements of my shoulder managed to shake him. I looked resentfully at the massive bulk of the Ukrainian, tilting Hiro sideways towards me, and thought to myself that there was no chance in the world that Hiro could fall in the other direction. Sometimes I would get a glimmer of hope when a bend on the road would pull the head away from me. The relief was always temporary, as he would inevitably sway back in my direction again, and the mixture of rumbling snore and stale breath would fill my senses once more.

At a scheduled stop at a gas station, the Swiss woman came up to me and said, 'You poor man, would you like me to swap seats with you for a while?'

I should have taken her up on the offer but pride wouldn't let me admit that it bothered me in the slightest. I assured her that all was fine in my universe. I knew she didn't believe me.

If I thought that the stop would make a difference, I was sadly mistaken. I tried to imagine different heads on my shoulder but Hiro continued sleeping, oblivious to my anguish.

I was distracted by the beautiful scenery. Extreme stillness and extreme activity define this wilderness. We had entered the world of glaciers and snowy mountains. Some of the glaciers were enormous and they seemed to push the mountains apart as they flowed through them. John pointed out miles and miles of bare rock at the edge of some of the glaciers; testimony to a different power. Global warming was pushing back the glaciers at an amazing speed, producing large changes in just a few years. This is an ongoing battle that spans millennia. These giant, silent and seemingly static rivers of ice carved their way through the mountain ranges. You could sense their motion and power, even if it could not be seen.

A different though related power was also flowing through these mountains. Rivers like the Copper River are virtual torrents of activity. Their cold, grey, surging waters cut their way through mountain and forest. Floodwaters have stripped the riverbanks bare and carved steep gullies, down which undermined trees topple. Majestic snowy peaks soared into the sky, some surrounded by black cloud, others in clear sunlight. A frock of green tundra forest crept up the flanks of the mountains before coming to the wall of altitude that repelled further advance; this green was a sign of the tenacity of life in a frozen wilderness. I took it all in while Hiro snored, and it was in this cosy manner that we reached Anchorage at eleven that night, roughly seventeen hours after leaving Whitehorse.

I was heading home.

21

Home

Mící recounted that on many occasions, when sitting around camp-fires, conversation inevitably turned to home and a yearning to return there again. It was like a hot water bottle that kept them warm during the cold, hostile nights. Of all the immigrant nations in the US how-ever, the Irish were the least likely to return. Most had no option but to stay, and, like an icy leaf on a branch, the immigrant's image of home became frozen in time. They in turn passed on this static pic-ture to succeeding generations. This was often a sentimental image of life in Ireland, tainted with anger because they had to leave. This isn't unique to the Irish. You only have to think of the Cubans, Jews and African-Americans who have similar perspectives. This frozen image often forms the basis for radical views in succeeding generations, and becomes intertwined with American political life.

Mící, however, had been successful, and this opened the door for him to return home. It is so much easier to return as a hero. He booked a first-class berth on a liner, which was a long way removed from the glorified coffin ship he had arrived in. It didn't stop him getting sick though! Like many immigrants in America, Mící had led a restless existence with no affinity to the places in which he worked. His life, full of risk and toil, allowed no roots to settle. It was no wonder then that when he turned his face to home again, he was looking forward to a land where he could 'take his ease', something he claimed he had not done since he left, sixteen years previously. It brings to mind the words of William Faulkner, 'How often have I lain beneath rain on a strange roof, thinking of home.'

Mící, however, was uncertain about the Ireland he would encoun-ter. On landing in Derry, his first impression was that everyone was in a hurry. The railroad had arrived and every household had bought a clock. He claimed that this was why roosters had become redundant.

Other things had changed too. The raw edge of people's suffering had been blunted by the actions of the Congested Districts Board. Working conditions had improved for fishing families, weavers and farmers. Schools, roads and bridges had been built, grants had been provided for the construction of new houses and movements such as the Gaelic League were giving people 'heart again'. Walking was redundant too. The new Derry to Burtonport train brought him near to his home in West Donegal.

After receiving a great welcome, Mící now faced a dilemma. He loved home, but could he find a way of fitting in again? It was as if he was on the outside, looking in at a familiar world that had moved on without him. Tired of being restless and placeless, he tarried, looking for an excuse to stay. That excuse arrived when he fell in love with and married a young woman called Maire Dixon. The path became clear. He bought his ex-landlord's property and built a big house which became a home for eleven children. Immersed in the local community, many eminent people came to stay with him, including Roger Casement. His wheel of life had come full circle. The image of home he had taken with him on his journeys had sheltered him from chaos, but now he had found his point of reference: a new home, where all journeys begin and end, a place where he could, in his own words, 'draw his breath'.